Raised in Dallas, *Ronald L. Davis* received his B.A., M.A. and Ph.D. from the University of Texas in Austin. He is a member of Phi Beta Kappa and Phi Alpha Theta (the national honorary history fraternity), and has been the recipient of a Colonial Dames Fellowship for American History. Currently he is Assistant Professor of Humanities at Michigan State University.

Ronald L. Davis

A History of Opera in
the American West

Prentice-Hall, Inc. ❖ *Englewood Cliffs, N.J.*

Library of Congress Catalog Card Number: 65–12168.

Printed in the United States of America—C. 39052

For MARILYN
with
a husband's love
and
an author's gratitude

PREFACE

The definition of the West suggested here is a rather unconventional one, covering everything west of and including Chicago and New Orleans. This is strictly an arbitrary delineation, made to embrace the *major* American opera companies outside the eastern fringe, and does not pretend to be based upon geographical or historical considerations. Only the most significant, or in some cases representative, organizations have been dealt with here. No attempt has been made at completeness. To those cities boasting operatic enterprises, either historical or contemporary, not mentioned in this survey, I apologize and ask them to count the pages of the text. The omission stems from necessity, not intent.

The story which follows has taken me through some fifteen states and has been responsible for my meeting a host of gracious people. While the list of those who rendered a helping hand is much too long to relate in full, gratitude must be expressed to Gus G. Jaquet of the New Orleans Opera House Association, Herbert Scholder of the San Francisco Opera, Carol Fox of the Lyric Opera of Chicago, Lawrence Kelly of the Dallas Civic Opera, Frank Magee of the Santa Fe Opera, and Clinton Norton of the San Antonio Symphony for taking time out from busy schedules to answer countless questions; to Lucine Amara and Edith Mason Ragland for sharing with me the singer's viewpoint on opera production; to Alfred Frankenstein of the *San Francisco Chronicle* for giving me significant insights into California's operatic life, both historic and current; to Ronald Seeliger of the University of Texas library for his advice on a multitude of plaguing technicalities; to Arlene Webster Ross of Detroit for her careful proofreading and typing of the final manuscript; to William A. Larsen of Dallas and Nancy Brouwers McNiff of Lansing for further proofreading; to my wife, Marilyn Bowden Davis, for her endless patience and willing assistance; and to Michigan State University for financial assistance

vii

through an All-University Research Grant. Finally, I am especially indebted to Professor Joe B. Frantz of the University of Texas for his thorough reading and constructive criticism of the manuscript.

R. L. D.

CONTENTS

One   Tuning Up on the Mississippi   1

Two   The Ballad of Bourbon Street   15

Three   Opera on the Great Lakes   36

Four   Chicago's Chords and Discords   61

Five   Lyric Gold in California   83

Six   San Francisco's Operatic Nugget   101

Seven   A Texas Success   113

Eight   Summer Festivals Along the Divide   134

Nine   The Finale   148

Notes   155

Index   169

ILLUSTRATIONS

French Opera House, New Orleans.
  Theater Collection, The University of Texas.

Interior of French Opera House, New Orleans.
  The University of Texas Library.

Rice's Theater, Chicago, 1850. Painting in water color by Justin Herriot.
  Courtesy Chicago Historical Society.

Crosby's Opera House, Chicago.
  Courtesy Chicago Historical Society.

Interior of Auditorium Hall, Chicago. View from the balcony.
  Courtesy Chicago Historical Society.

San Francisco Opera's 1959 production of Bizet's "Carmen."
  Act I—The square in Seville with Gloria Lane as Carmen and Jon
  Vickers as Don Jose (Sets and costumes by Howard Bay).
  Courtesy San Francisco Opera Association.

Central City Opera House.
  Denver Public Library Western Collection.

Interior of Central City Opera House.
  Denver Public Library Western Collection.

Dallas Civic Opera's "Daughter of the Regiment." Eugenia Ratti and
  Giuseppi Taddei.
  Courtesy Dallas Civic Opera.

Dallas Civic Opera's "Alcina." Joan Sutherland as Alcina.
  Courtesy Dallas Civic Opera.

Remains of the Tivoli Opera House, San Francisco.
  Theater Collection, The University of Texas.

San Francisco Opera's 1963 production of Rossini's "The Barber of
  Seville." Dr. Bartolo's house (designed by Alfred Siercke and
  Thomas L. Colangelo, Jr.).
  Courtesy San Francisco Opera Association.

San Francisco Opera's 1957 production of Poulenc's "The Carmelites."
  Dorothy Kirsten as Blanche de la Force and Blanche Thebom as
  Mother Marie (Sets by Harry Horner).
  Courtesy San Francisco Opera Association.

San Francisco Opera's 1963 production of Richard Strauss' "Capriccio."
Elisabeth Schwarzkopf as the Countess and Thomas Stewart as her
brother the Count (Sets and costumes by Leni Bauer-Ecsy and
Thomas L. Colangelo, Jr.).
Courtesy San Francisco Opera Association.

Santa Fe Opera Theater. A view from the loggia at the rear of the
theater. The theater is located about five miles north of Santa Fe
between the Jemez and the Sangre de Cristo mountains.
Courtesy Santa Fe Opera.

War Memorial Opera House, San Francisco, California. Foyer.
Courtesy San Francisco Opera Association.

A History of Opera
in
the American West

Tuning Up
on the Mississippi

Mention opera today to the average American, and he immediately thinks of New York City and the Metropolitan. To have suggested the same topic to a sophisticate of Andrew Jackson's day would have brought to mind not New York, but New Orleans. So long has New York been recognized as the cultural and musical center of the United States that recent generations have almost forgotten it was New Orleans that supported the nation's first opera company, possessing for years the largest and most elegant theater on the entire North American continent.

The thread of operatic history in New Orleans goes back to the latter part of the eighteenth century, when George Washington was President of the United States and Estevan Miró was Governor of Louisiana. The city, then a bare 5,000 persons, diverted itself in those days at *Le Spectacle de la Rue St. Pierre,* a theatrical establishment located, as best can be determined, at 732 St. Peter Street.

At that time, and until 1803, Louisiana was a part of the colonial empire of Spain; the area had been explored and colonized earlier by France. Culturally, New Orleans became a French city with a Spanish overlay. So deeply entrenched was this Latin heritage that its influence has continued in the city through the decades. Even today New Orleans is still loyal in many respects to its Latin traditions, particularly the French.

I

As early as 1791, Louis Tabary, an impresario of considerable talent, brought to *Le Spectacle de la Rue St. Pierre* direct from Europe a troupe of French comedians and singers, presenting something approximating drama, opera, and ballet. These Tabary productions were at first simply given in the street—sometimes under a crude tent, often *al fresco*, and frequently six inches deep in Louisiana mud. It was not until some time later that an unadorned wooden building was constructed on St. Peter Street to house *Le Spectacle*, but even then the structure was a far cry from the plush, velvet-cushioned, acoustically perfect theaters of today. The edifice was humble at best and, more realistically, downright primitive. The roof invariably leaked, and the interior was always in need of repairs.[1]

It was here—amid the mud bogs of the Mississippi, to the accompaniment of croaking frogs and whining mosquitoes—that the first opera in the United States was heard, at a time when the economically dynamic region to the north was given to nothing more sophisticated than ballad and hymn singing. Exactly what the nature of this earliest opera was we are not sure, for the source material on the subject is too sparse and scattered. We do know that by 1793 an orchestra was used in connection with the performances given at *Le Spectacle*. Other than that, these productions remain cloaked in mystery; nothing definite is known about either the company or the repertoire. Nevertheless, historians agree that there can be little doubt that opera was given in the theater from at least 1793 on, for it seems unlikely that the Louisiana-born Frenchmen, or Creoles as they were called, would have supported a theater with an orchestra unless the operas of their day were presented there.[2]

In 1799 a group of refugees fled to New Orleans from Santo Domingo, where a slave rebellion was raging. The insurrection had assumed alarming proportions when the mulatto element of the island, having recently been denied preciously won civil liberties, joined forces in an attempt to overthrow French authority. To escape the resulting chaos and bloodshed, refugees flocked to the Crescent City in droves, among them a troupe of actors and singers. As the performers soon found themselves in financial straits, they decided to exhibit their talents at *Le Spectacle de la Rue St. Pierre*, rendering comedy, vaudeville, drama, and comic opera.[3]

During the next three years, however, the local citizenry grew rather indifferent toward theatrical enterprises, and most of the performers moved on to a more profitable locale. The condition of *Le Spectacle* had rapidly deteriorated, and this dilapidated state, coupled with an internal dispute between the city's civil and military authorities, resulted in the theater's being closed by officials for two years. By 1804 substantial repairs had been made, and *Le Spectacle de la Rue St. Pierre* was again opened for public amusement. Nevertheless, the following year saw another examination of the theater by the authorities, who now found that "water to the depth of five or six inches" stood beneath the structure and that the hall was inclined "to lean very much on one side." Once more the ultimatum was given: the theater would either be repaired or closed.[4]

Early 1807 finds *Le Spectacle* still in operation but, as usual, in an extremely dilapidated state. The building, as it stood then, was described as "a long, low, wooden structure, built of cypress, and alarmingly exposed to the dangers of fire."[5] The tubs of water which the management strategically scattered around the auditorium offered little, if any, reassurance. Toward the end of the year, the local rabble got into a wrangle with the police at 732 St. Peter Street, and, consequently, *Le Spectacle de la Rue St. Pierre* was once again closed. By now the building was in such deplorable condition that general complaints had been evoked, and the authorities were eager for an excuse to terminate the theater's activities permanently.[6]

Early the following year the old theater was completely demolished, and a syndicate built a new one on the same site. This new showplace was *Le Théâtre de la Rue St. Pierre*, which opened on September 14, 1808, with a three-act melodrama entitled *Le Prince Tekeli* or *Le Siège de Mantgatz*, followed by a one-act opera, *Le Secret*. Later newspapers reveal that operas by Gaveaux and Méhul were also given at the theater and that the majority of the operatic pieces presented there were of the contemporary French school, tending to be of the lighter vein, generally one- or two-act works.[7] One author estimates that between 1806 and 1811 some seventy different operas were staged in the 700 block of St. Peter Street.[8] However, the *Théâtre St. Pierre* was destined for a short life, because at noon on Friday, December 28, 1810, the land, the building, and all of the theater's contents were sold at public auction in the nearby auction exchange.

Nevertheless, New Orleans was not without its opera, for in the intervening years a much more elegant theater had been erected. This was the *Théâtre St. Philippe*, raised during the latter part of 1807 on the corner of Royal and St. Philip Streets at a cost of $100,-000. The new theater had a seating capacity of 700—a rather sizable audience in those days—and opened on January 30, 1808, with *Les Fausses Consultations*, followed by *D'une Folie*, a two-act opera by Méhul. Louis Tabary, absent from the city for some time, was back, playing the role of impresario.[9]

During the years to follow, the *Théâtre St. Philippe* was the scene of many operatic delights. The custom then was to combine drama and opera on a single bill. As a rule a drama or melodrama would begin the evening's entertainment, and a one-act or two-act opera would bring the program to a close. On March 12, 1811, a significant event occurred when Cherubini's *Les Deux Journées* was staged at the *St. Philippe*, the city's first three-act opera.[10]

Normally, the amusement offered by the *St. Philippe* management was received in a highly sophisticated manner, and an evening at the theater was marked as a great social and cultural event. Occasionally, however, a performance ended in complete chaos and disorder, for the New Orleans Creoles followed the contemporary French habit of showing strong approval or disapproval of artists in no uncertain terms. A tenor who was in poor voice was often obliged to compensate for his vocal shortcomings by being swift-of-foot.[11]

In those days there were no printed programs, and it was customary for the manager to give curtain talks about the opera and the cast. The mayor, who had unlimited powers of censorship, insisted on reading every play and libretto before the work was staged. It was also the mayor who set the day and the hour for the performance and determined the order in which carriages would arrive and depart. Laws stated that the interior of the theater had to be swept between performances, and that oil lamps must be kept burning until the last patron had gone. Artists who failed to appear were subject to fine and anyone caught sneaking into the theater without a ticket might be jailed. It was unlawful to carry canes, swords, sabers, or sticks into the auditorium; and throwing oranges or anything else was strictly forbidden.[12]

Later, the *Théâtre St. Philippe*, once so elegant, degenerated into a kind of circus and, finally, into a notorious dance hall of ill repute, known as the Washington Ballroom. Its days of housing opera were then only a dim memory.

Back in 1809, however, the *Théâtre d'Orléans*, far surpassing any amusement place the city had previously known, was built by gambler-impresario John Davis. On November 30 of that year the *Théâtre d'Orléans* opened with a comedy entitled *Pataques*. Rapidly the opera house became the cultural center of New Orleans. But four years after its completion, this theater which had started its career so illustriously was in ashes, totally destroyed by fire.

At the time of the holocaust, John Davis was in Santo Domingo, scouting for talent. When he returned to New Orleans and learned of the catastrophe, he vowed to rebuild the opera house immediately —"bigger and better than ever." And in 1816 the *Théâtre d'Orléans* came to life again more splendid than before. Designed along Doric lines, the building was an architect's dream, one of the most harmonious structures ever to grace the *Vieux Carré*. At the time it was built, the opera house, erected at a cost of $180,000, was considered the finest in the country. Eventually a ballroom was added to the theater, and here, under gorgeous chandeliers, suppers were served on gala occasions to the city's social elite. The sight must have been a glorious one when the auditorium, the foyer, and the ballroom were all opened onto one another to form an uninterrupted vista of splendor.

It was in the *Théâtre d'Orléans* that the first serious opera was staged in the river city, and this is the theater that focused the eyes of the nation and the world on New Orleans as the first American opera capital. Here the entire operatic spectrum was run, from *opéra bouffe* to *opéra comique* to grand opera, all presented in a lavish and sumptuous manner. The *Théâtre d'Orléans* took opera in New Orleans out of the mud bogs and shabby dwellings and put it on a grand and lofty artistic scale. This was to be opera worthy of the name.

The interior of the new theater was elegant throughout, containing a parquet, two tiers of boxes, and *loges grillées*, or latticed boxes. These *loges grillées* were occupied by persons in mourning, women who were noticeably pregnant, or anyone else who simply preferred not to be seen. The boxes allowed spectators to view the performance comfortably without arousing gossip, criticism, or comment. An added advantage of the *loges* was that they concealed their occupants so thoroughly that one might sit in them, eavesdropping on all of the local gossip, without fear of being apprehended. To an inevitable circle, this naturally had great appeal.[13]

John Davis had high artistic aspirations for his *Théâtre d'Orléans*, most of which were eventually realized. Each year the impresario paid a visit to Paris, where he recruited artists for his company at the Paris Opera House. He succeeded in getting many of Europe's outstanding singers to cross the Atlantic and perform in the *Orléans*, although at first most of them were highly skeptical of what they would find there. But within a few seasons they hesitated no longer and even came eagerly. Davis hoped ultimately to present opera in a manner worthy of the leading opera houses of Europe.

The French repertoire particularly fascinated the New Orleanians, and at no time was the *Théâtre d'Orléans* far behind the Paris Opera House in presenting the new and distinguished works of the day. The river city became an American Paris, and the opera house emerged as the matrix of the city's social and cultural existence. Opera became an integral part of the city's life, not for just the wealthy and the social elite, but for the humblest citizens as well. Everyone in New Orleans went to the *Théâtre d'Orléans*, for opera was a popular institution here, one which all enjoyed and took pride in. Annually the townspeople awaited the announcement that was a major event—the list of operas and singers to be presented that year. On the day the notice was issued, excitement ran throughout every corner of the city. Men stopped one another on the streets, and women visited their neighbors to discuss plans for the coming season. As the artists began arriving from Europe, the press reflected the city's enthusiasm, which by then had reached fever pitch.

"Has the troupe left Le Havre yet?"

"Yes."

"When is it due?"

"Within the week."

"Are you going to the reception?"

"Of course!"

When the ship finally arrived, it was a day of great rejoicing; hundreds went to meet the boat at the dock.[14]

By the 1820's New Orleans heard three or four performances of opera each week during the season. Nor was this opera relegated to drama or melodrama as had been the case earlier and as still was the practice throughout the rest of the United States. The *Théâtre d'Orléans* presented full-fledged grand opera, as pure as that given in Europe. In 1825 the Marquis de Lafayette, the French revolutionary leader, visited New Orleans and attended a performance at the *Orléans*. Lafayette stated without hesitation that the theater, the singers, and the audience could compete with those of the most famous opera houses of Europe. He was particularly impressed with the elegant dress of both the men and the women and with the beauty of the Creole ladies, who sat in their boxes in a "truly queenly fashion."[15]

The *Théâtre d'Orléans* came to receive other distinguished visitors as the years went by. Three presidents of the United States were entertained there—Andrew Jackson, Martin Van Buren, and Zachary Taylor. "Certain it is," wrote a contemporary music critic, "that an evening passed at the *Théâtre d'Orléans* is an era of delight for anyone with a musical ear."[16]

By the 1820's the companies and the orchestras were large and of superior artistic caliber. The public, as well as the critics, growing more appreciative of the lyric theater, became exceptionally judicious in its musical tastes. The Creoles demanded the highest standards possible and tolerated no cutting or tampering with the score. Once a production of Rossini's *Semiramide* was offered with the last act omitted. The audience broke into a demonstration, "shouting, shaking fists, and throwing canes at the magnificent gas chandelier."[17]

Not only was this New Orleans opera significant in its home locale, but it also served as a stimulant to other American cities. Especially is this true of Philadelphia, which was introduced to opera by a New Orleans company in 1827. During that same year, a troupe from the *Théâtre d'Orléans* gave New York City a sampling of French opera and went on to tour several other major Eastern cities, bringing opera to many audiences that had never experienced the art before.[18]

After the death of John Davis, his son Pierre took over the management of the *Théâtre d'Orléans* for twenty-five years. Remarkable as the later efforts were, they rarely surpassed the productions given by the elder Davis in those early years. The operatic masterpieces of Rossini, Spontini, Mozart, Méhul, Grétry, Gluck, and other great composers of the time were presented under the Davises, always in a grandiose style. As the years passed, a surprising number of operas received their first American production here in the *Orléans*. Time and again, musical reference books list American premiere dates for operas in New York or Philadelphia when in reality a careful examination of contemporary newspapers will reveal that these works had been staged years earlier in New Orleans. For example, when the Metropolitan staged Spontini's *La Vestale* in 1925 for Rosa Ponselle, rumor had it that the United States was seeing the opera for the first time. Early newspapers, however, show that *Vestale* had been presented in New Orleans as early as February 17, 1828.[19] According to most sources, Bellini's *Norma* was given for the first time in the United States at the Chestnut Theater in Philadelphia on January 11, 1841. But New Orleans had heard the opera at least fifteen times before that date, and in 1836 alone the Bellini work received ten performances there.[20] That same year another Bellini opera, *Il Pirata*, received its American premiere in the Crescent City.[21] Meyerbeer's *Les Huguenots*, which was to become the most popular opera of all with the Louisiana Creoles, was given its first American performance in the city in 1839, only a few months after its world premiere in Paris.[22] Dozens of European singers came to New Orleans to display their talents and returned to the Continent without having sung a note in any other city in the United States.

An opening night in New Orleans was anticipated for months in advance, and the event always proved dazzling. The 1838 season, for example, opened with Rossini's *The Barber of Seville*, sung, as usual for this city, in French. The house was filled to capacity, and "a most brilliant galaxy of beauty and fashion . . . graced the boxes and dress circles."[23] To assume, however, that these fashionably-attired first nighters had come to the theater merely for ostentatious purposes would be to err. Music, undoubtedly, was the paramount interest. The Creole audiences were as intelligent and courteous as any likely to be assembled. Complete silence was observed during the performance, and no artist was ever interrupted in the middle of an aria by the cheers and applause of an unsophisticated house. Neither were "the ears of a lady pained by coarse expressions from the upper boxes."[24]

Outsiders were inclined to feel that New Orleans was music mad, so intense was the Creole enthusiasm. Casual visitors to the city were baffled by the fact that these people went to the opera at six o'clock in the evening and left the theater only in time to attend midnight Mass at the Cathedral. To northerners particularly, this could spell nothing short of insanity.[25]

And yet, glorious as the *Théâtre d'Orléans* was, for years something was missing. The romantic New Orleanians yearned for a glamorous prima donna to adorn their stage. In 1837 their dreams were realized in the form of twenty-two-year-old Julia Calvé. Madame Calvé, blessed with a petite figure, a magnificent head of black hair, and eyes described as "the most beautiful in the world," was every inch the prima donna. With her debut as Rosina in *The Barber of Seville* she was an immediate sensation. Overnight New Orleans fell in love with this stunning soprano, and she, returning the city's affection, promptly took up permanent residence there. Before long the diva met local businessman and social dandy Charles Boudousquie, who began taking a deeper interest in both opera and La Calvé. Shortly the two were married, and the city bubbled with the excitement of a story-book romance. Boudousquie eventually became the manager of the *Théâtre d'Orléans*, following the successful Pierre Davis, and under her husband's direction Mme. Calvé went on to even higher goals and even greater successes.[26]

Meyerbeer's *Les Huguenots* and Donizetti's *Anna Bolena* and *Les Martyrs* (the French version of *Poliuto*) all served as vehicles for the Calvé talents. But of Julia Calvé's many triumphs, none was more complete than her creation of *Lucia di Lammermoor* in the opera's American premiere, December 28, 1841. The opera, presented in French, two years before its initial staging in New York, was received with great enthusiasm by the Creoles, and Calvé's "Mad Scene" was a vocal gem which the city treasured for many years.[27]

Almost all of the operas given in New Orleans at this time were sung in French, although many of them were actually penned by Italian composers. The sets and costumes for the operas were generally imported from Paris. The prima donnas—Calvé, Fleury-Joly, and Borghese, to name a few—were reputedly as poised, as glamorous, and as talented as any to be found on the European continent. The conductors were the best to be had. Maestro Eugene Prevost, whose *La Esmeralda* was a favorite in the city, was an operatic composer of no little merit himself. Nor were the productions staged in a provincial manner, for the Creoles were particularly taken with operatic spectacle. During the second act of *Les Martyrs*, for instance, the Proconsul Severus entered in a triumphal chariot, followed by soldiers, magistrates, banners, slaves, and a horde of extras —much to the delight of both public and critics.[28]

Early in 1851 the music-loving New Orleanians saw real operatic history made when the notorious showman P. T. Barnum brought Jenny Lind, the Swedish Nightingale, to the city. When word spread that the soprano was to appear, the city was thrown into a frenzy. Virtually every shop in the *Vieux Carré* buzzed with rumors and gossip concerning the event. The Pontalba Apartments were prepared for the diva, and in the midst of the furor the city kept a watchful eye on the pier at Jackson Square, where the singer's boat was to dock.

When the good ship *Falcon* finally dropped anchor with the prima donna on board, the whole town must have crowded the docks to greet her. Mme. Lind took one look at the clamoring throng and refused to budge from her cabin. To placate her Barnum sent out several ladies as decoys, but the enthusiastic populace was not so easily fooled. The showman, however, had another plan. This time an elegantly dressed lady wearing a green veil was escorted down the gangplank, ceremoniously placed in a carriage, and driven to the Pontalba Apartments. Most of the crowd fell for Barnum's deception and anxiously joined the procession. But alas, when the gallant lady emerged from the carriage, she proved nothing more than the soprano's maid.

Returning to the docks, the crowd shortly saw Barnum himself escorting another veiled damsel into a fine carriage. Once more the mob followed in eager anticipation. But again deceit. This veiled one knew no music whatever. She too was a fraud. The patience of the normally good-natured New Orleanians was rapidly becoming strained to the point of riot when, appearing on the balcony of the apartments, was none other than Jenny Lind herself. The aroused tempers were soon soothed as Mme. Lind blew a traditional kiss to the crowd and thanked her admirers for the honor they had paid her. It seems that during the turmoil, the singer, inconspicuously attired, had calmly boarded a dilapidated cab and arrived without ado at Mme. Pontalba's establishment.

Seats for the first night of the Lind engagement were auctioned off, the first being bought by a Mr. D'Arcy, proprietor of a hat shop at Canal and Chartres Streets, for a price of $240. Opera lovers from all over the South came to hear her performances, and planters even designated "Jenny Lind" cotton bales to pay for the trip to New Orleans. Charlotte Cushman, the great American tragedienne, who normally played to packed houses in the city, found 1851 to be her poorest season there. Not even Miss Cushman's Lady Macbeths and Meg Merilleses could compete with the golden voice of Jenny Lind. Theatrical managers made a fortune from the diva's appearances. The total receipts have been figured at $135,000, and this, keep in mind, was at pre-Civil War prices.[29]

Local critics found their vocabularies inadequate to describe the Lind voice. The *Weekly Picayune* reported: "She is a true artist in the most exalted sense of the word; with a voice cultivated in the very highest school of art, till cultivation can improve it no longer or bring it under more control."[30] During a single evening, the soprano sang arias from *Robert le Diable*, "*Casta diva*" from *Norma*, and the "Mad Scene" from *Lucia di Lammermoor*. After each performance the ovations were thunderous.

For sheer drama the 1853–54 season was one of the most eventful in all New Orleans' musical history. Artistically, it is fairly typical of the operatic diet which the city had almost come to take for granted. The pre-season excitement was climaxed on November 4, when the ship *Belle Assise,* arriving from Le Havre, docked with members of the French opera troupe on board. During the summer months the *Théâtre d'Orléans* had been completely redecorated and was now ready for the grand opening.[31]

The season was launched on November 15, with *The Barber of Seville*, headed by "a new and talented cast . . . selected for the occasion."[32] Then in rapid succession were staged a number of works which had become Creole favorites: Rossini's *Otello*, Donizetti's *La Favorita*, Halévy's *Charles VI*, Meyerbeer's *Le Prophète*, and the perennial favorite *Les Huguenots*.

On Sunday, February 26, 1854, an afternoon performance of a new vaudeville piece, *La Petite Fille de la Grande Armée,* was being given. The *Théâtre d'Orléans* was crowded to capacity, as Mr. Carrier, a popular comedian of the day, was starring. The first act had been performed to the amusement of the house, and the second was drawing to a rollicking close. Then suddenly, "a sharp report, like that of a musket," startled the audience. Most of the spectators at first thought that the noise was a part of the action on stage and prepared themselves for another hilarious episode. "But, in another moment, a universal cry of alarm—a general rising—a rush—the crackling and crashing of timber—the screams of women and shouts of men told too plainly another tale."[33]

The third gallery, the one to the left of the stage, had given away under the weight of the packed house. This gallery, occupied mainly by Negroes, was attached by iron columns to the one immediately below it. Until this season the second gallery had been supported by additional columns which rested on the first tier, but with the recent remodeling these had been removed, and the dress circle extended out for some distance. Consequently, when the third gallery fell, the second was doomed to go with it.

The struggle of the crowd to escape the destruction was a scene of total bedlam. Survivors described it as "something utterly paralyzing and horrifying—exceeding any steamboat explosion, or conflagration, or railroad catastrophe they ever witnessed."[34] Fortunately, not all of the iron supports broke at once, "else, instead of slowly setting down like the leaves of a table, both galleries would have gone straight down on the dress circle and parquette, crushing all in them."[35] Also, the second gallery fell so that it rested at a wide angle against the wall and the back row of boxes in the dress circle, therefore leaving a sort of roof over the passageway behind the boxes which afforded an avenue of safety to many.

The events of that Sunday afternoon were more tragic than any operatic drama. The calamity left the city stunned and mournful. However, opera at the *Orléans* was quick to revive; within a short time, the theater was repaired, and the debris of the disaster cleared away. Even before the end of the 1853–54 season, the theater was flourishing again on a grand scale.

By the mid-fifties ticket prices at the *Théâtre d'Orléans* ranged from $1.50 to fifty cents, with seats in the dress circle, the latticed boxes, the parquet, and the second balcony all most expensive. The theater's seating capacity by that time had been expanded to 1,350 persons.[36]

Then, early in 1859, the *Théâtre d'Orléans* was sold to a new owner, Charles Parlange, who promptly boosted the rental fee on the house by a rather sizable amount. M. Boudousquie, who had been the opera manager for several years now, was infuriated by this price increase and in a fit of rage stormed out of Parlange's office, vowing he would build a new theater rather than submit to such unreasonable demands. On March 4, a stock company with a capitalization of $100,000 was organized for just that purpose.

The company lost no time in purchasing a building site, at the corner of Bourbon and Toulouse Streets, while M. Boudousquie set out to find an architect. The impresario first called on the famous Pouilly, designer of the St. Louis Hotel. But this was March, and Boudousquie insisted that the house be ready for the opening of the season in December. Pouilly felt the deadline impossible and would have no part of the project. Next the manager went to James Gallier, Jr., whose father had created the Pontalba Buildings, City Hall, and the St. Charles Hotel. After much discussion young Gallier agreed to the demands, and the contracts were signed.

Actual construction on the building began in June, with the workers laboring in shifts day and night. City officials even consented to the building of huge bonfires to assist in the night-time operations. After a frantic race against time, on November 28—just 233 days after the first plans were made—the finishing touches were put on the French Opera House, shortly to become "the lyric temple of the South."[37]

The theater, built at a cost of $118,500, was designed in an Italian Renaissance style and constructed chiefly of plastered bricks. The edifice contained four stories, with four curved tiers rising one above the other, each gradually receding. The interior color scheme was white with red and gold decorations. Strategically placed were magnificent chandeliers, and two broad staircases led up to the boxes. On the ground floor of the auditorium, upholstered armchairs offered the ultimate in comfort, while each of the theater's 2,000 seats permitted a perfect view of the stage. On either side of the proscenium, a huge mirror added to the sweeping effect of the interior panorama.[38]

The French Opera House, the crowning achievement in the history of the lyric theater in New Orleans, was the climax of a long, illustrious operatic tradition. With its completion the new theater at Bourbon and Toulouse Streets dominated the city's musical life. Not even the stately *Théâtre d'Orléans* could compete. While the

Orléans did linger for a number of years, with Parlange for a time staging opera regularly, it soon became obvious that the old establishment was no match for its youthful rival, a theater more modern and ambitious. On December 7, 1866, a fire was discovered in the wardrobe room, and shortly the old structure was engulfed in flames.[39] For over forty years the *Théâtre d'Orléans* had maintained standards of artistry unsurpassed in America and only slightly below those of the best opera houses of Europe. It had been the home of beautiful, ennobling music, but progress and a series of unforeseen misfortunes had forced the theater to a premature grave. The French Opera House was now the undisputed center of opera in the South.

The Ballad
of Bourbon Street

On Thursday, December 1, 1859, the French Opera House was formally opened with a gala production of Rossini's *William Tell*. The management had selected the opera because it permitted as many members of the company as possible to appear on stage. Eugene Prevost, the noted New Orleans composer, conducted. "This long-looked for event," reported the *New Orleans Daily Crescent*, "was ushered in with a large, brilliant, and fashionable audience, . . . every available position being occupied and the house positively jammed."[1] The first-night audience was ecstatic over the new theater, calling it "superb indeed." And the company outdid itself, giving a beautiful rendering of the Rossini masterpiece. One critic reported: "If I may premise this first night as a guarantee for the future representations, the lovers of good music may rest satisfied of having some rich treats in store."[2]

And how rich those treats were. The season at the French Opera House generally ran for three months. The singers, the orchestra, and the *corps de ballet* were all recruited from France, just as in the days of the *Théâtre d'Orléans*. As a rule forty subscription performances were presented each year, given on Tuesday, Thursday, and Saturday nights. A matinee performance of either grand or light opera was usually staged on Sunday afternoons, while Sunday nights were devoted to operetta. As in the case of all good opera,

15

the enterprise was carried on at great expense and rarely proved financially successful. The lack of funds was seldom a deterring factor, however, for benevolent patrons of the arts always underwrote deficits.[3]

Although the first season at the French Opera House proved highly successful, the second ran into difficulty. The operas the city normally found so fascinating seemed to lack appeal this year. The vocal fire was simply not catching hold. Largely because of the sectional crisis which was soon to tear the nation to shreds, the audiences seemed preoccupied, distant, and nervous. Their minds and hearts, it seemed, were not on grand opera.

On the morning of November 23, 1860, however, the New Orleanians picked up their copies of the *Daily Picayune*, thumbed through the first few pages, glanced at the steamship ads, and discovered in the amusements column an announcement that made them sit up and take notice—Adelina Patti was to make a series of appearances in the city.[4]

Adelina Patti, a slight, dark, Italian girl, yet to see her eighteenth birthday, had given a concert in New Orleans five years before and, child though she was, had made a profound impression. The girl possessed a captivating child-like beauty and, more important, a thrilling soprano voice.

There could be little doubt that M. Boudousquie was badly in need of a thrilling voice at the moment, for a whole chain of mishaps had marred his second season at the French Opera House. Once more a prima donna was lacking. The impresario's wife, Julia Calvé, had retired from the stage by now and was teaching voice. Before the season opened, the manager had contracted with a mysterious diva who he hoped would prove a sensation. But a sensation she was not. Some writers claim that the singer playfully jumped on a chair and broke her leg, while others lament that the lady had no voice.[5] Yet without a prima donna the French Opera House was only half an opera house. Couple that with the impending war crisis, which loomed larger each day, and the season seemed doomed.

Suddenly M. Boudousquie recalled Adelina Patti, whose earlier concert had been such a triumph. Could this mere child do what more experienced artists had failed to do? Was it possible that she could spark the excitement necessary to save Boudousquie's season?

If the laws of musical nature ran true, this child prodigy, like most child prodigies, would fall flat in young womanhood. It was a game of chance that Boudousquie played, a calculated risk at best. The results were dubious; the impresario held his breath.

On the night of December 19, 1860, the New Orleanians flocked to the French Opera House, eager to hear what the young diva could do with Donizetti's *Lucia di Lammermoor*. Throughout the introductory scene, the audience sat nervous. The tension mounted. Then at last, a harp interlude, a long moment of expectant anxiety, and suddenly Patti was on stage. At her entrance "the debutante was courteously, though not extravagantly greeted."[6] It was obvious that the soprano was to be tried on her merits and that she would not win an ovation until she had earned it. The trial, however, was a short one. Patti sang the difficult, ornate passages with complete ease and brilliance. By the time she came to the florid *cabaletta*, the audience was at her mercy, responding to her every note and gesture. At the close of the first act, all the pent-up emotions were unleased, and the house went wild. The soprano was called before the curtain again and again. States' rights, secession, the slavery issue, the growing threat of civil war were all momentarily forgotten. As far as New Orleans was concerned, Adelina Patti was the gem of all vocal jewels; nothing else mattered.

M. Boudousquie had his star, and a brilliant one she was, too. Like the opera-going public, the critics genuinely fell under the spell of her delightful musical witchcraft. The *Daily Picayune* reported: "Adelina Patti is gifted with a voice of singular sweetness, purity, capacity of volume, and range of register. It is of the most delicious quality of soprano, and as smooth, even, equable, and true as possible." And, the critic went on, "She is a born actress as well as singer."[7]

Patti's singing had a tonic effect upon the city, and, if ever a stimulant was needed, it was now. On the day after the diva's debut, South Carolina by a unanimous vote of the Charleston convention seceded from the Union. The war clouds were drawing thicker; decisions would have to be made soon. If the South declared itself independent, Louisiana had no choice but to follow. And yet many in the state had grave misgivings about such a path—a path strewn with unforeseen dangers and obstacles. Had any times been more troubled than these? During that winter of 1860 the perplexed New Orleanians felt not. The only solace the city seemed to find was in that petite Italian girl at the French Opera House. Her voice had the power to make people forget, at least for the moment.

On December 29, Patti sang the lead in Flotow's *Martha*, and two nights later she was Rosina in *The Barber of Seville*, singing the "Echo Song" and the Scottish ballad " 'Twas Within a Mile of Edinboro' Town" in the "Lesson Scene."[8] Two evenings later, January 2, 1861, the young artist did the impossible. She sang Leonora in Verdi's *Il Trovatore* only eight days after she began learning the part. Not only had Patti been singing three nights a week, but at the same time she had mastered one of the most demanding roles in the Italian repertoire. The soprano did *Il Trovatore* at the French Opera House without ever having rehearsed it. When she sang Leonora on stage that night, it was for the first time full voice. Yet, according to the *Daily Picayune*, the performance "was almost faultless throughout, both in singing and acting."[9]

Originally Patti had been scheduled for only six performances in New Orleans. The enthusiasm for her, however, was so great, and the size of the audiences she commanded so large, that Boudousquie quickly re-engaged the singer for several extra performances. On February 6, she sang Gilda in Verdi's *Rigoletto* for her first time on any stage and received tremendous ovations. The press declared: "M'lle Adelina Patti's Gilda is one of the finest things she does."[10] On March 4, Meyerbeer's new opera *The Pardon of Ploërmel* was given its American premiere, with Patti in the role of Dinorah.[11] Every time the diva sang, the results were the same— exuberant ovations, repeated curtain calls, and praise from the critics. In the years ahead Adelina Patti would go on to even greater acclaim, appearing in all the music capitals of the world, but New Orleans (in spite of the fact that she had sung earlier in New York, Boston, and Philadelphia) always felt that it had discovered the singer and given her her initiation to fame.

The sectional controversy which had been raging for well over a decade had reached a climax now. On January 26, 1861, less than a fortnight before Patti's first *Rigoletto*, Louisiana seceded from the Union. Eleven weeks later Fort Sumter was fired upon, and President Lincoln issued a call for troops to squelch the Southern rebellion. Within a year New Orleans was in northern hands.

French Opera House, New Orleans

Interior of French Opera House, New Orleans

Rice's Theater, Chicago, 1850

Crosby's Opera House, Chicago

Following a fierce battle on land and sea, the infamous Benjamin F. Butler entered the city with an army of occupation 18,000 strong.

During the turbulence of war no one, not even the New Orleans Creoles, could think of opera. For four long, unhappy years the Opera House was dark. But shortly after Lee's surrender in 1865 the New Orleanians began longing more than ever for amusement and grand opera. Before the year was out three theatrical brothers named Alhaiza reopened the French Opera House with a company on tour. Their venture proved so successful that they decided the following season to import a full company from Europe.

To realize their plan, Charles and Marcelin Alhaiza sailed for Paris. A company was recruited; the arrangements were all made; and the troupe awaited departure for America. But on the eve of the sailing, Marcelin died. His brother Charles, however, boarded the ship with his company of artists, determined to continue the project as outlined. The ship arrived in New York City, where on September 29, 1866, the troupe embarked on the steamer *Evening Star* for New Orleans.[12]

The destination was never reached. On October 3, the *Evening Star*, with some three hundred persons on board, was caught up in a storm and foundered at sea, about 180 miles southeast of Tybee Island, off the coast of Georgia. Only a handful of passengers survived the disaster, and the entire troupe for the Opera House, along with its manager Charles Alhaiza, perished. The elder Gallier, father of the architect who designed the French Opera House, was among the victims, along with a number of other noted New Orleanians.[13]

The surviving Alhaiza, Paul, still had aspirations of returning opera to the river city. Shortly he arranged an engagement with the Ghioni and Susini Italian Opera Company, which opened a brief season at the Opera House on Monday, November 19, 1866. The visit lasted only six nights and was most notable in introducing to the city Amelia Patti, Adelina's contralto sister. Later that same season, Alhaiza brought in the Italian Company of the Grand Theatre of Mexico for a few performances,[14] and gradually the offering became more regular. By the early seventies the French Opera House was back in full operation.

As much as the New Orleanians loved the old French favorites, the Meyerbeer works particularly, they were always delighted by the prospects of a local premiere. In the seventies and eighties new works, like Gounod's *Romeo and Juliet*, Thomas' *Mignon*, and Bizet's *Carmen*, were introduced to the city and heard with keen interest.

For the Creoles any premiere or opening night performance at the Opera House was an experience never to be forgotten, an event of unparalleled importance, and an occasion which one could not afford to miss if he chose to maintain his reputation as a lover of good music. Virtually all of New Orleans turned out for the event, irrespective of financial position. The humble opera-goer with fifty cents in his pocket rubbed shoulders with wealthy gentlemen whose wallets bulged with hundred-dollar bills. Opera in New Orleans was a democratic institution; a love for music was the unifying link.[15]

By three-thirty in the afternoon on the day of an opening, a few enthusiasts could already be seen standing in line for seats in the third and fourth tiers. Opera among the New Orleans Creoles was serious business. It was not a luxury item, but one of life's basic essentials. "The housekeeper," says Harnett Kane, "planning her week, might omit meat from a meal or two; tomorrow, soup and nothing else. But seldom would she fail to set aside the twenty-five-cent pieces for the family's visits to the temple of music."[16]

Young up-and-coming men with ambition never hesitated to borrow formal dress from their wealthier relatives, or they might mortgage their salaries or even borrow money from friends in order to rent a tuxedo for the gala occasion. In any event the youths were there on opening night, "mingling with the rich, the intellectual, the critics, the snobs, and discussing with them the merits or the failings of . . . the singers with as much sapience and with the same degree of authority and fervor which they themselves possessed."[17] The very fact that one was present for this grand event seemed to give him the right to fraternize with people he ordinarily would not have approached and to discuss—and even argue—the fine points of the performance with them.

On such an occasion the parquet was filled to capacity with the established ladies and gentlemen of the city, dressed in their most formal attire. The proscenium boxes were filled by the regular occupants, along with their guests, and were the center of attention. The horseshoe on the first tier was occupied with "the most beautiful girls of New Orleans and the vicinity, in *décolleté* and wielding fans of rare plumage and variegated colors, wearing in their hair or around snowy white delicate throats dazzling pieces of jewelry."[18] The second tier was also filled with spectators in formal dress, and up in the third and fourth tiers, the *paradis,* as it was often called, sat people in business suits, less elegantly dressed perhaps, but no less astute in their musical judgment.

Between acts the first-nighters would visit from box to box, and some might even climb up to the higher galleries to talk with their poorer relatives. In either case the discussion concerning the strong and weak points of the performance continued. Had the tenor sung with the proper phrasing? Was the soprano's range equal to the demands of the score? The entire production was analyzed by an audience whose musical tastes were the highest.[19]

By far the majority of the New Orleanians walked to the theater, in fair weather or foul, and on the way home after an exciting performance, one could catch snatches of the opera's melodies being hummed or whistled by the young men as they walked homeward along the dark streets.[20]

For days after a premiere or season's opening, the city bustled with talk concerning the latest triumph at the French Opera House. Political issues, business affairs, even such all-important topics as fashion and weather, were momentarily pushed aside by the chatter over the latest operatic display. And this was not a matter to be passed over lightly, nor was it a subject the Creoles could joke about. "One would have thought that the very existence of the city hung in the balance," writes André Lafargue, "as these discussions went on . . . sometimes degenerating into fights or acrimonious remarks."[21]

Not even the dedication of the modern-day television addict, bloodshot though his eyes may be, surpasses that of the Creoles for their opera. A favorite anecdote among New Orleanians concerns a Creole belle who came dangerously close to being born in one of the boxes at the French Opera House. It seems that not until the middle of the third act of *Faust* did her mother, Mme. Blanque, turn to M. Blanque and somewhat excitedly state, "Pierre, I do not think I can wait for the ballet!"[22]

Another often repeated story centers around a small, middle-aged woman who lived in the French Quarter and had long ago reconciled herself to a life of spinsterhood. For years the little lady had earned her modest living at one service or another, sometimes clerking, sometimes working in a millinery shop, sometimes making Mardi Gras masks, but never did she meet any man who would show her the least bit of attention. Then in the 1870's a cousin gave up her concession stand at the French Opera House, allowing her spinster relative to take it over. Suddenly the pallid little woman was besieged by a horde of eager suitors, and within a month she had become a bride, taking her choice of several marital proposals. The explanation lay in the fact that the man who married her would get free admission to the Opera House, a boon worth even such a sacrifice![23]

As one walked about the French Quarter in the days of the French Opera House, he found himself in a world truly entranced with music and, especially, grand opera. "Melody showered the streets. From the window of this galleried house rose the notes of an aria; Madame was repeating a second-act number from last night's opera. Over there, carrying a basket of crabs on her head, a *marchande* sang still another solo."[24] The Creoles knew their music and were as severe and quick in their criticism as today's college sophomore is of the Saturday football game. As one continued his walk through the *Vieux Carré*, he might well find on any corner an argument raging over the qualities of this or that voice. "Ah, good—yes, but not so good as La Dauterive. When I was a boy . . . that divine trill, the way she held it, two minutes—no, three! And who could ever die of consumption so well?"[25] The baker from Lyon and the grocer across the alley both boasted of not having missed a week at the Opera House in the last fifteen years. The little sewing woman who lived in the cubbyhole down on St. Anne Street and her husband, the barber's assistant, were as poor as the proverbial church mouse, but they loved their music and attended the French Opera House regularly.[26]

To satisfy these tastes, the management staged opera with the highest standards possible. Never was a new work presented until it had been thoroughly rehearsed and until the production weaknesses had been ironed out. Perfection was the aim at the Opera House, and rarely was the attainment far below the goal set.

Early in 1885 New Orleans enjoyed another of its truly great operatic experiences when the legendary British impresario James Henry Mapleson brought Her Majesty's Opera Company to the city. With him Mapleson brought not one, but two prima donnas, Emma Nevada and Adelina Patti. Mme. Patti had become the toast of the musical world since her fabulous 1861 season in the river city, but was still relatively young and in her vocal prime. American-born Emma Nevada had recently skyrocketed to fame and at this time was one of the leading singers in Europe.

Mapleson opened his New Orleans engagement with Bellini's popular *La Sonnambula,* featuring Emma Nevada as the night-strolling Amina. The following evening Patti revived old memories and gave the city some new ones with a sensational interpretation of Violetta in Verdi's *La Traviata.* Patti's triumph in fact was so complete that near disaster resulted. Just before the last act of the opera, some plaster fell from the front of the dress circle, causing a moment of panic. In the confusion someone shouted "Fire!"—a cry which was repeated throughout the house. A general stampede to the doors began, and several ladies actually fainted from the shock and excitement. Fortunately a few calm souls, veterans, perhaps, of the great gallery collapse of '54, kept their wits and eventually managed to quiet the fleeing crowd. It seems that the stamping of feet and the unrestrained applauding for Patti had loosened the plaster and caused it to fall.[27]

For two glorious weeks Her Majesty's Opera Company played at the French Opera House. Mme. Patti brought sheer vocal magic with her appearances in Rossini's *Semiramide,* Donizetti's *Linda di Chamounix,* and Flotow's *Martha.* Emma Nevada was no less the vocal sorceress in *Faust, I Puritani,* and *Lucia di Lammermoor.* One critic even wrote, "Mlle. Nevada excells all the Lucias that ever appeared on the New Orleans lyric stage, taking everything together."[28] And what praise this was; for, if the judgment were correct, it would include the *Lucia* which Patti herself gave in 1861, a performance which by now had reached mythical proportions.

Her Majesty's Opera Company finished its 1885 season in New Orleans in a blaze of glory and remained the talk of the town for weeks to come. But Mmes. Patti and Nevada had not won their ovations easily, for the artistic competition had been ruthless indeed. Playing in the city at the same time was another popular theatrical spectacle, Buffalo Bill's Wild West Show. Who but Adelina Patti and Emma Nevada, even in New Orleans, could hope to compete with Buffalo Bill's sharpshooters, his herd of thundering horses, and his pack of commercially savage redskins? A prima donna of any less stature would simply have had to recognize the box-office facts of life, pack up her bag of operatic tricks and leave.

The 1885–86 season at the French Opera House was rather unusual in that the entire season was devoted to *opéra bouffe*. The two outstanding stars that year were Alice and Tony Reine, who thoroughly delighted audiences with their melodic capers.[29] With the close of this comic interlude, however, the management returned to a more serious and varied lyric diet.

With the 1890's came another host of American premieres for the Crescent City. Massenet's *Hérodiade*, Lalo's *Le Roi d'Ys*, and Saint-Saëns' *Samson and Delilah* were just a few of the works to receive their first American staging on the boards of the French Opera House.[30]

One of the most exciting premieres ever staged in New Orleans was that given Gounod's *La Reine de Saba* on January 12, 1899. The work had long been a favorite on the concert stage, but the scenic effects and stage mechanism of the opera were so difficult and complex that most managers simply were afraid to mount the piece. The story centers around Adoniram, a famous sculptor and molder of bronze, who is asked by King Solomon to decorate the palace in honor of his bride, the Queen of Sheba. The opera is spectacle from start to finish. In the second act, for instance, the Queen of Sheba makes her grand entrance into the city of Jerusalem in a scene that requires unlimited stage grandeur. But the third act is even more demanding, for here Adoniram's workshops are shown, complete with a visible furnace burning full blast.

As presented at the French Opera House, this scene was a magnificent piece of stagemanship. The fire effects were so realistically carried out that many of the spectators began to fidget and look anxiously toward the nearest exit. The center of the stage was occupied by a huge blast furnace which smoked and rumbled most authentically. When the signal was given, the door of the furnace opened. At once a stream of molten metal poured forth and slowly ran into a mold. Suddenly, with a rumble the furnace burst, and the burning metal poured out upon the floor. "The stage, which a moment before had been trodden by swarms of people, was gone, and in its stead a billowy sea of crimson fire."[31]

So impressive was the scene that the audience immediately rose to its feet, applauding joyously and crying "Charley! Charley!"—M. Charley being the manager of the Opera House at the time. Finally, not only the impresario, but also M. Gaston Noblet, the mechanical director responsible for these spectacular effects, appeared on stage, as the house broke into a frenzy of enthusiasm. Poor M. Noblet was so confused by the unprecedented curtain call that he came dangerously close to falling into the fiery furnace which he himself had created!

The production was a sensation. The public loved it, and the critics called Gounod's music "masterly." The visual effects were said to be "the acme of scenic splendor on the operatic stage in New Orleans."[32] The management was well pleased with itself and pleased, too, that it had not been necessary to use the fire engine that had been standing at the stage entrance all during the performance on the chance that M. Noblet's creation might be guilty of overacting.

Another impressive premiere came on January 25, 1900, when Reyer's *Salammbô* was presented for the first time in the United States. The production was one of the most sumptuous ever staged by the Opera House, with lavish sets imported from France and a stellar cast. The opera's grand ballet was deemed the most gorgeous displayed in many a year. But the climax occurred in the last act, when Matho, the barbarian leader, appeared at the top of a long flight of stairs, wounded and bleeding, lashed relentlessly onward by his tormentors. He fell, rolling down the great staircase, and lay in a faint at the feet of his beloved Salammbô. The performance of M. Gauthier, the tenor to whom this vocally and physically demanding role was allotted, left the audience spellbound, so realistically did he act the part.[33]

The 1900–01 season brought Puccini's *La Bohème* to the city for the first time, a year after its first Metropolitan performance. The New Orleans opera-goers were deeply moved by the production, but during the last act especially a "flood of emotion" swept through the Opera House, so touching was the death scene. "Mimi's silent passing away with her hands still clasping the little muff," wrote one reviewer, "will haunt one for many a day."[34] The composer's *Tosca*, heard in New Orleans for the first time in 1905, was less favorably received. "*Tosca* is better as a drama than as an opera," reported the *Times-Democrat*. "The strongest proof of the dramatic mastery was that in the tremendous climax—the killing of Scarpia by Floria—music acknowledged its failure, and the action developed as pantomime." It was even suggested that the work might have been just as effective, if not more so, "had the original [Sardou] drama been retained and Puccini's music played as instrumental accompaniment."[35]

In 1909 an event occurred at the French Opera House which still causes tears to come to the eyes of those who recall it. During a performance of Verdi's *Il Trovatore*, M. Escalais, a tenor widely acclaimed in Paris, came to the famous aria *"Di quella pira,"* containing its three high C's. Escalais, who was having an especially glorious night, sang the aria magnificently, hitting all three C's head on. The audience showed its approval with a rousing ovation, and eventually M. Escalais was forced to step out of dramatic position and take a bow. Then resuming his pose, the tenor began the aria again, and again he hit all the high C's, perhaps more richly than before. Once more the audience broke loose with cheers and applause. But in a moment the tenor had again taken his dramatic stance, and the spectators held their breaths. He was going to try the taxing aria a third time. But again the singer hit all three high C's squarely and beautifully. The audience repeated its storm of applause, and for a fourth time the C's were brilliantly hit with apparent ease. The New Orleanians could not believe their ears. The enthusiasm was unparalleled, as the standing audience applauded and shouted in a frenzy. And then, as the house gasped, Escalais raised his hand for silence. He was going to try the notes a fifth time. It seemed impossible!

All in all, the tenor hit fifteen consecutive high C's without a dodge or a slur. A Creole descendant recalls the evening to this day. He and his brothers and sisters were at home in bed, when their father burst into the house, shouting to them wildly as he climbed the stairs to their rooms. The children were panic-stricken, assuming that some terrible tragedy had struck. As they ran to their papa, the man's face was red, and his voice was shaking: "Fifteen high C's, I tell you—fifteen!" The whole French Quarter was thrown into a commotion by the episode, and the story has been repeated over and over to each new generation.[36]

The productions at the French Opera House at the dawn of the twentieth century were as sumptuous as any given in the theater's long, illustrious history. Nougues' *Quo Vadis*, for example, introduced to the city in 1913, contained a scene representing the arena of the Colosseum so elaborate that it took the stage crew twenty minutes to mount it.[37] New operas, like Massenet's *Don Quichotte*, which had its American premiere in New Orleans in 1912,[38] were staged each year, and standards remained unexcelled.

And yet something was wrong. A mysterious blight had begun to attack the theater just before the outbreak of World War I. Each season the effort seemed greater, and the results less successful. Production costs were constantly on the increase, and the theater was urgently in need of repairs. The management had recently undergone a tremendous expense in compliance with the new rat-proofing ordinance. At the same time that operating costs were increasing, the Carnival organizations, which for years had served as a major source of income for the house, began demanding a reduction in the rentals charged them. As the debts mounted, the Opera House began to fade. Suddenly it seemed old-fashioned and out-dated.

With the coming of the war in 1914, all seemed lost. Now France, the source of the theater's very lifeblood, had been cut off. No singers, directors, scenery, costumes, or anything else could be imported. As if these trials were not enough, on September 29, 1915, a storm wracked the city, leaving the French Opera House in a sad state. As a result, the theater was closed, and the opera association passed into the hands of a receiver.[39]

Soon the old structure at the corner of Bourbon and Toulouse Streets began to suffer from neglect. Fortunately, William Ratcliffe Irby, a wealthy tobacco manufacturer and noted philanthropist, purchased the building and presented it to Tulane University. In addition to the building itself, a significant sum of money was given to the university to repair the edifice and bring it back to life.[40]

After four years of darkness, the French Opera House was re-opened. Louis P. Verande now acted as impresario, and Harry B. Loeb as general manager. Both men were determined to restore opera in New Orleans to the high plane the city had known so long. When the curtain rose on November 11, 1919, everything pointed to a successful season, and hopes were flying high. The Great War was now over; the financial problems of the Opera House seemed under control; and opera appeared to be reviving.[41]

On Tuesday, December 2, 1919, New Orleans saw a restaging of its favorite opera, Meyerbeer's *Les Huguenots*. The city's opera-goers, as in days of old, were enthralled by the opera's spectacle and passion. The old enthusiasm, it appeared, had been sparked and was catching hold.[42] On the evening of December 3, a new production of *Carmen* was rehearsed. It seemed that the management had some real treats in store for the operatic public,[43] but in the early morning of Thursday, December 4, someone smelled smoke in the old theater. By dawn the entire structure was reduced to nothing but a heap of smoking ruins, surrounded by partially-destroyed walls.[44]

Half the population of New Orleans must have rushed to the scene of the holocaust, as the news of the disaster spread throughout the city. Novelist Harnett Kane, then a boy of nine, recalls being taken to the scene: "I remember the steaming wreckage, and my surprise that the ladies with odd foreign accents were crying so hard. This one had been the company's Delilah, that one the Gilda. This singer had lost jewels in her dressing-room, that one a complete wardrobe."[45]

As the New Orleanians stood before the smoking debris, many of them found memories of past happiness rushing through their minds, all of which were closely linked with the French Opera House. There were few men in the throng who did not have recollections of evenings "when they sat in the dreamy darkness of the old building, listening to the voices of great singers blending with the orchestra, and thrilling at the touch of a bit of gauze, as it brushed their cheeks."[46]

How the fire started no one is sure. It is highly probable that the flames originated in an overheated stove of the adjoining restaurant. But whatever its source, the disaster was complete. Not only was the Opera House destroyed, but countless costumes, scores, and instruments had burned as well, not to mention irreplaceable records, pictures, programs, and other items of historic interest.[47]

For sixty years the French Opera House had stood "like a great beacon of light and cultural encouragement."[48] The Opera House had been as important a part of New Orleans as Canal Street, the Cathedral, the Cabildo, the Pontalba Buildings, or Jackson Square. Not only had the structure been a music center of unparalleled importance, but it also had served as the setting for

most of the city's carnival balls and social functions following the
Mardi Gras parade. It had witnessed political conventions, bazaars,
scientific meetings, benefit concerts, and innumerable other events
significant in the social, political, and intellectual life of New Orleans. "It is no small wonder," wrote André Lafargue, "that we
who know so well what the edifice represented and what it stood
for in our midst, wept unashamed when we saw the walls of the
famous old building totter and fall with a dismal crash."[49]

At the time of the fire, there was a great deal of talk about building a new opera house, but this was to remain nothing more than a
vague and distant dream which continues to the present day. Tulane
University, which still held title to the property, carried only $57,-
000 worth of insurance on the building, and architects estimated
that to rebuild the theater would cost at least a million dollars.[50]
Consequently the opera house was never rebuilt. The famous site at
the corner of Bourbon and Toulouse Streets today is a parking lot,
frequented mostly by tourists thirsty for the entertainment and
drink which abound in the surrounding "nite spots."

The 1919–20 opera season, in progress at the time the theater
burned, was continued at the Athenaeum, a concert hall, with costumes from carnival wardrobes and storehouses. But this feeble attempt to keep the city's opera alive proved fruitless. The task of
reviving the old days of operatic glory had been difficult enough at
the Opera House. Now with the "lyric temple" no more, there
seemed no hope at all.[51]

And yet why did grand opera, which for so long had been the undisputed queen of all art forms in New Orleans, suddenly lose its
appeal? For decades the Creoles had cherished their opera as an integral part of the city's cultural life. Why, after all of these years,
did the art go out of vogue? Why had the French Opera House
begun to decline a few years before its destruction? Why was the
theater never rebuilt? Why was a quarter century to pass before
New Orleans could again boast a resident opera company—and that
one only a reflection of the city's past operatic glory?

A new generation of Creoles, second- and third-generation Americans, had appeared in the *Vieux Carré*. The youngsters, more Amer-
icanized and therefore further removed from the European traditions
than their parents, simply preferred a different type of music. As

early as 1900 the old opera-lovers were rapidly becoming a minority in the French Quarter, as a new attraction—jazz—revolutionized the city's musical pattern.

The new century brought life to Dixieland jazz and fame to the first great jazz artists. The legendary streets of the old French Quarter—Basin, North Rampart, Bourbon, all of which became virtually synonymous with jazz—were the locale for the birth of this new musical phenomenon. New Orleans shortly was hailed as the jazz capital of the world. By 1912 jazz had reached adolescence in the city and had taken the younger generation by storm. In 1914 W. C. Handy composed the "St. Louis Blues," one of the early classics in the field, and three years later the Original Dixieland Jazz Band made the first recording of "Tiger Rag." By 1917 the Jazz Age was definitely in full "swing," and the entire nation was rapidly falling under its spell.[52]

The history of opera in New Orleans and that of jazz stand essentially in converse proportions. As the new musical sound was developing, grand opera and the French Opera House were declining. That jazz usurped much of the enthusiasm for opera there can be little doubt. Opera remained the lifeblood of New Orleans' musical existence only as long as the city's Latin traditions outweighed the Anglo-American. Once the latter became supreme, it was to be expected that the French and Italian operas which the city had once loved so dearly would suffer. A new musical medium, one more consistent with the Anglo-American culture pattern, was bound to emerge.

While talk of rebuilding the Opera House continued, New Orleans saw little of the lyric theater during the twenty-five years following the great fire of 1919, relying solely on touring companies for its occasional operatic pleasures. For ten years, 1920–30, the city was deprived of any opportunity to hear truly grand opera. Finally, in 1930 the Chicago Civic Opera paid a short but brilliant visit to New Orleans, during which Mary Garden was heard in Massenet's *Le Jongleur de Notre Dame*. In 1935 and 1936, the San Carlo Opera Company gave performances in the Crescent City, while the Salzburg Opera Guild made a local appearance in 1937. For three consecutive seasons, 1939–41, the Metropolitan presented a series of operas there, playing to rather sizable audiences and receiving enthusiastic receptions.[53]

Strangely enough it was in the middle of World War II that resident opera returned to the city. A group of energetic music-lovers, headed by Walter L. Loubat, a local businessman and lifetime opera enthusiast, felt that the time had come—war or no war—to break this operatic fasting. Consequently, with Loubat as president, the New Orleans Opera House Association was organized, having as its ultimate goal the rebuilding of the old French Opera House. During the summer of 1943 the new organization went into action, staging an outdoor season of popular-priced opera in the scenic City Park. The enterprise operated on a financial shoestring, but "Opera under the Stars," as it was called, met with considerable success. The repertoire was made up of standard works (*Pagliacci, Carmen, Il Trovatore*), staged with artists of modest repute. For almost every performance the City Park Stadium was filled to capacity, proving that the city had not lost complete interest in the lyric theater after all.

Walter Loubat and the New Orleans Opera House Association, encouraged by this showing, were now determined to undertake a regular winter season, beginning the next fall. It was decided that, rather than give the whole season in a few crowded weeks, it would be wiser to stagger the productions over a period of about six months, beginning in October and ending in April. Each work would be presented twice, and there would be an interval of at least three weeks between operas. This arrangement would permit more rehearsal time, and with the scattered season more people would be able to attend every production. Also, the interest in opera could be kept up for a larger part of the year than if the offering were concentrated in a short span of time. Then too, the staggered season could be arranged so that the productions would not conflict with either the Christmas holidays or the Mardi Gras season, both of which were traditionally unprofitable for any type of cultural enterprise.[54]

As conductor and musical director of the new organization, Walter Herbert, of Vienna *Volksoper* and San Francisco Symphony fame, was brought to the city. The difficult behind-the-scenes work was finally completed; the Municipal Auditorium was rented for the productions; and the city's opera-lovers waited expectantly for opening night.

On October 29, 1943, the project was launched with a production of Verdi's *Rigoletto*. The results were almost disastrous! "If opera returned to New Orleans under the stars at City Park Stadium last summer," the *Times-Picayune* bluntly stated, "it all but stole away again at the Municipal Auditorium Friday night."[55] Within the traditional confines of the theater, the company appeared completely inadequate. The voices failed to deliver the proper emotions; the acting was generally forced and weak; and the twenty-nine-piece orchestra proved entirely too small. It was quite obvious that the demands of producing opera without the aid of microphones, amplifiers, and the effects of outdoor floodlights had strained the young company to the brink.

A few weeks later, however, the Association's reputation was considerably enhanced with a production of Bizet's *Carmen*. By this time the orchestra had been augmented and now even included a harp. The cast, headed by Viennese contralto Maria Mayhoff, was adequate and at times even rose to vocal heights.[56] The season of six productions continued with the same type of repertoire as had been presented the summer before—all safe, standard works. When the curtain fell on the final production that spring, the company's artistic ledger showed a number of definite weaknesses, but these were insignificant compared with the financial shortcomings.

And to a great extent this has been the history of the New Orleans Opera House Association. The company has repeatedly been wracked with budget problems, and from time to time bankruptcy has been far too close for comfort. In 1949, for example, Hugh M. Wilkinson, then president of the Association, preceded a performance of *Carmen* with a personal appeal for funds, warning that there would be no season the following year unless the company received additional backing.[57] Several crises later, the Association was forced to cancel the first two operas of the 1956–57 season, when the list of subscribers took an appreciable drop. The season opened that year a month late and had weathered only two productions when disaster struck again. In March, with a scheduled performance of *Faust* only a week away, the Opera House Association had a bare $122 in the till. On the eve of complete calamity, Fred Bultman, a member of the company's board of directors, went into action, and between Tuesday, March 12, and Thursday, March 14, raised over $40,000.[58] A message from Bultman in the programs the following season made the situation clear: "This is a year of decision

—we cannot go into another opera season with a deficit. . . . Our mothers sang arias from operas for lullabies to our children for more than a hundred and sixty-five years and will continue to do so for many years if we make our decision NOW."

By the spring of 1958, it was obvious that the old organizational machinery had broken down and that a new plan would have to be devised. A few months later, the Greater New Orleans Opera Foundation was organized to solve these financial difficulties. The Foundation consisted of one hundred members and a governing board of fifty trustees, which would work in conjunction with the Opera House Association, handling all the financial affairs of the company. The Opera House Association would be responsible only for the artistic aspects of production. All funds would be held in trust until actually needed by the Association. Then just before each of the season's six productions, one-sixth of the sum available would be released to meet expenses. Fortunately, this new business arrangement, aided by a rigid bookkeeping system, seems to be working out rather well.[59]

In view of these financial difficulties, it might be anticipated that the repertoire of the Opera House Association has been pretty routine. In the early years especially, this was quite true. *La Traviata*, for instance, was presented during five of the company's first six seasons. And for the most part the old war horses, particularly the Italian, have continued to dominate. French works are given occasionally, but the German operas, and even Mozart, have very little appeal here. This does not mean, however, that the city has not enjoyed an impressive list of novelties. Rossini's *La Cenerentola*, Massenet's *Werther*, Montemezzi's *L'Amore dei Tre Re*, and Carlisle Floyd's *Susannah* are just a few of the departures which the Association has taken through the years. The old French favorites, even *Les Huguenots*, once so popular in the city, are not done any more, partly because of the shortage of singers nowadays with the particular voice necessary to sing them and partly because the works seem to have lost their appeal, here as elsewhere. It would almost seem that these works perished with the French Opera House in 1919.

Most of the lead artists for the Opera House Association's productions come either from the Metropolitan or the New York City Opera. However, since the fees demanded by the well-established stars are often prohibitive, the company has devised a means for partially developing its own talent. From the very beginning, the Association consciously pursued a policy of promoting local singers —Marguerite Piazza and Norman Treigle among the more successful. Since 1955 the New Orleans Experimental Opera Theater has served to train young singers for subordinate roles and occasionally to groom a particularly brilliant youngster for leads. Each year Renato Cellini, who took over as the Association's artistic director when Walter Herbert resigned in 1954, supervises the interviewing of some five hundred to six hundred students, selecting the top twenty to take part in the Experimental Theater's spring operations. Those chosen to participate in this project will also be given subordinate roles in the regular winter season. In 1957 the Association received a grant of $165,000 from the Ford Foundation to assist in this elaborate training program.[60]

While the Experimental Theater supplies a portion of the chorus for the regular season, most of the choristers are recruited from local colleges and universities. Once the chorus is selected, it begins rehearsal in July under the direction of an experienced teacher. Since this is valuable training for these youngsters, they are not paid until the winter season actually begins. Then, everyone is paid on a union contract basis. The same is true of the ballet.[61]

In the early days of the Association, scenery, props, and lighting all served as artistic and monetary liabilities. Commenting on a 1945 production of *Traviata*, the *Times-Picayune* reviewer found the sets "entirely out of keeping with the tone of the production and . . . [the] props obviously . . . gathered from here and there."[62] Somewhat later a critic complained of the lighting, "We're developing a squint trying to discern what's going on."[63] Vast improvements were made in visual effects in the early 1950's, however, when the company established its own scenic studio for the designing and execution of sets and scenery. Since many of these basic sets are interchangeable, the cost of production was thus greatly reduced. Not only that, but these sets have frequently been rented to other companies. Tampa, Shreveport, Philadelphia, Fort Worth, and Houston have all borrowed scenery from New Orleans, an arrangement to the financial advantage of all concerned. The lighting equipment used in the Opera House Association's productions is also owned by the company now. Costumes are still rented, although most of the lead artists bring in their own.[64]

While the New Orleans Opera House Association has succeeded in returning opera to the river city, the organization has never come close to its ultimate goal, the rebuilding of the old French Opera House. The company's tenuous financial status has, of course, been a limiting factor, forcing a constant battle for mere existence. The not so simple task of producing opera has been all that the organization could possibly handle. And certainly the Association is to be commended for its valiant effort to carry on the great operatic tradition of the city's past.

Noble as the project is, however, it must be admitted that for the city that witnessed the first opera in the United States, thrilled to the marvelous productions of the *Théâtre d'Orléans* and the French Opera House, joyed to the golden voices of Jenny Lind and Adelina Patti, the present is only faintly representative of the past. Yet the city continues to dream. Perhaps André Lafargue put it best: "We still need a home for our new operatic productions, and that home must be a resurrection of the never to be forgotten French Opera House. Again we look to the corner of Bourbon and Toulouse Streets for a beacon of operatic endeavor. *En Avant!*"[65]

Opera on
the Great Lakes

When New Orleans was enjoying its first opera, on the shores of Lake Michigan there were hardly half-a-dozen whites outside the walls of Fort Dearborn. The closest thing to opera here was an occasional hymn or folk-tune, most probably sung to the accompaniment of a Kickapoo war drum. For the Northwest Territory this was a time of colonization, hard physical labor, and war, a time when its settlers were struggling for possession of the very soil on which they dwelt. Those willing to brave the unpleasantness of this prairie wilderness were rugged pioneers, having little time or interest for such gentlemanly frivolities as grand opera.

But as the years went by, this wilderness was transformed into a booming center of trade and commerce. What had once been a rustic frontier stronghold soon became the nucleus of a thriving community, a community destined to develop into a great industrial city. For where Fort Dearborn stood during the War of 1812, the city of Chicago appeared in the 1830's, noted first as a commercial terminal for lake traffic and later as the crossroads of the nation's railway system.

By mid-century Chicago had a population of about 28,000 and could boast of having heard its first opera. It was in the summer of 1850 that a small touring company was brought to J. B. Rice's Chicago Theater to give a series of Italian operas. The company landed on Monday, July 29, and, despite having just spent three hazardous days making its way by boat along the coast from Milwaukee, prepared to sing its first performance that very evening. The opera was Bellini's *La Sonnambula*, with Eliza Brienti singing the title role. The Chicago Theater's orchestra, the quality of whose playing sparks the imagination, served in the pit, while local singers were recruited to form a chorus. Despite an occasional crudity here and there, the performance was an emphatic success, and a repeat was scheduled for the following night.[1]

Next evening, everything went well through the first act. The curtain had just gone up on the second when the audience was alarmed by the smell of smoke. A fire had broken out in an adjoining stable, and within a matter of minutes the theater itself was ablaze. Fortunately, manager Rice succeeded in getting the small audience out of the burning building, and no one was injured. But before the holocaust could be brought under control, twenty buildings had been consumed, the Chicago Theater one of them.[2]

For the next three years, Chicago heard no opera, for there was no theater to house it. Then, in 1853 the ballroom of the Tremont House was converted into a concert hall, and interest in the lyric drama revived again. That October a company known simply as the Italian Opera Troupe was brought to a second Rice Theater, with Rose de Vries as its prima donna. *Lucia di Lammermoor* and *Norma* were both received so enthusiastically that the company decided to stay over an extra day to give *Sonnambula* as an encore. With the conclusion of these three performances, however, the theater was turned over to a troupe of acting dogs, and Chicago went through another five-year lyric dearth.[3]

In September, 1858, it was announced that arrangements had been made for a New Orleans English Opera Troupe—which, incidentally, did not come from New Orleans—to give a two-week season of opera in English. One of the more interesting characteristics of this company was that most of its tenor roles were taken by *Miss* Georgia Hodson, a situation which apparently left something to be desired. On opening night the inevitable *Sonnambula* was presented with Rosalie Durand as Amina and Mme. Hodson as Elvino.[4]

In 1859 Chicago enjoyed its first really outstanding opera season when a company headed by Maurice Strakosch and his wife Amelia Patti (Adelina's sister) came to town and staged an extensive repertoire, including *Traviata*, Donizetti's *Lucrezia Borgia, I Puritani*, and *Don Giovanni*.[5] Six years later, the city heard its first German opera from a company which presented fifteen performances at Mc-Vicker's Theater, among them productions of Wagner's *Tannhäuser* and Beethoven's *Fidelio*.[6]

Of even greater significance was the completion of the Crosby Opera House in 1865, erected on the north side of Washington Street between State and Dearborn. The new opera house was a sumptuous structure for those days, more elegant than anything the city had previously known. Originally, it had been planned to open the theater on April 17, 1865, but when the management learned of President Lincoln's assassination two days before, the inaugural was postponed until April 20. When the doors of Crosby's Opera House were at last flung open, the occasion was a gala one. Everyone who was anyone in Chicago was there, with carriages lined up for blocks before the theater's entrance. Despite miserable weather, every seat in the house was taken, and cloaks and jewels were out in full force. On stage for the occasion was the Grau Italian Opera Company, performing *Il Trovatore*. The whole event was an unprecedented success, both artistically and socially.[7] Later in the season, Grau's company put on Verdi's *La Forza del Destino*, just four months after the opera's American premiere at the Academy of Music in New York.[8]

But times were not always so glorious at Crosby's Opera House. In 1867 the theater was rescued from financial disaster when Crosby sold lottery tickets in order to raise the funds necessary to pull his enterprise out of difficulty. Then in the great fire of 1871, the opera house was destroyed along with virtually every other significant building in the city.

Nevertheless, between 1850 and 1870 Chicago had heard thirty-six different opera seasons, a total of 433 performances. *Martha* had been given twenty-eight times; *Trovatore*, twenty-seven; *Faust* twenty-one; Balfe's *The Bohemian Girl*, nineteen; and *Norma*, seventeen. Since the ticket prices for these productions averaged about twice those for purely dramatic works, one may surmise that the opera was attended chiefly by persons of some financial means. Certainly by the time of the fire, opera-going had become the fashionable thing to do, and most of the city's "better" families had a regular box at the Opera House.[9]

Not all of Chicago's lyric excitement, however, was limited to grand opera, for shortly after the Civil War *opéra bouffe* became quite popular. As was the case all over the country at this time, the old Italian works which for years had been favorites were now running into stout competition from the more frivolous music of composers like Jacques Offenbach. So popular in fact were the Offenbach operettas that many a French troupe was encouraged to cross the Atlantic to capitalize on some of this American enthusiasm. In September, 1868, Chicago was taken by storm by the notorious Tostée, the most risqué of all the Parisian *opéra bouffe* stars. As George Upton recalls it, "She dressed alluringly, glittered with jewels, contorted vulgarly, sang as raucously as a raven, and skated over very thin ice."[10]

While grand opera and its more vivacious sister, *opéra bouffe,* continued to vie with each other for the attentions of the handsome Chicago public, the city's interest in both became more serious throughout the 1870's and 1880's. And yet, for the eighteen years following the fire, Chicago had no appropriate theater to house its musical productions. From time to time there was talk about building a new music center, but finances always served as a stumbling block. Then in 1885 Ferdinand W. Peck began to realize his dream of giving the city a great hall where "the multitude" could gather for all sorts of events, including opera. But Peck's big fear was acoustics, for he understood that success here was more or less a matter of chance. Eventually, he sought out architect Dankmar Adler, who with his celebrated partner Louis Sullivan spent four years working on Peck's project.[11]

The result was the now-famous Auditorium Building, consisting of a theater, a hotel, an office building, and a twelve-story tower, built at a cost of eight million dollars. The 4,250-seat theater, with its gilded proscenium, marble-pillared foyer, handsome murals, and impressive staircases, at last gave Chicago the setting for opera it had needed so long. And, much to Peck's delight, the acoustics in the house were superb.

On Monday, December 9, 1889, the Auditorium was dedicated with a lavish ceremony and the usual multitude of speeches. A now middle-aged Adelina Patti sang "Home, Sweet Home," plus a Swiss song by Eckert as an encore, receiving $4,000 for her efforts. Among the dignitaries present were President Benjamin Harrison and Vice-President Levi P. Morton. Theodore Dubois, considered then one of the finest contemporary French composers, had been commissioned by the management to write a Triumphal Fantasie for organ and orchestra especially for the occasion.[12]

The next day the Italian Grand Opera Company, managed by Henry Abbey and Maurice Grau, took over the Auditorium, presenting a four-week season of opera with Mme. Patti and Lillian Nordica as its two major prima donnas. The first work presented by the company—and therefore the first given in the new theater—was Gounod's *Romeo and Juliet*, Patti singing the role of Juliet. The performance seems to have been somewhat disappointing, and even Patti herself, apparently, lacked much of her usual vocal sheen. Nevertheless, the diva received her customary $3,500 a performance, in addition to 10 per cent of all box-office receipts over $5,000.[13]

Toward the end of the season the company ran into more serious trouble. Virtually the whole troupe came down with influenza, "la grippe" as it was known then. Francesco Tamagno, the company's prize tenor, was out of commission. Nordica was in bed at her hotel suite, as were Mmes. Giulia Valda and Maria Pettigiani. Only Patti remained on her feet. It seemed she was the management's only hope. But would the soprano agree to substitute for her ailing colleagues? A committee representing both the Auditorium and the Abbey and Grau company went to her suite at the Richelieu Hotel. When they entered, they found Patti busily eating marshmallows, which she claimed were good for the throat, and warming her feet over a coal fire.

"You are well, are you not?" asked the committee spokesman.

"Perfectly," replied La Patti.

"Then you can sing tonight!"

"For $4,000!!"

The committee returned to the Auditorium in despair. Abbey, his hands in his pockets, paced the floor angrily, while Peck sat with his face in his hands and moaned. Milward Adams, the house manager, was so disgruntled that he kicked a man who approached him for a free pass.

At the eleventh hour, a couple of principals agreed to sing despite their indisposed condition. *Les Huguenots* was staged in place of *Otello*, and the company was saved. Mme. Patti continued eating her marshmallows.[14]

The Auditorium's first season consisted of twenty-two performances, played to over 100,000 persons, and took in some $232,952
through the box-office. The season's largest audience was its last,
when Adelina Patti again held the stage, now as Rosina in *The
Barber of Seville*. For her "Lesson Scene" Patti interpolated the
"Shadow Song" from *Dinorah* and the popular "Home, Sweet
Home," both of which brought down the house.[15]

In the twenty years following the completion of Peck's Audi-
torium, the theater was visited by most of the outstanding opera
companies of that time, among them the Metropolitan, the Walter
Damrosch Company, the New Orleans French Opera, the Maurice
Grau Company, the Savage English Opera, and the Boston Opera
Company.[16] And the city heard its share of famous singers, too.
During the Chicago World's Fair in 1893, for example, the golden-
voiced Nellie Melba was heard for the first time in the United
States.[17] Later in the 1890's, during a performance of *Romeo and
Juliet* while Melba and Jean de Reszke were singing the "Balcony
Scene," a religious fanatic jumped onto the Auditorium stage and
tried to speak, completely interrupting the performance. The au-
dience, which included a young Chicago schoolgirl named Mary
Garden, was terrified by the sudden action.[18]

For the most part, however, opera at the Auditorium appears to
have been a grand social display, for from 1889 until 1895 the programs there invariably carried the urgent plea: "The audience, especially the ladies, are requested to leave their seats during the
intermission."[19] That one statement probably did more to increase
the local sale of feminine finery than a score of calculated advertise-
ments.

In 1909 the Metropolitan Opera, under the management of Giulio
Gatti-Casazza, paid a call on the Chicago Auditorium, one which
saw the local debut of both Arturo Toscanini and Emmy Destinn
in the opening-night *Aïda*. The following year the Met offered
there such vocal gems as Destinn's Gioconda, Caruso's Rodolfo,
Scotti's Iago, Slezak's Radames, Farrar's Butterfly, and Fremstad's
Elsa.[20]

Certainly in the sixty years that had passed since Chicago heard
that first *Sonnambula* back in 1850, the city had seen a multitude
of operatic glories. Since the building of the Auditorium, the city
had sponsored an opera season almost every year, playing host to

some of the most illustrious companies ever to tour the United States. But these visits were always erratic and uncertain. By 1910 Chicago had grown artistically, economically, and numerically, to warrant a regular season with its own company. After all, the city had had a symphony for two decades now, one of the finest in the country. Why then could it not support its own opera company as well? Civic-minded Chicagoans began putting their heads together to see what could be done, and as the talk continued, enthusiasm rose.

Meanwhile in New York cigar-smoking Oscar Hammerstein, reputed to have the only tongue quicker than Mary Garden's, had recently built the Manhattan Opera House and founded the Manhattan Opera Company. His purpose—brazenly enough—was to drive the Metropolitan out of business. The Met, however, was somewhat timid about playing Hammerstein's game and entrenched itself for a fight. The battle was to the death, and both sides knew it. In the resulting struggle, the two opera houses gave some of the finest performances New York has ever seen, the Manhattan concentrating on French opera, the Metropolitan on Italian and German. In the end the Met held the decisive weapon, a deeper treasury to draw on. Hammerstein was eventually forced out of business, signing a written promise that he would not re-enter the American operatic arena for a period of ten years. In exchange the Met paid him a cash settlement of $1,200,000 for scenery, costumes, the rights to several operas, and contracts with several of the Manhattan artists.

Yet Hammerstein had literally scared the Metropolitan into this settlement. Even though he was obviously losing the war in New York, what was to keep the enterprising Oscar from going to one of the nation's other major cities—say Chicago—and setting up an opera company there? Perhaps, after catching his financial breath, the impresario might try to continue his war from a point outside New York. And Hammerstein, realizing his ace, gave the Met every reason he could for thinking just that. After all, any man who could handle Mary Garden surely knew how to deal with a mere opera company. So one morning Hammerstein, accompanied by two assistants and a pack of newspaper reporters, showed up in Chicago, spending the day driving around the city, conspicuously stopping from time to time for a closer look at what appeared to be a promising building site. He even went over to the lake front to take a look at a huge pile of stone, the remains of a demolished building, carefully taking measurements and jotting them down in a notebook.

If Hammerstein was merely playing a practical joke on the Met, he must have laughed himself silly. For with the impresario's show of interest in Chicago, the New Yorkers panicked. After desperately racking their brains for a way to stall off this potential threat, the Metropolitan backers finally hit upon a scheme. Why not buy Hammerstein out and lend a helping hand to the ambitious Chicagoans in the process? Surely if Chicago already had some sort of operatic organization, Hammerstein would forget his plans, if plans he had, for building an opera house there. Consequently, the New Yorkers and the Chicagoans, for totally different reasons, began pooling their resources. The end product was the formation of the Chicago Grand Opera Company, with Harold F. McCormick as president and Charles G. Dawes as vice-president. Andreas Dippel, formerly of the Metropolitan, became the organization's general manager, while Cleofonte Campanini, recently of Hammerstein's Manhattan Opera, was chosen musical director.

Poor Oscar Hammerstein had been foiled again. Or had he? With the birth of their own company, the Chicagoans now needed a supply of costumes, scenery, and muscial scores. What better place to obtain them than from the defunct Manhattan Opera House? The Met had bought these properties with the intention of transferring them immediately to Chicago. Thus, Hammerstein had created a market for several thousand dollars worth of assets which in all probability would have been worthless had the Metropolitan not become so instrumental in the formation of the Chicago Grand Opera. Perhaps there had been some business method to the impresario's note-taking that day in Chicago.[21]

When the company's artistic roster was drawn up, it consisted primarily of former Manhattan Opera artists, with a few guest stars from the Metropolitan. In addition, the Hammerstein technique of production was essentially taken over lock, stock, and barrel by the Chicago organization, with French opera again the predominant ingredient in the repertoire.

On Thursday, November 3, 1910, the Chicago Grand Opera Company was christened with a gala production of Verdi's *Aïda*. Its success was overwhelming. "Chicago," wrote Edward Moore, "took its opera, and took it hard."[22] The performance, of course, was staged in the Auditorium, the interior of which had recently been re-decorated.

Two evenings later, Mary Garden, who was to dominate the Chicago operatic scene for twenty years, made her local debut in Debussy's *Pelléas and Mélisande* before a sold out house.[23] The opera, which received its world premiere in Paris eight years earlier with Garden in the lead, had been introduced to the United States by Hammerstein at the Manhattan in 1908, also with Mary Garden. Although the Chicago public at first found the work "difficult" and "obscure," it shortly became recognized as the masterpiece of the Garden repertoire.[24] Debussy himself had coached the soprano for the role and, incidentally, is supposed to have fallen madly in love with her.

Undoubtedly, no one knew how to make news in her day like Mary Garden. She came to Chicago in 1910 supposedly engaged to a Turkish pasha; he was never heard from after that season. The diva is quoted as saying that she thought Chicago was "rotten" and that suffragettes were worse. She strongly disapproved of cigarettes, and stormed out of a performance of *The Mikado* when the usher asked her to remove her broad-brimmed, plumed hat. "Why, the idea!" she bellowed. "I would not take off my hat for the King of England unless I just felt like it."[25]

Although Mary Garden was born in Scotland, her childhood had been spent largely in Chicago. While still a young girl, she went to Paris to study music, making her operatic debut at the *Opéra-Comique* in 1900 as Louise. Seven years later, she made her American debut in Massenet's *Thaïs* at the Manhattan Opera House. From her first performance on, the soprano remained a highly controversial figure on the Chicago scene. To one group, La Garden could do no vocal wrong; for another she was totally unsatisfying in everything she did.

Following her success as Mélisande, Mme. Garden turned to Charpentier's *Louise*, another work she had sung for Hammerstein. Then, a few evenings later, she assumed the title role of Strauss's *Salomé*, and here trouble began. Mary Garden, with her great dramatic flair, always insisted upon realism in her art. Her Salomé, performed in French, was strictly according to the Oscar Wilde formula—"a monstrous oracle of bestiality."[26] As Mary herself describes her "Dance of the Seven Veils," "I had on enormous veils, which I took off one by one and threw in Herod's face. With the very last veil I enveloped myself entirely. . . . Under that last veil was just the thinnest, thinnest muslin. As I ran from the cistern over to Herod, I thrust the last veil at him and knelt and said, 'I want the head of Jokanaan.' "[27]

The morning after Garden's first *Salomé*, Chicago found itself embroiled in a violent controversy over the nature of art and morals. The Chicago chief of police, Leroy T. Steward, after viewing the performance, said, "It was disgusting. Miss Garden wallowed around like a cat in a bed of catnip. There was no art in her dance that I could see. If the same show were produced on Halsted Street the people would call it cheap, but at the Auditorium they say it's art." Mary Garden responded with the comment, "Any one whose morals could have been corrupted by seeing *Salomé* must already have degenerated." Each viewpoint had its determined supporters. When the opera was given a second performance a few nights later, the house was packed, and ticket scalpers had a heyday. But the opposition remained firm. "Performances like that of *Salomé*," declared Arthur Farwell, president of Chicago's Law and Order League, "should be classed as vicious and suppressed along with houses in the red light district." Finally in the face of this controversy the company's board of directors ordered a third performance of the opera canceled. And so the battle ended with *Salomé*'s withdrawal from the Chicago scene for over a decade, not heard again until Mary Garden herself came to the helm of the Chicago Opera.[28]

Less controversial were Geraldine Farrar's *Madama Butterfly* and Nellie Melba's *La Bohème*. Mary Garden took another turn on the Auditorium stage in the local premiere of Massenet's *Thaïs*, making a dramatic first-act entrance scattering roses. And Enrico Caruso came out from New York during the latter part of the season to sing Canio and Dick Johnson.[29]

The Chicago Grand Opera's first season ran for ten weeks. During that time, sixty-three performances of twenty-one operas were given. Still the season was not long enough for the company to attract the artists it sought, nor would it allow the organization to produce the caliber of opera which its backers envisioned. In order to broaden the company's activities, an extensive tour was worked out, with Philadelphia as the major stop. Actually, since the organization drew its financial support from both cities, it was more correctly known for the first three years as the Chicago-Philadelphia Grand Opera Company, the season in the East being nearly as long as that in Illinois.[30]

The company's second season was highlighted by the introduction of pint-sized Maggie Teyte, who possessed a voice several times larger than she was, and musical director Cleofonte Campanini's famous sister-in-law, Luisa Tetrazzini. Mme. Tetrazzini, of course, is one of the all-time greats in the art of coloratura, and in her day the Tetrazzini name was almost a household word. "Physical illusion," writes Edward Moore, "was not in her line at all; she was the size of three or four Maggie Teytes. But what a voice!"[31] During her first season in Chicago she sang five roles in two weeks—Lucia, Violetta, Gilda, Rosina, and Lakmé.

After Tetrazzini left town, these coloratura assignments were taken over by the petite Jenny Dufau, a situation which sent the economics-minded wardrobe department into a real dither, as they hurriedly set about remaking the costumes just vacated by the bulky Tetrazzini. On the night of Dufau's first *Lakmé*, the house sat waiting for the first-act curtain, which was held long overdue. With each passing minute, the front office grew more and more uncomfortable about the delay. When a representative was finally sent backstage, Mme. Dufau was discovered in tears. The costumer was wrapping the Tetrazzini girdle twice around her waist instead of once, and even at that it was falling over her slim hips. Several precious minutes and a couple dozen safety pins later, the performance got under way, but it was noticed that for some time La Dufau was "measurably and pardonably preoccupied."[32]

Mary Garden was back that year with some new roles, among them *Cendrillon*, *Le Jongleur de Notre Dame*, *Carmen*, and Victor Herbert's *Natoma*. The latter is laid in California during the days of Spanish occupancy, and Garden portrayed the Indian maiden Natoma. The Chicagoans longed to introduce the first really successful American opera, and it was hoped that *Natoma* would give them their chance. The audience was highly enthusiastic about the work and eager to pronounce it a smash hit. After the first performance, the cast received a whole string of curtain calls, one of which saw Miss Garden toss a wreath of flowers over the head of composer Victor Herbert.[33]

While the production was in rehearsal, Maestro Herbert had been concerned about Mary Garden's "Dagger Dance." It seems that while the soprano was engaged in her terpsichorean routine, on another part of the stage a man was busily abducting a beautiful young girl. Herbert felt that with this touch of racy misconduct as a distraction, no one would notice the "Dagger Dance." But Joe Redding, who wrote the book for *Natoma*, consoled the composer: "Why, Victor, that man could be taking his pants off and nobody would see him when Mary's on the stage."[34]

The annual wrangle over morals was left that year to Wolf-Ferrari's one-act *The Secret of Suzanne*. The secret is that of a bride, trying to hide her cigarette habit from her husband. Consequently, during the course of the opera Carolina White, singing the title role, was called upon to smoke a number of cigarettes on stage, much to the disgust of the city's Anti-Cigarette League. "Horrible!" exclaimed the league's president. "Perfectly horrible. One after another! I saw her with my own eyes."[35]

At the close of the 1912–13 season, the company, 300 strong, went on tour, first to the East (including New York), then down to Dallas, and finally on an extensive trip through the West and Midwest. It was during this western tour that Mme. Tetrazzini and her brother-in-law, Maestro Campanini, had their big falling out. It seems that the two had clashed over some artistic point or another, and the argument ended with Tetrazzini's declaring that she was the star and he merely a conductor. Campanini, sensing that he had come out second best in the squabble, was determined to get even. In Los Angeles he had his chance. Madame had just ended Gilda's "*Caro nome*" with her usual cadenza, but in the midst of the vocal frills had managed to lose her pitch, ending several notes away from where she should have been. Campanini saw his revenge. "He took a firm grip of the baton, signaled the orchestra, and produced a crashing chord that jarred the roof and showed every one in the opera house the discordant, spinechilling distance that she had removed herself from the correct pitch."[36] This marked the last occasion that the two worked together, for Mme. Tetrazzini refused to sing in Chicago again until after Campanini's death.

Shortly after the troupe returned home, Andreas Dippel, very suddenly, and without notice, resigned as the company's manager. No explanation for the resignation was given at the time, but it seems to have been a part of the company's throwing off of eastern influence. At any rate Cleofonte Campanini was elevated to general director.[37] Also, by the fall of 1913, Harold McCormick, president of the Chicago Grand Opera, had purchased all of the stock remaining in the hands of the eastern shareholders, thereby placing full control of the organization in Chicago.[38]

Now with Campanini as the artistic head, the Chicago Grand Opera entered its fourth season, producing thirty different operas within the first six weeks. Rosa Raisa and Cyrena Van Gordon were the sensations that year, both making their debut in *Aïda*. While the success of the two debutantes was unqualified, the performance had its share of mishaps. One unexpected incident occurred during the "Nile Scene" when two Negro gentlemen from South State Street, who had served as supernumeraries in the preceding act, came casually strolling up the bed of the Nile, derby hats and all. They had mistaken the stage for the theater's exit. Pooling their resources, Radames, Aïda, and an army of Egyptian soldiers finally managed to chase them off, but it is said that Maestro Campanini's remarks from the pit established some sort of record. "Meanwhile," writes Edward Moore, "the audience laughed as no grand opera audience is ever supposed to laugh."[39]

There were new operas that year too. Massenet's *Don Quichotte* was given with Vanni-Marcoux in the title role. Franchetti's *Cristoforo Colombo* was staged with Titta Ruffo as Columbus and Rosa Raisa as Queen Isabella.[40] And Leoncavallo, whose earlier *Pagliacci* was now standard fare in the repertoire, came to the city to conduct his *Zingari*, a story about a wronged tenor who lures an unfaithful soprano and her baritone boyfriend into barn, locks them in, and sets fire to the place. "The thought of broiled prima donna and toasted baritone was a little too much for . . . [the Chicago] public," recalls Edward Moore.[41]

In the summer of 1914, Europe was thrust into the depths of the First World War. Almost immediately the Chicago Grand Opera gave up plans for a season that year. The company had just suffered a tremendous financial loss (the tour itself had brought a deficit of nearly $250,000), and the war simply made a bad situation impossible. But now the management found itself with contractual obligations and no season with which to fulfill them. There appeared to be only one way out—to declare the corporation bankrupt. Thus, the first of Chicago's opera companies came to an abrupt end.[42]

Nevertheless, the following March an announcement was made that a new organization had been formed, this one incorporated as the Chicago Opera Association. Harold McCormick was again president of the company, with Charles G. Dawes as vice-president. Maestro Campanini continued as general director.

Since this reorganization had not taken place until the spring of 1915, Campanini was considerably rushed to get a season lined up by November. Not only that, but by the time the director had been given the green light, many of the artists whom he wanted to engage already had previous commitments. Mary Garden, Rosa Raisa, and Titta Ruffo were just a few of the major singers whom the company found unavailable. Consequently, more than once that year, Chicago had to be satisfied with second best.[43] Despite the European war and the strong anti-German sentiment building in the country, Campanini heavily emphasized the Wagnerian works that season, including a complete *Der Ring des Nibelungen*. Each of the epic's four component operas was given on a successive Sunday, marking the first consecutive *Ring* the city had heard in over twenty-five years.[44]

The following season, while it had its problems, was considerably less hectic. Geraldine Farrar gave one of her most charming performances in Humperdinck's *Die Königskinder*, sharing honors with a flock of squawking geese, who despite having given their histrionic all to the production, were slaughtered at the end of the season and given to the stagehands. Mary Garden took the lead in Massenet's *Grisélidis*, a work which the company abandoned after this one staging, and Rosa Raisa gave the city its first opportunity to hear Giordano's *Andrea Chenier*.[45]

But the undisputed sensation of this 1916–17 season was quietly revealed on Saturday afternoon, November 18, without any particular ballyhoo from either the press or the opera management. Most everyone in the Auditorium that day expected just another pleasant performance of Verdi's *Rigoletto*. And for the first scene and fifteen minutes of the second, that's exactly what the audience heard, a routine performance. Then suddenly a vocal bomb exploded. A young, unknown soprano with a rather prominent nose came on stage and sang Gilda's "*Caro nome*" as Chicago had never heard it sung before. The name of the velvet-voiced interpreter was Amelita Galli-Curci.[46]

As the singer came to the end of her coloratura display, holding the final note for several measures, the audience broke into the most spontaneous ovation the Auditorium had ever seen. What a minute before had been a highly sophisticated assemblage suddenly turned into a frenzied mob, yelling, shouting, screaming, stamping its feet, some zealots even standing on their seats to cheer more enthusiastically.[47] Chicago had discovered a vocal treasure who was shortly to become renowned throughout the musical world.

Campanini had initially contracted the soprano for only two appearances at a slight $300 a performance, maintaining that any further engagements would depend upon her reception in these two. After the thunderous ovation following *"Caro nome,"* Maestro Campanini lost no time in scurrying back to the diva's dressing room to sign her for as many performances as she would sing, at a sum over three times that of the original agreement. And a wise move it was too, for every night that the name Galli-Curci appeared on the program that season, whether the opera was *Rigoletto, Lucia, Barber of Seville, Traviata,* or *Romeo and Juliet,* the Auditorium was filled to capacity.[48]

Less fortunate for the company was a strike precipitated by the male chorus on December 10, just before the curtain was to go up on Wagner's *Die Götterdämmerung.* The choristers had been receiving twenty-four dollars a week and two dollars extra for Sunday performances, and they were now seeking five dollars for their work on Sundays. Campanini held that their demands were not justified and refused the raise. Consequently, while the strikers argued their cause in the stage alley, *Götterdämmerung* was presented with supernumeraries standing in for them and Octave Dua and Desiré Dufrere, the tenor and baritone, supplying the choral vocalism. Most of the audience, as a matter of fact, was not even aware that anything was amiss.

Manon and *Königskinder* were both given with just the female choristers, while *Rigoletto* was staged with a few soloists serving as the chorus. But finally, the strike was broken when Maestro Campanini threatened to recruit a new chorus in New York if the delinquent one did not return to the job. With this, the strikers came around, blaming the agitation on two Russian members of the group, Russia at this time being on the verge of its Bolshevik revolution.[49]

Interior of Auditorium Hall, Chicago

San Francisco Opera's 1959 production of Bizet's *Carmen*

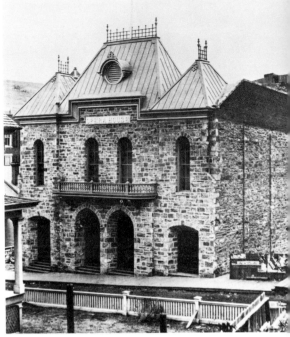

Central City Opera House

Interior of Central City Opera House

On the happier side, however, Charles G. Dawes, vice-president of the Chicago Opera Association and later vice-president of the United States, announced in December that wealthy friends of the opera had guaranteed the company a sum of $100,000 a year for the next five years. In addition, Harold McCormick, the association's president, promised to make up any deficit not covered by the other guarantors.[50]

In 1917 the Chicago Opera opened its season in a newly-decorated Auditorium with the American premiere of Mascagni's *Isabeau*, based on the Lady Godiva legend. The opera, according to *Musical America*, "was . . . sumptuously staged and well sung, and it agreeably disappointed those that had heard unkind things about Mascagni's score."[51] Rosa Raisa starred in the production, receiving an ovation surpassed only by that given Galli-Curci the year before. Lady Godiva's famous ride, which could easily have caused *Isabeau* to go the way of *Salomé*, was handled most tactfully. For a moment when Mme. Raisa threw off her cloak and ran off the stage, the audience gasped, thinking that she had completely disrobed. Then, as she came riding by on her mount, it became obvious that the diva was wearing flesh-colored silk tights.[52]

Galli-Curci continued to be the company's number one sensation, invariably commanding sold-out houses. One of the soprano's most charming moments came in the "Lesson Scene" from *The Barber of Seville*, where she interpolated "Home, Sweet Home" and "The Last Rose of Summer," playing her own accompaniment on the spinnet.[53] A new role for the singer that year was Meyerbeer's *Dinorah*, and the first performance proved even more exciting than the Chicago management had hoped. Some apparently demented individual had set a bomb under a seat near the stage. During the performance it began to fizz and give off an alarming odor. A local fireman, sitting nearby, hurriedly carried the bomb outside. Meanwhile to avoid panic (this was wartime and nerves were on edge), conductor Campanini struck up "The Star-Spangled Banner," summoning Galli-Curci before the footlights. "Sing, Madame!" he ordered. And sing she did, even though she did not know the anthem's words. While the audience joined in the singing, outside the bomb sputtered and went out. Fortunately, it was a dud.[54]

Soon the Great War was over, and the Chicago Opera Association celebrated by adding a new conductor to its staff. He was Giorgio

Polacco, later musical director of the company. Campanini's health had begun to fail, and his doctors had ordered him to slow down. Polacco, who had gained a wide reputation for his musical ability and for his lack of patience with troublesome singers, was brought in to take over part of Campanini's load. A native of Venice, Polacco's career had taken him to almost every major opera house on three continents, and at one time he had served as Arturo Toscanini's assistant.[55]

The Chicago Opera was now probably at its zenith. Mary Garden still headed the French wing; Amelita Galli-Curci took care of the coloratura; and Rosa Raisa handled the dramatic works. Each was tops in her field, and yet, since their roles seldom overlapped, there was little or no real competition among them.

While Raisa was an artist of the first magnitude, one of her *Tosca*'s in 1919 ended with the audience in stitches. The Mario of the production was Alessandro Dolci, a talented young tenor who was extremely unpopular with his associates. Raisa had taken all from her operatic "lover" that she could stand and vowed vengeance. In the last act, she had her chance. Mario had just been shot by Scarpia's firing squad, and Tosca was to fling herself across his body in a fit of anguish. Sensing victory, Raisa "managed to fling herself in such a way that two vigorous elbows bored into what can be best described as his equatorial line. With a grunt that could have been heard out in the lobby, Dolci's feet went up in the air and he deflated like a burst football." Then as the soprano got up to run over to the parapet, she stepped on the palm of the tenor's hand with the sharp heel of her shoe. The audience broke into a gale of laughter. Giorgio Polacco nearly lost his composure in the pit, for the stage was blocking his view, and he could not see what the audience was laughing at.[56]

About a month deep in the 1919–20 season director Cleofonte Campanini died. The impresario had arrived in Chicago that fall with a severe cold which he had contracted on his way over from Europe. Shortly, his condition grew serious, pneumonia set in, and he was confined to his bed. On Friday morning, December 11, he was dead.[57]

Campanini's funeral was as theatrical as his life had been. His coffin was placed in the center of the Auditorium stage with the brilliantly lighted sets for the "Transformation Scene" from *Parsifal* about it. On either side of the casket was placed a burning candle, the conductor's baton and one of his scores resting nearby on a stand. Flowers were massed all over the stage. After a musical service by the company, the Chicago public was allowed to file by the coffin, a procession which continued for three solid hours. "After that," Mary Garden recalls in her autobiography, "the curtain came down slowly, and that was the last we saw of Cleofonte Campanini."[58]

In the spring following Campanini's death, Gino Marinuzzi, one of the company's conductors and a composer of some note, was appointed the organization's artistic manager, while Herbert Johnson, the association's former business comptroller, was named executive director. Both of these positions were newly created in an attempt to cover the duties formerly performed by Campanini as general director.[59] The announcement was also made that Harold McCormick, who had generously promised three years ago to make up any deficit in excess of the $100,000 stipulated by the other guarantors, had reconfirmed his pledge to back the opera for two more years. "What we're trying to do," McCormick explained, speaking for himself and his prominent wife, Edith Rockefeller McCormick, "is to make the opera company an attractive proposition for the guarantors who will have to relieve us at the end of two years. Others will have to do their part. It won't be difficult. Even now the annual deficit is not large and in two years it will be still smaller."[60]

And so the Chicago Opera Association entered its 1920–21 season with financial confidence, if without the guiding hand of Cleofonte Campanini. The opening night production was none other than musical director Marinuzzi's own *Jacquerie*, a tale of a revolt of French peasants in the fourtenth century. Sets and costumes alone for the production cost $50,000.[61] Rosa Raisa scored a success a little later in Wolf-Ferrari's *The Jewels of the Madonna*, although at the last minute the production was denied the services of Andreas Parley, who was to have interpreted an apache dance with Mme. Ada Nemeroff. Parley's dance was found to be "too realistic and too rough for Chicago." Herbert Johnson, who was immediately responsible for the artist's withdrawal, philosophized, "Art is art, but enough is enough."[62]

This 1920–21 season also saw the first Wagner produced in the

Auditorium since the United States entered the war against Germany. And even then, two years after the Armistice, it was not considered apropos to present the composer's works in German. By some odd logic, however, it was deemed discreet to sing them in English. So, lest they be considered un-American by an age which doted on emblematic superficialties, Rosa Raisa, Cyrena Van Gordon, and Edward Johnson were forced to sing *Lohengrin* in President-elect Harding's native tongue, and what once had been fondly known as *Die Walküre* was now billed as *The Valkyrie*.[63]

On the last day of 1920, Mary Garden arrived in Chicago from France, shortly launching into her first role of the season, Erlanger's *Aphrodite*. She sang a *Faust* opposite Lucien Muratore, and then settled down to prepare for *Monna Vanna*, one of her favorite vehicles. In the meantime, however, an even more interesting drama was taking place backstage at the Auditorium, a drama from which Mary Garden would emerge with the starring role.

First, on December 19, the vocally-limited Ganna Walska, known as the world's wealthiest prima donna and later wife of Harold McCormick, stormed out of her apartment in the Blackstone Hotel and returned to New York, because of personal and artistic reasons. A production of Leoncavello's *Zaza,* planned for Mme. Walska, was indefinitely postponed.[64] Then, on January 6, Gino Marinuzzi resigned as the company's artistic director, maintaining that he simply could not tolerate the behind-the-scenes wrangling any more. The musician said that he planned to return to his old position as conductor, a job which he hoped would allow him to get some much-needed sleep. The squabbling singers, he said, had given him nothing but sleepless nights. "Their voices have been in my ears twenty-four hours a day," Marinuzzi complained. "Each one with a grievance, each one objecting to a role I have assigned to someone else."[65]

A week later, Mary Garden was elected general director of the Opera Association by the company's board of directors. While the soprano would continue as one of the organization's leading performers, she was now to be in complete supervision of both the company's artistic and financial affairs. It was agreed that the diva would accept no salary for her managerial duties, receiving payment only for the performances in which she starred.

Since Mme. Garden was scheduled to sing *Monna Vanna* the evening following her appointment as director, she remained in her

Blackstone Hotel suite all the next day, unavailable for interviews.[66] After the performance, however, the company's new head met with reporters in her dressing room, receiving them with the famous Garden charm. Yes, she was happy over her new position. She would give fewer operas, and thus better ones. "We must be the best company in the world bar none," she declared. She would pay big salaries only to the stars who could draw big audiences. Half of the operas given would be Italian, 35 per cent French, and 15 per cent English. She detested translations and would not present German operas until they could be sung in their original language. What about Mme. Garden's own *Tosca*, which she always sang in French, rather than Italian? Well, nobody had the nerve to ask about that.[67]

On January 22, George Spangler was selected as the company's new business manager, having served for a number of years as the convention manager of the Chicago Association of Commerce. Giorgio Polacco was named musical director.[68]

The coming season, 1921–22, was to be the Harold McCormicks' last as the principal sponsors of the Chicago Opera Association. In 1916 they had agreed to pick up the tab on any excess deficit which the company might incur for the next five years. Now, the McCormicks were coming to the end of their costly period of beneficence, and they wanted to close their regime with the greatest opera season Chicago had ever known. Consequently, it had been largely at the insistence of the McCormicks that Mary Garden was chosen as the company's new director. "We want to go out in a blaze of glory," McCormick had confided to La Garden, "and we need your name."[69] The tycoon had even agreed that next year's deficit might run as high as $600,000, as compared with the high of $350,000 for the season just concluding.[70]

And so, shortly after the close of the 1920–21 season, director Mary Garden—the "directa," as she always insisted upon being called —was off for Europe, where she would spend the next several months scouting for talent in all of the more fashionable summer resorts. George Spangler, who had been appointed by McCormick to keep a financial eye on Mme. Garden, lest she become too extravagant, spent his summer trailing Madame all over the continent, trying desperately to keep some sort of tally on expenses. But Spangler was soon to learn that trying to curb Mary Garden was sheer folly. Frequently, in the course of a business transaction, the diva would turn to her financial shadow and ask, "Have we reached the $600,000 mark yet?" When the negative response was given, she would return to her spending with renewed vigor. On one occasion, the soprano was engaging a young artist who was perfectly willing to come to Chicago for $200 a performance. "Why $200 per performance?" La Garden asked in surprise. "You are worth $600!" And while Spangler cringed, the contract was signed for $600 a performance.

By fall Garden and company had lined up one of the most formidable arrays of operatic talent ever assembled. The final artistic roster showed seventeen sopranos, nine contraltos and mezzo-sopranos, thirteen tenors, eight baritones, nine basses, and five conductors, about twice as many of each as the company actually needed and would be able to use. When the initial reports of the season's line-up and proposed expenses began coming in to the board of directors, George Spangler suddenly found himself among the ranks of the unemployed.[71]

On November 15, 1921, the flamboyant Mary Garden year got under way with a performance of Saint-Saens' *Samson and Delilah*. Lucien Muratore was Samson, Marguerite D'Alvarez Delilah. The Auditorium was filled to capacity, and the celebrities were even more numerous off stage than on. Mme. Garden herself occupied a box in the diamond horseshoe, accompanied by her parents. Cyrena Van Gordon was there. So were Edith Mason and Claire Dux. All went well, except for Mme. D'Alvarez's first-act entrance. As the mezzo started down the steps of the temple, she slipped and fell, sliding almost to the middle of the stage. Miraculously enough, she rolled to her feet without missing a note, even managing to stay on pitch.[72]

Two nights later, Chicago saw a gorgeous portrayal of *Madama Butterfly*, when Edith Mason appeared on the Auditorium stage for the first time. Although Mme. Mason had enjoyed a great reputation in Europe, had sung at the Metropolitan, and for four summers had even appeared at Chicago's own Ravinia Park, it was not until now that her talents were displayed by the city's downtown opera management. On the night of her Auditorium debut, the air was filled with expectancy, every ear in the house eagerly awaiting Butterfly's entrance. Finally, as the magnificent Puccini music throbbed through the hushed theater, a pure, brilliant voice was heard floating out above the strains of the orchestra. By the first-act love duet, the audience was well aware that here was a Butterfly to reckon with, and Chicago had a new operatic sweetheart. At the conclusion of the final scene, the Auditorium "thundered and rocked with applause, while the stage became a huge bank of flowers."[73]

Serge Prokofiev's opera-burlesque *The Love of Three Oranges* was given its world premiere on December 30, with the composer himself conducting. The work was beautifully mounted by the company, for an extravagant $100,000. While the public was generally confused by Prokofiev's "advanced" music, the critics were impressed. *Musical Courier* pronounced it a "stupendous new opera."[74]

Meanwhile, "Madame Directa" herself was having a busy time, performing one of her favorite roles at least twice a week. *Carmen*, *Pelléas and Mélisande*, *Thaïs*, *L'Amore dei Tre Re*, *Monna Vanna*, *Louise*, and *Le Jongleur de Notre Dame* were all done that season, and then La Garden announced that *Salomé*, which had been carefully tucked away in moth balls for the past eleven years, would be revived. Once again the city prepared to be shocked, while tickets for the opera sold like bourbon on New Year's Eve. When the work was presented, the reaction was much less violent than it had been a decade earlier. Critics, at least, seemed to have become more sophisticated during the intervening years. Emil Raymond, writing for *Musical America*, found the performance "weighty, thrilling, majestic."[75] René Devries, who eleven years earlier had found the Garden portrayal disgusting, now professed, "No censor, no member of the Baptist Church, or of any other congregation, could, even with field glasses, find anything depraving or even degrading in her Salomé—a role in which Miss Garden's artistry finds its best debouche."[76]

Devries was a little too optimistic, however. There were those who could find immorality in Garden's Salomé and did. Preachers and professional bigots all over the Chicago area, most of whom never actually saw the performance themselves, rose up in anger. One clergyman urged his congregation to demonstrate against such debauching of grand opera.[77] Billy Sunday, that venerable saver of souls, took up the crusade, violently denouncing Mary Garden in his tent-meeting revivals with a vocal tirade that only a baseball-player-turned-evangelist is capable of delivering. "Let's put one over the plate for Jesus," he used to shout (reverently, of course) in this case with the intent of "striking out" sin of the Auditorium.

Mme. Garden, however, loved a good fight almost as much as she enjoyed the artistic limelight. One day she took it upon herself to sit in on one of Sunday's demonstrations, just to hear what he had to say about *Salomé*. After the service, the diva sauntered back to her denunciator's tent, much to the revivalist's surprise. When he regained his composure, Sunday invited the soprano to stroll with him down to the corner drugstore. There, perched at the counter atop two high stools, the two sipped ice-cream sodas and discussed *Salomé*. By the time the evangelist had tossed off his "creme de fizz-water," he was completely under the Garden charm, even admitting that perhaps he had been wrong about her portrayal. They parted friends and for several years after that corresponded regularly.[78]

About this time a smoldering backstage feud burst into open flame. Johanna Gadski, who had been engaged by the management for a number of performances of *Tristan und Isolde*, was informed, after several weeks of waiting for rehearsals to begin, that her services would not be needed. Something was muttered about her husband's questionable war record, and she was handed a check for $7,500 and blithely sent on her way. Mme. Gadski immediately brought suit against the company for $500,000 worth of damages, listing slander as one of her grievances.[79]

Shortly other artists began to discover that they had been signed for more performances than they could possibly fulfill. One singer had been contracted for forty-five appearances, but thus far had sung only a half-dozen times. Another was scheduled for twenty-five performances, but as yet had sung only one role. Midway through the season *Samson and Delilah* was dropped from the repertoire, and Marguerite D'Alvarez was paid for the remainder of the appearances called for in her contract and dismissed. Tito Schipa left Chicago in a huff, having been called upon for only one performance during the first three weeks of the season.[80] Lucien Muratore resigned from the company in a rage, declaring that he would never return to Chicago so long as Mary Garden was director of the opera there. Among other things, the tenor claimed that when he performed with Miss Garden, she would mockingly hiss "Pretty boy!" at him while they were singing what was supposed to be a love duet.[81] In addition, Charles Marshall, Amelita Galli-Curci, Edith Mason, Rosa Raisa, and Giorgio Polacco were all peeved about one thing or another and were on the verge of walking out.

Essentially the trouble boiled down to the fact that directress Garden had engaged too many singers and promised them too many appearances. There simply were not enough operas and parts to go around. Consequently, some big stars found themselves, for the first time since their cub days, warming the bench. On the other hand, "Madame Directa" herself was giving two, sometimes three, performances a week, having a fine time singing everything that she thought was fun. While the operas presented that year were generally of a superior caliber, the backstage scene was a seething mass of dissension, brought on largely by too much idle talent. Edith Mason, one of the season's busier artists, recalled some forty years later that in reality Mary Garden had two companies that year. "One was singing; the other was out walking the streets."[82]

After the close of the season in Chicago, the company moved on to New York for a five-week engagement. In April Mary Garden resigned as the organization's general director. "I am an artist," the diva declared, "and I have decided that my place is with the artists, not over them."[83] The McCormicks had ended their era of patronage, as they had promised, in a blaze of glory. Mary Garden had seen to it that the end was a glorious one. That the productions of this last year were excellent no one could deny.

Then in the spring of 1922, when the final figures were tabulated, McCormick was handed the bill for his final operatic spectacle— $1,100,000.[84] The tycoon's gentlemanly moan could be heard in every speakeasy in Chicago.

Vincent Sheean recalled many years later, "It was a remarkable opera season. . . . An opera might be given once only—two performances was rather a long run—and a singer might make a debut which was simultaneously a farewell. . . . Garden conducted her whole season . . . like the triumphal scene in *Aïda*."[85] Mary Garden's final comment on the season in her autobiography was, "If it cost a million dollars, I'm sure it was worth it."[86]

Nevertheless, with the end of Mary Garden's lavish year as director, the Chicago Opera Association became a thing of the past. The company was totally reorganized on a different basis. No longer would one man carry the burden of the inevitable operatic deficit. Now under the new plan, several hundred citizens would contribute to the support of Chicago's lyric drama, thus turning the project into a truly civic enterprise. Consequently, when the fall of 1922 rolled around, the city's resident opera had been re-formed into the Chicago Civic Opera Company.

Backed by the McCormick millions, Maestro Campanini and his successors had built up an operatic organization renowned the world over. Chicago became the second American capital of French opera, coming into prominence about the time that New Orleans was forsaking opera for jazz. The Metropolitan still had no French wing worth speaking of, and the Chicagoans gave the nation a chance to hear a number of operas and singers that the Met never got around to presenting. And for the next decade, the city continued to boast a company of real lyric accomplishment, a company second only to the Metropolitan.

Chicago's Chords
and Discords

At the same time that Mary Garden's colorful display of operatic fireworks was keeping Chicagoans agog in the winter of 1921–22, very quietly in the background a significant fund-raising drive was in progress. In order to insure the existence of the city's opera after the last of the McCormick dollars were gone, a plan had been devised whereby 500 guarantors would each contribute a sum not to exceed $1,000 a year for the next five years. Thus ended the days when Chicago's opera was financed by a select group of wealthy benefactors, for with the recent alteration in the nation's tax structure, it became more and more impossible for a few leading citizens personally to underwrite losses. Now the burden was spread out, and the idea of civic opera developed.

Financed by this broadened plan of support, the newly formed Chicago Civic Opera went into operation in 1922, with Samuel Insull president and Charles G. Dawes again serving as vice-president. Harold McCormick and Edith Rockefeller McCormick, whose marriage incidentally had gone the way of their operatic patronage, were relegated, by choice, to seats on the board of trustees.[1] The new management made it quite clear that hereafter the Chicago Opera would be run on a businesslike basis, with a strict accounting system. By summer it was officially announced that the $500,000 a year needed to support the opera for the next five years had been raised, plus an additional $25,000 for good measure.[2]

Artistically, the Chicago Opera under the Insull regime continued in much the same vein as it had during the McCormick days, although gradually it became more and more Italianate. The new company took over all of the physical properties of the Association, and most of the major artists stayed on. Giorgio Polacco was reinstated as musical director.

There were new stars, of course, from time to time, like Feodor Chaliapin, who appeared on the scene in 1922 to sing the title role of Boïto's *Mefistofele*. The singer showed up for the first rehearsal and promptly made it known that he thought the company's production was totally inadequate. While the stage director looked on in amazement, Chaliapin proceeded to tear the staging apart and put it back together again. The results are legendary. In the "Brocken Scene," under instruction from the star, the normally subdued chorus became "a whirling, shrieking crew of minor devils on a diabolical spree."[3] Standing over them was Chaliapin himself, over six feet tall, half-naked, as commanding a demon as ever appeared on earth.

Claudia Muzio, who also made her debut in 1922, shortly became one of the company's most valuable assets. Everything Muzio did, she did well, but Madeleine in *Andrea Chenier* particularly suited her talents, and she played it to the hilt. So completely did the soprano enter into her hysterical outbreak in Act III (when her lover is sentenced to the guillotine) that she often appeared before the footlights to accept her curtain calls still in a noticeable daze. During one performance in 1923, she actually fainted on stage when she was torn from the arms of the condemned Chenier.[4]

Mary Garden continued as one of the company's feature attractions, now and then scandalizing the city as only she could. A 1923 production of Massenet's *Cléopatre* was considered by many to be even more daring than the notorious *Salomé* of two years before. But Farnsworth Wright concluded in *Musical America*, "The dresses of the feminine cast were wholly adequate, being not nearly so thin as Massenet's score."[5] More successful, mainly because they served as excellent vehicles for the Garden acting ability, were Alfano's *Resurrection*, based on Tolstoi's novel, and Honegger's *Judith*, said by some to make *Salomé* look like a nursery rhyme.

The familiar Garden roles, which Chicago had come to love, were given often, although many of them contained rather pallid scores. *Monna Vanna*, for instance, was done repeatedly by the company, and Mary always managed to pull it off, despite the fact that composer Henri Fevrier had given her little with which to work. For this role the diva always wore a jewel-studded tiara throughout the whole opera. Even when Pisa was besieged by the enemy and its citizens were dying of famine, La Garden went about her business adorned by her elegant headpiece. This was a little too much for the critics, and they said so. On the other hand, no one could deny that the soprano, now definitely middle-aged, had fully mastered the art of makeup. With a few skillful touches, deep lines were gone and her Monna Vanna became the adolescent girl which the libretto demanded.[6]

Unhappily, 1923–24 marked Amelita Galli-Curci's last season with the Chicago Opera. A dispute had arisen just before the season began between the coloratura and Maestro Polacco regarding the vehicle for her first appearance that year. Galli-Curci preferred *Dinorah*, while Polacco insisted on *Lakmé*. Upon receiving notice that the management's choice had been scheduled, the soprano lost no time in telegraming Samuel Insull that she was obliged to accept his decision inasmuch as she was bound to the company for that season, but that she would not be with the company the next season.[7]

The news of the singer's resignation brought anguished cries of protest from Chicago's opera-lovers, who had virtually worshipped the diva ever since her first *Rigoletto* back in 1916. On January 4, 1924, the celebrated Galli-Curci gave her last performance with the company. The opera was *Romeo and Juliet*, and the Chicago public packed the Auditorium to bid her a fond farewell. The demonstration after the last act rivaled that which followed *"Caro nome"* seven years earlier. The curtain calls lasted a full twelve minutes. Certainly, the soprano had been one of the most popular Chicago has ever known, playing to more sold-out houses than any artist in the history of the city's resident opera.[8]

Rosa Raisa, however, remained until the end of the Civic Opera and even after, invariably giving a good performance. She opened the season in 1924 with Ponchielli's *La Gioconda* amid cries of *brava* from both public and critics. "Unforgettable is Raisa as La Gioconda," wrote René Devries. "A better piece of acting than that in the last scene . . . has not been seen in many a year on the so-called legitimate stage."[9] The following year the soprano starred in the world premiere of W. Franke Harling's *A Light from St. Agnes*, a work which holds the distinction of introducing jazz into grand opera, its music containing frequent syncopations and often demanding solo work from the saxophone and banjo. The opera was met with considerable enthusiasm, but failed to win more than a fleeting place in the repertoire.[10]

Financially, the Chicago Civic Opera seemed to be holding its own about as well as can be expected in this perilous business of opera production. At the close of the 1924–25 season President Samuel Insull announced a deficit of $400,000, but quickly stated that attendance was growing faster than expenses.[11] Insull had hopes of eventually putting the company on a self-supporting basis, and in December, 1925, he revealed his plans for how this could be done. The dream which Insull had harbored for years was to build a new opera house within a huge skyscraper. The opera house would occupy the ground floor, while the top levels could be leased out as office space. The rental would be used to cover the inevitable operatic deficit. If the scheme were successful, as Insull was certain it would be, in time the Chicago Opera could actually be self-supporting.

Plans for such a building were discussed for two years. In the fall of 1927 they became final. The structure would be built at 20 North Wacker Drive, construction beginning early the next spring. If all went according to schedule, the house would be ready in time for the November 1929 opening. The local press inundated the city with architects' drawings and details of the new building, while popular interest began to surge.[12]

On Saturday, January 26, 1929, the company gave its last performance in the old Auditorium. The opera was Gounod's *Romeo and Juliet*, the first work presented in the theater nearly forty years before. Edith Mason and Charles Hackett portrayed the Veronese lovers, and they both sang their finest. The occasion was a sentimental one, for as the opera-going Chicagoans entered the Auditorium for that last time, their thoughts were inevitably torn between the future and the past. While there was real excitement regarding the new opera house being readied down on Wacker Drive, a certain nostalgia over leaving the old Auditorium could not be denied. The city's operatic past, which the old theater symbolized, was too glorious to let go without an occasional thought. And so, after the curtain was rung down, Maestro Polacco signaled the orchestra to strike up "Home, Sweet Home," the song Adelina Patti had sung at the dedication of the house four decades before. The audience spontaneously rose to its feet and, brushing an occasional tear from the eye, sang the words with heart-felt emotion.[13] Then, as the song was ended, sentimentality was put aside. The days ahead took on new proportions, looming larger as the months progressed, and Chicago's musical public began looking forward to an era of even greater operatic splendor.

By the fall of 1929 the giant structure at 20 North Wacker Drive was complete. The site itself is only a few feet south of where the old Wigwam stood, the scene of Abraham Lincoln's nomination for the presidency in 1860. Now, nearly seventy years after Lincoln's political victory, the area was to become a center for the arts, the realization of Insull's dream. The new edifice, consisting of forty-two stories, contains on the ground level both the Civic Opera House and the smaller Civic Theater. In the tower is housed some 739,000 square feet of office space, which, according to the plan, would serve as a perpetual source of revenue for the Chicago Civic Opera. The cost of the building came to a total of $20,000,000. Half of the sum was raised by subscription; the other half was borrowed from the Metropolitan Life Insurance Company at 5 per cent interest.[14]

Prefacing the entrance of the Opera House (the home of the present Lyric Opera of Chicago) is a colonnade of octagonal piers, affording protection from the weather. Five doors of bronze and marble lead into the outer lobby, where a series of marble columns rise to a vaulted ceiling of gold. The auditorium, seating 3,471 persons, consists of a main floor, two balconies, and thirty-one boxes. The decorative scheme, executed primarily in rose and gold, is keynoted by rich simplicity throughout. The lower walls are covered by oak paneling, while above, the sides are formed by bays which gradually step back to give greater width at the rear. The ceiling is fashioned of panels, at the back of which are coves concealing the lighting and ventilating grilles.

Between acts, a great steel curtain, measuring thirty-five by fifty feet, is brought down over the stage, rather than the usual drop.

Painted on this curtain is a panorama of some thirty noted operatic characters in costume. The stage itself measures seventy-five feet in depth, 120 feet in total width, with a working stage area fifty feet wide. The gridiron for the changing of scenery towers 140 feet above the stage, clear up to the fourteenth floor of the building.[15]

On November 4, 1929—just eleven days after the great stock market crisis on Wall Street—the Civic Opera House was dedicated with a production of Verdi's *Aïda*, starring Rosa Raisa, Charles Marshall, and Cyrena Van Gordon.[16] While the performance itself was largely of secondary interest, it did point out several significant features of the new opera house. The acoustics, although at first somewhat controversial, were close to perfect. Even an ordinary speaking voice on stage could be heard way up in the last row of the top balcony. In addition, every seat in the house permitted an unobstructed view of the stage. And one of the greatest reasons for rejoicing was the stage's lighting system, one of the severest limitations offered by the Auditorium all these years. Now, light could be directed to any area of the stage from any angle, with the result that the old scenery took on new life and dimension.[17]

Most of the artists were delighted with the new house, although some of them claimed the deep auditorium and distant boxes limited audience contact. Lotte Lehmann, who made her American debut in Chicago in 1930 as Sieglinde, was highly excited about it: "The stage is fitted with the most modern devices. The dressing rooms have their own bathrooms."[18] Actually Mme. Lehmann had preferred to sing at the Metropolitan that season. But the Met at this time had very little interest in the German wing of the repertoire, and therefore for the next three years remained rather passive toward Mme. Lehmann and many of her colleagues. However, the diva writes in her autobiography, "We gave very fine performances" during that first year in Chicago.[19]

The 1930–31 season marked Mary Garden's last year with the Chicago Opera. And, unlike many of her associates, the soprano did not just quietly fade off the American operatic scene. Mary Garden never did anything quietly. She left as she had entered—a controversial figure with her name in the headlines.

The big Garden production that year was *Camille*, an opera composed by a twenty-seven-year-old Chicago ex-office boy named Hamilton Forrest. The work had never been heard anywhere, and it was staged now primarily because Garden wanted to do it. Insull himself was somewhat skeptical about the whole affair, concerned, as always, with balancing the budget. La Garden, as we well know, understood nothing of this budget business and insisted that the opera must be staged, lavish in every detail. And so, rather than martyr himself, Insull consented. *Camille* would be given its chance.

Then in the fall of 1930, as the bills for the production began pouring in, the impresario found himself nervously thumbing the pages of his financial ledger, gasping harder with every page. The cost of the scenery alone came to over $42,000. For the first act a massive set was created, dominated by a huge twenty-eight foot staircase. La Garden had no more than arrived in Chicago from Paris when she ordered the *Camille* sets mounted. Upon arrival at the Opera House, the diva took one look at that first-act colossus and shook her head. While poor Samuel Insull grabbed for his wallet, Madame explained that it simply would not do. The whole thing would have to be done over.[20]

On December 10, after many long, expensive hours of rehearsal, *Camille* was given its world premiere before a sold-out house. The opera consisted of three acts and a prologue. When the initial curtain went up, there was nothing on stage but a huge book on which was written "Camille." Then a young man came out and opened its pages, displaying first the entrance of the Paris *Opéra Comique*. With the turning of another page, Marguerite Gautier was discovered sitting in her box at the opera, being introduced to the handsome Armond. Act I took place in a fashionable gambling house two years later, the second was played in Marguerite's salon, and the last in her boudoir.

The production (except for the sets which everyone agreed were gorgeous) was received with mixed emotions. The first-night audience gave the opera an enthusiastic send-off and declared that Mary Garden had done it again. René Devries, of *Musical Courier*, states that he stopped counting the curtain calls after the first ten but he is sure some sort of a record was set.

Professional critics, on the other hand, were less enchanted with both *Camille* and La Garden. Except for her dramatic last act, Devries found the diva totally disappointing: "Poorly made up with a wig that did not fit her, she did not look the demimondaine, but a sort of caricature of Zaza, a courtesan of the low class and not the one who would stroll through the Bois with the Count de G and his friends."[21] Forrest's score, which Mary Garden herself admitted "just screeched with modernism,"[22] was received even less favorably by the critics. *Musical America*'s Albert Goldberg flatly stated, "We were bored."[23]

At the end of the season, Mary Garden left Chicago, having decided to retire from the American scene. For twenty years the soprano's name had been linked almost synonymously with that of the Chicago Opera. While her art remained somewhat controversial, no one could deny that the diva had caused more excitement, both on stage and off, than any other artist of her day. It is no exaggeration to say that the soprano's retirement marked more than the end of a brilliant career; it did in fact herald the closing of a whole glorious era.

The following year saw the beginning of several changes for the Chicago Opera. First, the company acquired a new artistic director when Herbert Witherspoon, later to serve briefly as general manager of the Metropolitan, was brought in to replace ailing Giorgio Polacco.[24]

Next, the 1931 season would see the end of a second five-year period of financial guarantee. Another fund-raising drive would have to be waged. But the prospects of raising the necessary $500,-000 were at best slight, for by now the economic crisis which had started on Wall Street in October 1929 had spread to every artery of the nation's fiscal blood stream. Prices and incomes not only had dropped alarmingly, but were continuing their rapid decline. Banks were failing, and the lists of bankrupt businesses grew daily. Millions were unemployed. In some areas starvation was an ever-present threat. In times as uncertain as these, the formerly generous supporters of the Chicago Opera were reluctant to commit themselves to guarantee any project, no matter how worthy the project might be. Perhaps next year after things have calmed down, but now they already had too many other commitments.

By the end of the season, it had become obvious that the guarantee fund necessary for the company to continue operations could not be raised. When on top of everything else Samuel Insull himself met with financial disaster, the company suspended the fund drive altogether. Consequently, in the spring of 1932 the Chicago Civic Opera Company collapsed. For the next two decades—the first dominated by economic disorder, the second by global conflict—Chicago operatic history was one of struggle and disillusionment. The spring of 1932 found Chicago with an attractive new opera house but no company to use it. Even the Ravinia Park project, which had produced beautiful open-air operas for the past seventeen summers, had been abandoned with the depression. For a city which had so recently possessed one of the two finest opera companies in the nation, such a sudden turn of events could only mean complete and utter civic frustration, a frustration intensified by the fact that many had believed that the realization of Insull's dreams at 20 North Wacker would mean a permanent economic panacea for the city's opera. To have come so close to Utopia, only to find all hopes dashed on the rocks of financial ruin, left the city's opera forces thoroughly demoralized.

Then, adding a sad denouement to an already tragic tale, in the early part of 1933 a federal grand jury indicted Samuel Insull on charges of fraud in connection with the bankruptcy of some of his utility companies, the collapse of which had ruined nearly 300,000 small stockholders. Insull, preferring not to face the charges, fled to Greece, where he was given legal sanctuary,[25] but was eventually brought home to trial.

Nevertheless, Chicago continued to dream of an operatic renaissance. From 1933 to 1940 an organization known first as the Chicago Grand Opera and later as the Chicago City Opera Company, under the direction of Paul Longone, staged a yearly season of modest-priced opera, mainly with Metropolitan stars. The productions generally left much to be desired, primarily because of financial limitations. Pinza, Mason, Martinelli, Lehmann, Pons, Moore, Melchior, and Flagstad all sang for Longone at one time or another, but only occasionally were the productions worthy of their talent. Rosa Raisa returned to the city in 1935 to take the lead in the American premiere of Respighi's *La Fiamma*, one of the company's bigger successes. *Musical America* acclaimed the work "the most important operatic novelty heard here since *Der Rosenkavalier* was first revealed."[26] Still, as *Time* magazine candidly pointed out, "It was not enough to make subscribers forget what they had sat through before."[27]

Longone's seasons were invariably plagued with financial difficulties, operating on a budget that had been cut to the bone. On more than one occasion it was highly improbable at six o'clock in the evening that the curtain would even go up at eight. The performances were more often than not ragged, sometimes making it hard to believe that they had been rehearsed at all. Many of the artists were totally unqualified for the roles they sang, for one of Longone's more questionable policies was his Italian custom of permitting wealthy would-be singers to purchase productions, a practice which the impresario defended on the basis that it helped balance the budget.[28]

In an attempt to make a go of its 1936–37 season, the company succeeded in talking the retired Amelita Galli-Curci into making a highly publicized reappearance. The diva had recently undergone a goiter operation, and it was now claimed that her voice was as beautiful as ever. The soprano maintained that the operation had given her voice new weight, and, consequently, she was through with the coloratura roles and was now planning to concentrate on lyric and dramatic parts.

The much-heralded return came early in December, with Mme. Galli-Curci singing Mimi in Puccini's *La Bohème*. The house was sold out far in advance, at gala prices, and the management was fairly beaming with excitement. However, except from the financial standpoint, the event was a sad disappointment. While the soprano was most enthusiastically cheered by an admiring audience, her voice was decidedly unsteady, lacking its former brilliance and color.[29]

Somehow Longone managed to keep his company together. Then suddenly, just as plans were being concluded for the 1939–40 season, disaster struck Chicago's opera again. Paul Longone died. Henry Weber, who for several years had served as one of the company's principal conductors, took over as musical director.[30] With Longone's death, however, the central pillar had been torn from under the Chicago City Opera. The manager's enthusiasm and hard work had provided the cohesive forces necessary for holding the company together through these most difficult years of depression. With his passing, the project, at least as a corporate body, shortly disintegrated, to be revamped as the Chicago Opera Company, Henry Weber now serving as general manager.

Weber remained with the new company one year, then resigned. The level of the performances under his management was higher than it had been, but so was the deficit. As a result financial patronage took a sharp drop. Weber withdrew at the end of the season, declaring that "conditions and circumstances are such that I feel the high excellence maintained last year cannot be repeated."[31] Fortune Gallo, well-known director of the itinerant San Carlo Opera Company and a man with an eye on the box-office, was appointed his successor. In his first season Gallo proved that if anyone could make opera pay, he could. The public flocked to see his productions, and capacity audiences seemed the rule rather than the exception. The attendance record at the end of the season showed sixteen sold-out houses out of a possible twenty-six, with an over-all attendance of 90 per cent.[32]

And yet, having won the financial battle, impresario Gallo soon found himself engaged in another, for by his second season the United States had been swept into World War II. The nation was finding the war effort more than a full-time job. Transportation facilities were buckling under the strain, and wartime priorities placed a sharp limitation on any nonmilitary endeavor. Gallo managed to stage a season in 1942, but the next year the company temporarily suspended operations, largely because of the difficulties in assembling an adequate company. The war situation had simply been too much, yet *Musical America* continued to remind its readers in large, bold type, "Music Maintains Morale! Music Must Go On!"[33]

During this operatic void the skyscraper at 20 North Wacker, including the Opera House, changed hands. The General Finance Corporation bought it, paying $266,000 to the Chicago Music Foundation (the charitable trust formed by Insull which controlled a lion's share of the stock in the building) and assuming a $9,885,000 mortgage. The funds received by the Chicago Music Foundation were set aside to help support the city's resident opera over the next ten-year period.[34]

Needless to say, the promise of an annual grant of over $25,000 for the next ten years served as an attractive impetus for reviving the idle Chicago Opera Company. On December 5, 1943, the board of directors announced that there *would* be opera in 1944. Fausto Cleva, noted Metropolitan conductor and musical director of the Cincinnati Opera, became the Chicago company's new general manager.

While Maestro Cleva's productions aroused considerable popular enthusiasm, by now the Chicago Opera had become practically a carbon copy of the Metropolitan. Met stars, whose names were powerful enough to attract large audiences, were brought in to sing essentially the same roles they were singing in New York at the time. Elsa Borowski, writing for *Musical Courier*, was out-spoken in her condemnation of this practice which she considered simply a poorly disguised Pandora's box. "The hasty borrowing of singers from the Metropolitan for an appearance or two," she wrote, "is a system which contains within itself the seeds of decay, as obviously a fine ensemble cannot be achieved by this means. No 'star,' however refulgent, can entirely carry a performance."[35] Still, as long as the war continued, it remained impossible to import gifted singers from abroad, therefore making Chicago's dependence on the Metropolitan almost inevitable.

One star whom the company did not borrow from the Met was Hollywood's Jeanette MacDonald, who in 1944, after a decade of making movies with Nelson Eddy, had decided to try her hand at opera. Most of the critics immediately chalked up this movie queen-turned-prima donna arrangement as nothing more than a shrewd box-office maneuver and were more than liberal with their snide comments on the subject. The afternoon of Miss MacDonald's debut, however, was accompanied by wholesale critical re-evaluation.

The opera was Gounod's *Romeo and Juliet*, and the house was sold out. Despite a sudden substitution in tenors (forcing her to sing opposite Captain Michael Bartlett, with whom she had not even rehearsed), a last minute change in staging (which saw most of the action shifted to the opposite side of the stage), and a brand-new conductor (who took the cadenzas slower than she had learned them), the soprano's performance was a remarkable success, artistically as well as financially. Contrary to predictions, no one laughed when Miss MacDonald sang, and except for one scene in which the audience mistook Romeo's dark head for a cat in Juliet's lap, no one laughed at all.[36]

As a matter of fact, the slim, red-headed star, youthful in voice and figure, gave Juliet a freshness which the operatic stage has rarely known. Dressed in a dazzling new costume for each of the opera's five acts, the singer's dramatic sense imbued the role with an unusual balance and smoothness. Even the *Tribune*'s Claudia Cassidy, never one to bestow idle praise upon any artist, agreed that Miss Mac-Donald had given a "charming performance in Gounod miniature which left us wondering what her beauty, charm, and good coaching could do to beguile us in the more taxing role of Marguerite."[37]

Miss Cassidy had only to puzzle that question a few days, for later in the week *Faust* was staged with Jeanette MacDonald as Marguerite. And again the singer met with amazing success. Having been coached in the role by Lotte Lehmann, Miss MacDonald proved that, though possessing no great volume, her voice was capable enough of meeting Gounod's vocal demands.[38]

Fausto Cleva had headed the Chicago Opera Company for three seasons when the company met financial disaster. The productions had improved with each season, and by 1946 the management disclosed "a standard of performance that Chicagoans had long ceased to expect from . . . [their] local company."[39] But again there was the old problem of deficits—over $150,000 in 1946.[40] And so the Chicago Opera, wrapped in a shroud of artistic glory, was given a pauper's burial. Once more, the Windy City underwent operatic starvation.

For the next eight years, Chicago heard no opera of its own, only touring companies. But in the spring of 1951, three musical wizards asked themselves why the second largest city in the United States, with one of the three finest opera houses in the country, could not support a first-rate opera company. The answer they gave was, "No reason at all." These three were Carol Fox, a young woman of some financial means who had studied to be a singer; Lawrence Kelly, who had inherited his father's real estate business, but had always had a keen interest in music; and Nicola Rescigno, a dedicated young conductor whose specialty was Italian opera. Their combined ages would scarcely have totaled more than a hundred.[41]

The whole thing started when Carol Fox returned to Chicago in 1950 from studying voice in Europe. A group that had been considering the possibilities of forming a new opera company there invited the young singer to join them in their project. It was hoped that the soprano might be interested in singing in some of the operas and—more important—that her wealthy family would be willing to pay for her productions. Although Miss Fox did not accept the offer, it did start her thinking about the possibility of shifting from opera singer to opera manager.

A few weeks later she was in Nicola Rescigno's office in New York. It was just a friendly call, Maestro Rescigno at one time having been Miss Fox's vocal coach. In the course of the conversation the telephone rang. Rescigno talked for some time, growing more and more excited. As he hung up, the conductor turned to his visitor and asked, "Do you know who that was? It was Fortune Gallo, and he wants to start an opera company in Chicago!"

To Rescigno's surprise, Carol Fox was something less than enthusiastic about his announcement. "Oh, Nicky, don't go in with Gallo!" she exclaimed at last. "I'm thinking about forming a company myself!" While Rescigno listened attentively, his former pupil bared her plans, nebulous as they were. Yes, he was interested. But how would they ever get the necessary backing?

Upon returning to Chicago, Carol Fox incorporated her proposed opera company as the Lyric Theatre of Chicago and then began an active campaign of electioneering. In the meantime she met Lawrence Kelly, a bright young businessman with enough nervous energy for a whole corporation. Kelly was intensely interested in seeing opera returned to Chicago, and before long he was invited to join the organization.[42]

In February, 1952, the three operatic dreamers met in New York to discuss plans. The meeting occurred in Box Eight of the Metropolitan Opera House, where the blissful trio chatted for hours. Eventually the conference adjourned to the Hotel Waldorf Astoria, where there was more stationery available to figure on. It was a crazy scheme, but it just might work.[43]

Back in Chicago, the would-be impresarios found their proposals received with mixed emotions. Local critics, like Claudia Cassidy, were as excited as they were encouraging. Equally enthusiastic were the officials of 20 North Wacker, who, incidentally, would receive a sizable tax advantage if opera were regularly staged in the Opera House. Many local businessmen also went out of their way to lend a helping hand to the nascent opera company. On the other hand, the opposition group hesitated to turn over $5,000,000 worth of sets and $7,000,000 in costumes, left over from the Insull regime, to three "kids."[44]

And so the youngsters decided to show their reluctant elders what they could do. After several months of work, the Opera House was reserved, and a "calling card" performance of Mozart's *Don Giovanni* was announced for February 5, 1954. Nicola Rossi-Lemeni was the Don, Eleanor Steber the Donna Anna, Irene Jordan the Donna Elvira, and Bidu Sayao the Zerlina. Nicola Rescigno conducted. The old sets from the Insull era were dusted off and graced with a brilliant chorus and ballet. As Claudia Cassidy put it, "It was an astonishing performance on the higher level, created out of hopes and dreams."[45]

Although the "calling card" performance resulted in a deficit of $922.34, it succeeded in convincing even the most skeptical Chicagoan that the Lyric Theatre's three promoters were musically wise beyond their years. With the nod to go ahead, Carol Fox left for Europe to scout for talent for a regular fall season.[46]

The array of artists which the three young impresarios lined up caused not only Chicago, but the entire operatic world to blink in disbelief, enough to arouse the interest of even the most casual American opera-goer. First they succeeded in capturing the reigning queen of opera, Maria Callas, convincing her that she should make her long-awaited American debut in Chicago. Then there was Giulietta Simionato, *La Scala*'s leading mezzo-soprano; Giuseppe di Stefano, *La Scala*'s principal tenor; and Tito Gobbi, *La Scala*'s chief baritone—to name just a few. Not only were these singers high-caliber talent (known primarily in this country through their recordings), but only two of the artists which the Lyric contracted—Eleanor Steber and Lorenzo Alvary—were on the current Metropolitan roster. Here then, was a fresh group of singers with a fresh approach to the lyric stage, who would give Chicago's resident opera its first really new look in over twenty years.

And so the Windy City prepared to launch its first season of local opera in nearly a decade, a season, which, largely because of its independence of the Metropolitan, immediately drew national and even international recognition. Thinking back, all three of the Lyric Theatre's promoters virtually tremble at their own daring. Lawrence Kelly recalled several years later that the company was launched with "eighty-seven sets in the warehouse from the Insull regime, a great many hopes, and even more guts."[47] Claudia Cassidy, who had seen more than one opera company in Chicago collapse, declared in retrospect, "Their necks were out so far they must at times have thought the chopping block inevitable."[48]

But Chicagoans took a look at the proposed season, shook their heads in amazement, and rushed to the box office. Of the sixteen performances given in this first season, twelve were sold out. Not only that, but ticket-orders came from every state in the Union, plus the territory of Alaska.[49]

Then, suddenly, it was opening night, November 1, 1954. The Civic Opera House "blazed with an electricity that had not been felt since Samuel Insull opened it in 1929." Old-timers and youngsters alike were bubbling over the prospects of an operatic renaissance in their city. From time to time one could glimpse a reminder of yesterday's glories simply by scanning the first-night audience, for Rosa Raisa, Edith Mason, and Giorgio Polacco were all there, eagerly applauding a new era.[50]

And certainly there was plenty to applaud. On stage was the illustrious Callas, making her United States debut in Bellini's *Norma*. By the end of the first act Chicago knew what Europe had known for several years, that here was not only an imposing singer, but a highly-skilled dramatic actress as well. "Don't wake me if I'm dreaming," wrote Claudia Cassidy. Then excitedly, she explained, Callas "has presence and style, and she sings magnificently. . . . Her range is formidable, and her technique dazzling. She sang the '*Casta diva*' in a kind of mystic dream, like a goddess of the moon briefly descended."[51] Ronald Eyer of *Musical America* declared, "The voice is excitingly big, vividly colored and meticulously schooled."[52]

Still, this was no one-woman show, for mezzo Giulietta Simionato as Adalgisa kept her audience enraptured every minute she was on stage. Not to be overlooked either were Nicola Rossi-Lemeni's Oroveso and Mirto Picchi's Pollione. Nor did the singers alone turn the trick, for the ensemble, the orchestra, the chorus, Rescigno's conducting, and the staging were all superb. It was in short as perfectly integrated a performance as Chicago had ever seen, rivaling the productions of the city's golden age.

A few evenings later, Maria Callas was again on stage, now as Verdi's *Traviata*, revealing three different voices to project the various moods of the role. For a second time in less than a fortnight, Chicagoans were entranced, both musically and dramatically, by the diva's commanding stage presence. Critics Dosha Dowdy and René Devries, without qualification, pronounced her "the greatest singer-tragedienne of the lyric stage."[53]

But the Callas pinnacle was not reached until Donizetti's old warhorse *Lucia di Lammermoor* was trotted out. Here the diva not only electrified her audience with an amazing display of virtuosity, but also imbued Lucia with a heart and soul, making the character for once a believable human being. At the end of a magnificent "Mad Scene" the audience rose almost spontaneously to pay the diva the greatest tribute an artist can receive. Such shouting, cheering, and foot-stomping the Opera House had not known in many a year. A casual observer might well have thought Donizetti had written the "Mad Scene" for the audience.[54] Edith Mason, an exuberant part of that standing ovation, confessed that only twice in her life had she seen such a demonstration for a singer. One was for Caruso; the other was for Callas after this Chicago *Lucia*.[55]

While Maria Callas was the greatest single sensation of this first Lyric Theatre season, there were a number of other triumphs as well. Giulietta Simionato and Tito Gobbi teamed for a highly successful *Barber of Seville*. Roger Dettmer of the *Chicago American* found a *La Bohème* with Rosanna Carteri superior to the Metropolitan's production "note for note, role for role, act for act."[56] And the world premiere of Victorio Giannini's *The Taming of the Shrew* was pronounced by the *Sun-Times* the "first really expert operatic score by an American that ever has been heard in this city."[57]

The one disappointment of the Lyric's first season was a *Carmen* which stubbed its toe rather badly. By that time, however, Chicagoans were so thoroughly elated with their new opera company that they could well overlook a single fiasco. As a matter of fact, one man who had earlier contributed ten dollars to the company's fundraising campaign, sent the management the following note: "I was beginning to think you were infallible when I saw your *Carmen*. Thank God you're not. Here's another $5."[58]

At the close of this glorious season, little doubt remained that Chicago had rejoined the opera capitals of the world. The combination of Fox (general manager), Kelly (managing director), and Rescigno (musical director) had proved artistic dynamite. *Musical America* concluded, "If respect for musical values, intelligent and imaginative casting and forward-seeking ideas of repertoire have any meaning, the success of this venture on artistic grounds is already assured."[59]

But what about next year? Could the company ever hope to compete with the standards it had set for itself? And what about its prima donna, Maria Callas—would she be back?

As plans were begun for the 1955 season, Lawrence Kelly drew the job of following Mme. Callas all over Europe with the goal to get her signature affixed to a contract. The two met, talked, discussed repertoire, casting, and terms until it seemed that nothing could possibly be left to talk about. Finally, after Kelly had agreed to all of Madame's requests, she agreed to sign. Then the diva turned to the Chicago impresario and made a suggestion which gave Kelly a real start. "You should sign up Renata Tebaldi," she announced calmly. "Then your audience will have the opportunity to compare us, and your season will be even more successful."[60]

At the time Tebaldi was Callas' only serious rival, and it was generally known that their relationship was anything but cordial. Aside from that, the prospects of having both Callas and Tebaldi on the Chicago roster were almost staggering. Nevertheless, the management began negotiations with Renata Tebaldi, and before long she too had signed a highly desirable contract.

Consequently, the Lyric Theatre's second season found the management offering Callas and Tebaldi in alternate performances for a ten-night stand unparalleled anywhere. Callas opened with Bellini's *I Puritani*. Tebaldi raised with an *Aïda*. Callas stayed with an *Il Trovatore*. Tebaldi called with *La Bohème*. It doubtless would have been a draw, except that Callas had a *Madama Butterfly* still to go. So great was the popular demand for tickets for this *Butterfly* that the soprano agreed to give an additional performance. An hour and thirty-eight minutes after the box-office sale began, every seat in the house was sold.[61]

The special performance was given, with Callas receiving a warm farewell tribute from her devoted Chicago admirers. Then, after her final curtain call, the real drama of that day took place. On her way back to her dressing-room, La Callas was greeted by a process-server, who had been lurking about for several days. It seems that back in 1946 an unknown Maria Callas had signed a contract with one Edward Bagarozy, giving him the sole managerial rights to her career. In the meantime, however, she and Bagarozy had gone their separate ways—she becoming the toast of Europe, without any assistance from her one-time manager. Nevertheless, the contract remained, and Bagarozy was determined to take full advantage of it. Consequently, when the diva walked off the stage after her final *Butterfly*, she suddenly had a summons thrust into her kimono.

La Callas, whose temperament is legendary, proceeded to top her Butterfly with an impromptu, but nonetheless impassioned, rendition of *Medea*, aided by her husband Giovanni Battista Meneghini. While the tirade continued, a wide-eyed Carol Fox and a dumbfounded Lawrence Kelly looked on in amazement. In the midst of the harangue, the two Lyric managers caught one verbal blast which made them livid. "Chicago will be sorry for this!" Madame shrieked. And sorry it was.[62]

Maria Callas left Chicago that year, vowing never to sing with the company again. The Lyric management had promised her protection against such an incident, and their defense had failed. And yet, stormy as this final scene was, the diva had served Chicago well, turning immediate international recognition upon a nascent company which, without her, might have been just another noble attempt at reviving Chicago's operatic tradition. As *Time* magazine put it, "She taught a new generation what it was like to catch opera fever."[63]

Meanwhile, the Lyric Theatre's 1955 season still had three more weeks to run. By now, however, both Callas and Tebaldi had left the city—Callas apparently for good, Tebaldi promising to return next year. Fine though the remainder of the season was, with its two luminaries gone, it was almost anticlimactic.

Enmeshed with these artistic glories, however, was a recurring note of foreboding, heralding an internal dispute which was soon to split the Lyric Theatre wide open. The trouble started when musical director Nicola Rescigno presented the company a contract in which he demanded the sole right of veto on all matters artistic. At first both Carol Fox and Lawrence Kelly balked, but eventually Kelly was swung over to Rescigno's side.[64]

The feud boiled down to a clash of opinion over production philosophy. Rescigno and Kelly, the idealists, felt that in all cases artistic standards and production dynamism were of paramount importance. Rather than settle for a repetitious "safe" repertoire,

Kelly had said, "I would go back to the real-estate business. I love music too much to be satisfied with that familiar old routine."[65] The more businesslike Carol Fox, on the other hand, was ever aware of the box office and guarantor support. In her mind artistic standards were fine, but the guarantors must also be satisfied. If this meant compromising, then compromise one must.

Eventually the schism degenerated into a prolonged court battle and name-calling session which saw both factions struggling for control. The board of directors, consisting of six members, was equally divided, three and three. After several months of stalemate, during which neither side could transact any business or make plans for the coming season, Carol Fox succeeded in gaining the necessary financial backing and consequently was given the legal nod to go ahead.[66] Kelly shortly received a bid from Dallas to become general manager of the newly-formed civic opera company there. Rescigno went to Texas also, as the Dallas Civic Opera's artistic director.

Meanwhile, the Carol Fox group had reorganized the Chicago opera under the somewhat redundant title Lyric Opera of Chicago, assuming both the assets and the liabilities of the former Lyric Theatre. The assets primarily consisted of several contracts with artists for the upcoming 1956 season. The major liability was a deficit of $50,000, hanging over from the previous season.[67]

If the Chicago Lyric has never quite regained its original verve, it has continued to produce highly creditable opera, boasting a particularly impressive artistic roster. Renata Tebaldi has returned to the company season after season, along with Chicago favorites Simionato, Gobbi, and Boris Christoff. These four have been offered in most of their best roles, and occasionally the repertoire has even been specially tailored to gratify their talents. But a host of new artists has been introduced too—Anna Moffo, Carlo Bergonzi, Renata Scotto, Ilva Ligabue, Régine Crespin, and others in their American debut. Every season the Lyric's productions contain a number of fresh voices, often before they have been heard at the Metropolitan. Leontyne Price, Birgit Nilsson, Eileen Farrell, and Leonie Rysanek all appeared with the Lyric before singing at the Met.

Undoubtedly, the strongest point of Carol Fox's company has been a depth in casting. All-star productions have almost become expected. Take for example a *Forza del Destino* in 1956 with Tebaldi, Simionato, Richard Tucker, Ettore Bastianini, Nicola Rossi-Lemeni, and Georg Solti conducting. The following season opened with *Otello*, featuring Tebaldi, Gobbi, and Mario del Monaco, with Tullio Serafin in the pit. *Falstaff* in 1958 had Gobbi, Tebaldi, Simionato, Moffo, and Cornell MacNeil. A 1960 production of *Marriage of Figaro* boasted Elisabeth Schwarzkopf, Rita Streich, Christa Ludwig, Walter Berry, and Eberhard Wächter, a cast then virtually unknown to the Metropolitan. True, these stellar casts have not always jelled as the management had hoped, but rare is the production which has not at least had its moments.

The Lyric has also been highly successful at spicing up the standard repertoire by mixing in an occasional unfamiliar ingredient. Such rarely given works as Rossini's *Cenerentola*, Cilea's *Adriana Lecouvreur* (with Tebaldi), Janácek's *Jenufa*, Massenet's *Thaïs* (with Price), Giordano's *Fedora* (with Tebaldi), Boïto's *Mefistofele* (with Christoff), Giannini's *Harvest* (in its world premiere), Borodin's *Prince Igor* (with Christoff), Verdi's *Nabucco,* and Donizetti's *La Favorita* have all been given with better than average success.

But the company has its weaknesses, which have often been painfully apparent. The fact that the company fell heir to a whole warehouse-full of scenery and costumes has been a mixed blessing. Since the organization does possess most of the essential sets, it has tended to slight new productions, instead allocating a large share of the funds to the importing of all-star casts. Consequently, Leontyne Price's *Thaïs* in 1959 was sung with the same scenery that had been used when Mary Garden sang the role. Even when new operas are mounted, their sets are often a composite affair, snatched piecemeal from other productions. The results are that all too often the Lyric's physical productions are almost shamefully ragged. Partially because of these antiquated sets, the company's lighting has repeatedly been weak, often consciously dim to hide the scenic relics on stage. Stage direction frequently has been perfunctory, at times even absurd.

Still, the Lyric Opera's contribution has been a great one. With the success of the Lyric, Chicago has at last regained its place as one of the world's leading opera centers. Despite its weaknesses, which in time may resolve themselves, the company has made remarkable progress toward entrenching itself as a permanent operatic organization. Certainly in its brief history the Lyric has already added a new depth to the American operatic scene, frequently operating on a plane with the Metropolitan and at times—particularly in casting and now and then in repertoire—anticipating the Met by several seasons.

Lyric Gold
in California

Although New Orleans was the scene of the first opera in the United States, New York has claim to the nation's oldest opera company still in existence, the Metropolitan. It was in 1883, largely in protest to the snobbish Academy of Music where the Astors insisted on nothing less than full dress, that the Vanderbilt clan sponsored the building of the Metropolitan. Within a few years the Met had earned the right to be crowned queen of American opera houses and had become the principal sporting ground of the *nouveau riche*.

Forty years later, the second oldest continuous opera group in the country was organized in San Francisco. Here the founding angel, Gaetano Merola, was not so much a man of wealth as a man of ability and vision. While still in his youth, Merola fell in love with the west coast, having made several extensive tours through the region. In 1923 the energetic young conductor took steps to form a permanent opera company in the area, the San Francisco Opera Association.

Merola's company often left much to be desired in its early days, but the organization steadily grew in strength and matured in production wisdom. Too dependent at first upon the Metropolitan for its own artistic good, it eventually managed to shake itself loose from the Met's protective apron strings to become an independent enterprise with its own roster of artists, its own repertoire, and its own production ideas.

Opera, however, was not suddenly thrust upon a musically untutored San Francisco in 1923 by Merola and his staff, for the city's operatic history extends back to the mid-nineteenth century, a history tinted with the dust from the California gold-fields.

In 1848 with the discovery of gold near Sutter's Fort, California virtually overnight became a name on the lips of an entire nation. The following year many an eastern worker told his employer all those things he had been wanting to tell him for some time and rather haughtily slammed the industrial door on his way west. Farmers all over the country threw down their plows, hitched up the covered wagon, loading in the wife and young ones, and headed for the golden west. Sailors struck with the gold fever were known to jump ship in their frenzy to strike it rich in California. Eastern misfits and malcontents—all the way from the lady in red to the labor agitator to the dissatisfied husband with the plumpish, aging wife—looked to the west and caught the scent of new hope, an opportunity to begin life over again. And so the migration to California began, bringing men and women from all walks of life. But the lure was always the same—gold.

California towns that, until now, had been nothing more than sleepy little Spanish villages, suddenly mushroomed into thriving, dynamic communities. San Francisco, at the gateway to the gold-producing hills, served as the main base of supply for a multitude of eager prospectors and became one of the more important of these mining boom towns. Here wooden shacks were hastily thrown up to house the shopkeepers, the bartenders, and the indispensable dance-hall girls. Plank sidewalks were built, giving the bustling town an air of permanency. By June, 1851, the first vigilance committee was created in a desperate attempt to bring some semblance of law and order to the uninhibited western town. What had been a couple of years earlier barely a town at all, now contained a population of nearly 25,000, about 90 per cent of whom were male.

Even amid the crudeness and turbulence of the gold-rush days, however, the San Franciscans possessed an almost religious awe for the culture of the eastern dude. In 1850, for instance, Henri Herz, a Viennese pianist, came west, and San Francisco heard its first notable concert artist. For some reason the local citizenry turned out in full force to hear the "fancy playin'," and Herz went home with enough gold dust to pay off most of the losses which he had suffered earlier on some unwise European investments.[1]

On February 12, 1851, just two years after the gold rush, San Francisco viewed its first grand opera, when the Pellegrini Opera Troupe presented Bellini's *La Sonnambula* at the old Adelphi Theater. A fortnight later, the same group gave *Norma,* and still later, Verdi's *Ernani,* with prices ranging from one to four dollars.[2] The San Francisco citizenry, a motley collection to be sure, flocked to the opera house, largely because they had heard this was something one did if he had wealth to spare. Yet while most of these frontiersmen came to the opera merely to acquire the trappings of eastern society, many of them actually went away intrigued by what they saw and heard there. Especially were they drawn to the early Italian operas. It seems that these westerners tended to identify themselves with the operatic characters of Verdi and Bellini, and in many respects life in the mining camp did have an operatic quality about it. "Overnight, new arrivals won fortune or suffered ruin. Classes were fluid; social differences fluctuated; individual bravura was applauded; sudden reversals of situations were experienced by almost everyone. The mood was grandiose. An air of triumph and unexpectedness pervaded the atmosphere."[3] Consequently, grand opera in many ways was consistent with this rather bizarre, melodramatic life of the West, and the lyric drama proved a highly satisfying medium of entertainment.

During the decade following the discovery of gold in California, a number of theaters—gaudy, architectural monstrosities in most cases—rapidly began appearing to house the operatic and dramatic productions which the well-paying San Francisco public demanded. In 1851, for example, the Jenny Lind Theater (Jenny herself was never there) was built opposite the Plaza, with a seating capacity of some 2,000. A year later, the American Theater, on Sansome Street, was completed, a worthy rival for the finest opera houses of the East. Although many of these early theatrical structures were destroyed by fire, they were generally rebuilt within a short time, the second version usually more elaborate and ornate than the first.[4]

On a rainy day in February, 1852, the semaphore atop Telegraph Hill signaled the San Franciscans that an ocean steamer was making its way into the harbor. On board was the first real prima donna the rustic coastal city had ever seen, Mme. Eliza Biscaccianti, widely known for her many vocal triumphs throughout the East. To a world still primarily limited to the male sex, as California was in the 1850's, the arrival of any woman was a notable event. But Mme. Biscaccianti, armed with a pair of dancing eyes, a winning smile, and a glorious voice, was no ordinary woman. Within a matter of hours after she stepped off the boat, the diva had captured the heart of the city with her glamor and charm. Under the management of the renowned P. T. Barnum, Eliza Biscaccianti, known as the "American Thrush," gave ten concerts during that visit in 1852, each of which was received enthusiastically by the San Francisco public.[5]

More and more frequently during the 1850's itinerant opera groups began wandering into California from Mexico, presenting either French or Italian operas. In 1854 the Italian Opera Troupe, the first really complete company to play San Francisco, visited the city with Mme. Clotilda Barili as its prima donna. That year alone eleven different opera seasons were given in the city, demonstrating that the San Franciscans had more than just a casual interest in the art of the lyric theater.[6]

By far the most sensational musical event that year was the appearance of Anna Bishop, who in midsummer sang the lead in Weber's *Der Freischütz* at San Francisco's Metropolitan Theater. The *Golden Era* maintained that this was "incomparably the finest operatic performance ever given in this city" up to that time.[7] The opera itself is quite a spectacle, but a rather grim tale about Lucifer's attempt to win a couple of souls for the cause of infamy. During the first San Francisco performance of the work, a bit of comic relief came when a supernumerary suddenly appeared on stage, carrying a blue bucket and a rusty tin dipper, and hurriedly began extinguishing the fire in the magic circle, which, through the negligence of a stage hand, had gotten a little out of hand.

On the last evening of Mme. Bishop's 1854 season in the city, the same opera ran into further difficulties. At the end of the second act the gas lights all over the theater suddenly went out—"with the result that the audience was obliged to do the same."[8]

In 1859 a company formed by Thomas Maguire gave the bay city performances of opera at prices ranging from fifty cents to one dollar. The company made a splendid showing at its opening, but shortly afterward the group dissolved, leaving poor Maguire holding his libretto. The impresario, still determined to carry out his ambitions, eventually imported the New Orleans English Opera Troupe, which staged a number of performances in the San Francisco area.[9]

To enumerate every opera company that played the bay city during the fifties and sixties would be difficult, for more companies came to the city during those two decades than during any other period of the same length. Yet touring in the West in those days was not without its problems. Time and again these troupes would meet with tragedy of one kind or another, forcing them to disband. Stranded artists whose funds had run short frequently were compelled to settle where fate left them, often becoming teachers, choir directors, or perhaps even music critics.[10]

San Francisco did not possess a resident opera group during these early days, as New Orleans did, but the abundance of touring companies which came through made sure that the young boom town never lacked musical opportunities. And the San Franciscans generally took full advantage of their chances to hear opera, particularly if the offering were of the early Italian school. "No city in the New World was more eager to hear the latest importation from Italy than the turbulent new town by the Golden Gate."[11] Donizetti was a particular favorite, especially his *Daughter of the Regiment*, which received more performances during the mining period than any other single opera. Nevertheless, the works of Verdi, Rossini, and Bellini also received their share of attention.[12]

These were the gold-rush days, and in this rustic era the enthusiasm of the westerners could be nearly as unrestrained in the opera house as it was in the dance hall or saloon. More than once a singer in the midst of a grand ovation found himself being pelted with pieces of raw gold which his admirers hurled on stage in a gesture of sincere tribute.[13] Perhaps artistic conditions were not ideal, but, on the other hand, one could hardly deny such ardent enthusiasm, especially when it involved gold.

During the 1860's there was little letup in San Francisco's rich operatic life. Eliza Biscaccianti, the city's first real prima donna, reappeared on the scene in 1861 and tried to establish an opera company using local talent, but the venture met with little success.[14] A few years later, the diva took to drink and was reduced to singing at the Bella Union, a famous variety hall, "where the customers did not mind if she leaned unsteadily against a wall or table."[15]

In 1865 Gounod's *Faust*, which had premiered in Paris only six years earlier, was given its first presentation in San Francisco by the Bianchi Opera Company. The next year, *La Traviata* was staged in the city for the benefit of Signora Brambilla. Shortly afterwards, Verdi's *Un Ballo in Maschera*, first viewed in Rome in 1859, was given its California premiere by another company imported by the ill-fated Thomas Maguire, a company which lost the impresario some twenty thousand dollars. But two years later, Maguire was back, presenting the famous soprano Euphrosyne Parepa-Rosa in Donizetti's *Don Pasquale*.[16]

The 1870's, however, saw a cooling of this interest in grand opera, partially because the seventies witnessed a period of economic hard times and partially because grand opera had now begun to lose ground to *opéra bouffe* and the rapidly developing musical comedy, both of which were becoming immensely popular with the San Francisco public. In 1871 the charming music of Jacques Offenbach took the city by storm, and during the following year the composer's popularity reached an even greater height when the Aimée Opera Company staged his melodic operetta *La Périchole*.[17]

In 1873, the year in which the depression of the seventies reached low ebb, Dr. Thomas Wade, a local dentist, built the Grand Opera House. Seating nearly 4,000 people, this was reputedly the third largest opera house in America at that time. Six years later, the more famous Tivoli, which housed light opera and musical comedy every night for almost three decades, began its illustrious, and now legendary, career. Both the Grand Opera House and the Tivoli were later destroyed in the great San Francisco earthquake and fire of 1906.

With the sporadic wave of national prosperity in the eighties, grand opera, to some extent at least, became fashionable again in the bay city. Nevertheless, the light opera of the Tivoli still remained by far the most popular of all entertainment forms.[18]

In 1884 interest in grand opera did reach a momentary fever pitch, when Colonel James Mapleson brought Adelina Patti to San Francisco (on the same tour that played New Orleans), touching off what became known as an "Adelina Patti epidemic." The diva's arrival in the city was preceded by one of the most elaborate press build-ups in California history, creating a situation which broke into mob frenzy when the soprano appeared on the scene. Crowds followed her carriage wherever it went, and at ten o'clock on the evening of Mme. Patti's arrival, a line of people which shortly extended for blocks began forming outside the offices of Sherman and Clay Music Company, waiting for tickets that sold for seven dollars each. All through the night the line grew, with some farsighted individuals bringing chairs and food along to make the wait a little more pleasant. Other enterprising souls struck up a profitable business selling hot coffee, while still others were in line for the sole purpose of selling their place at a later hour to the highest bidder. Places within thirty from the entrance are known to have sold for as much as ten dollars each.

When Sherman and Clay finally opened their doors for business, what during the night had been a ruthless crowd suddenly became a savage mob, for utter chaos broke out. Within a few hours the music company had suffered over $3,000 worth of damages. Window panes were knocked out, and the tops of the store's handsome new pianos were scarred by men standing on top of them in their hobnailed shoes, indignantly demanding service. After the initial shock of the disaster had worn off, Messrs. Sherman and Clay contacted Colonel Mapleson and begged him to allow someone else to handle the sale of tickets for Mme. Patti's San Francisco appearances.

On the night of the diva's opening, the theater was not only sold out, but every inch of standing room had also been bought. As a result of this over-crowding, Mapleson was fined seventy-five dollars for violating a fire ordinance, a fine which he was permitted to pay in opera tickets.[19]

Patti was an unqualified success during her San Francisco season, particularly in *La Traviata*. Always, of course, there was the mysterious wait before the first act curtain went up, while the soprano went about her customary habit of carefully counting the $5,000 cash which Mapleson paid her before each performance. But after this minor delay, all ran smoothly, clear through the final "Home, Sweet Home," with which she always ended her performances.[20] At the close of the season, the *San Francisco Bulletin* reported, "The most sanguine of people could not have predicted such a success as greeted the opera company. . . . The opera season has been the most brilliant known in San Francisco."[21]

During the nineties the bay city was entranced by the talents of Sembrich, Nordica, Schumann-Heink, and especially Nellie Melba. In April 1898, Melba appeared on the San Francisco scene, opening her season there with the inevitable *Traviata*. The critics and public alike were glowing in their reports of the diva's artistry. "Probably not since the advent of Patti," reported the *Bulletin*, "has there visited this city a prima donna of such unquestionable superiority as Melba. There can be no disparaging criticsm. She is thoroughly artistic, modest, and carries about herself a personality attractive in the extreme."[22]

Despite Melba's great personal charm and talent, however, the company had more than its share of trouble during its visit to the west coast. It all began during the third act of a performance of *Rigoletto*, when a steam pipe burst underneath the stage, causing great clouds of steam to ascend over the Verdian melodrama. The audience immediately was thrown into a state of panic, for it looked as if the entire back end of the theater were on fire. The curtain was finally brought down, and, while the orchestra frantically played the overture to Hérold's *Zampa* in an attempt to quiet the fleeing mob, the steam was turned off. Shortly, all was back to normal, the curtain went up again, and a valiant attempt was made to continue the lyric tale of dukes and court jesters. But by now, the plumbers had arrived to repair the trouble, and Verdi's music had to settle for second place against the discordant chorus of hammers which soon struck up beneath the stage. If only *Il Trovatore* had been playing that night!

A few evenings later, during the prologue of Leoncavallo's *I Pagliacci*, while Melba was standing in the wings awaiting her entrance, the audience again grew uneasy. This time, a nearby stable had caught fire. Again the audience thought that the theater itself was ablaze and stampeded to the nearest exit. Even the singers rushed out the back entrance. Melba, who had given up waiting for her cue, was carried to her dressing room in a dead faint.[23]

Then a question arose over the wisdom of staging a performance of Rossini's *The Barber of Seville*, which had been scheduled for April 21, 1898. Just two days before, Congress had declared war on Spain, largely over misunderstandings in Cuba. While it was assumed that Teddy Roosevelt and the boys would shortly have the situation well in hand, thanks to an irresponsible "yellow press,"

American public opinion had been so sharply turned against Spain that the management of Mme. Melba's opera company had grave doubts about how any work with a Spanish setting would be received by the patriotic Californians, innocent though the Rossini romp might be. On the other hand, since the opera had been scheduled for some months now, there was little choice but to go on with the work as planned and hope for the best. When the fateful night came around, Melba, as Rosina, went about her comic routine with considerable restraint, fearing that any moment the audience's placid veneer was going to crumble, as it had a few evenings before.

The first act passed without incident, but both the management and the cast still had serious misgivings about the whole affair. The famous "Lesson Scene" arrived in which Melba usually interpolated either "Home, Sweet Home" or "Old Folks at Home." On the night in question the soprano seated herself at the piano and on impulse struck up "The Star-Spangled Banner." Before the diva had finished the first verse, the entire house was on its feet, cheering. By the time the pro-American señorita was through the second refrain, the audience was in such a state of fervor that the singer herself became carried away with her own sentimentality. As she began the melody a third time, tears began pouring down her lovely cheeks, and in a moment she had lost her composure completely and was unable to continue. As the diva sat there in her gay, Spanish costume, sobbing, the audience responded with mixed emotions. Half was empathetically crying, while the other half gave forth with shouts of approval.[24] Needless to say, the management breathed a long sigh of relief.

With the dawn of the new century San Francisco's preference for light opera and musical comedy became even more pronounced. "While the public in the fifties and sixties found in the gaudy and grandiose art of the Italian opera a fit expression of its emotional world, the new twentieth century theatre-going bourgeoisie turned away from even the operatic dilution of *Faust* to give whole-hearted support to *The Toymaker*"[25] and to other works of a lighter vein. The opera season eventually dwindled down to a bare week or two, while the operettas of Offenbach, Gilbert and Sullivan, and Victor Herbert presented at the Tivoli were favorites all year long.

Late in the history of the Tivoli, the management did begin to pay increased attention to the more serious works. One of the greatest events to take place there occurred in February, 1903, when the noted Italian composer Pietro Mascagni conducted performances of his *Cavalleria Rusticana* and *Zanetto*.[26]

Two years later, the Tivoli's impresario, "Doc" Leahy, discovered in an opera troupe stranded in Mexico a young soprano named Luisa Tetrazzini. Leahy brought the singer to San Francisco, where her success was immediate. Later, the diva moved on to New York and Covent Garden, there to be acclaimed by the musical world, but the soprano made frequent returns to the bay city, and her early affection for the west coast continued. On Christmas Eve, 1909, Tetrazzini visited San Francisco, singing outdoors at Lotta's Fountain to a crowd of 250,000 people, without the aid of a microphone.[27]

Early in the twentieth century, New York's Metropolitan also paid several calls on the west coast. In fact the Met was on tour in San Francisco in April 1906, at the time of the great earthquake and fire. On the very evening before the disaster, Enrico Caruso sang Don Jose opposite Olive Fremstad's Carmen at the city's Grand Opera House. While Caruso's portrayal was nothing short of sensational, Mme. Fremstad's seemed somewhat pale and restrained. The diva later claimed that she had sung only with considerable effort, unable to shake a strange premonition of impending tragedy.

Caruso, however, experienced no such feeling of doom. The tenor entertained in his dressing room after the performance and then retired to his suite at the Palace Hotel. Early the next morning, he was shaken out of his slumber by a loud crash. Jumping to his feet, he dashed across the room and peered out the window. The scene he beheld made him tremble with fear, for buildings were toppling over like matchstick houses, and the shouts of terror from people in the streets were enough to chill the marrow in one's very bones. The tenor later said that as he stood there viewing this horrible spectacle, he seemed to sing the whole score of *Carmen* over again in his mind.

When Caruso finally broke out of his trance, he called for his valet, who helped him into some clothes. A moment later, as the two ran out into the hallway, they met Antonio Scotti, the noted Metropolitan baritone, who had been awakened by a feeling of seasickness.[28] After surveying the situation from the street, the musicians decided that the best course would be to get out of town as quickly as possible. Scotti, with some difficulty, managed to hire a wagon and driver for the tidy sum of $300. The singers' trunks and luggage were loaded on, and slowly the horse-drawn vehicle edged its way to the country estate of Arthur Bachman, well out of the danger zone. Bachman was a close personal friend of both Caruso and Scotti, and the performers had visited his home on several previous occasions.

That night, Caruso, whose nerves had been badly shaken by the events of the day, would have no part of sleeping indoors, preferring instead to spend the night under a tree in the Bachmans' yard.[29]

Meanwhile, back in San Francisco, Olive Fremstad had fled from her hotel room, careful to take with her the crimson roses given her after the *Carmen* performance the evening before. For several hours the soprano sat in a park across the street from her hotel, pressing the long-stemmed flowers to her breast. Marcella Sembrich, the little Polish soprano, ran crying from her hotel suite in her nightgown, convinced that the world had come to an end. Not until a gallant gentleman put his overcoat around her shivering shoulders did she come to her senses. Emma Eames, who was scheduled to sing the Countess in Mozart's *The Marriage of Figaro* that afternoon, was staying with friends on Taylor Street atop Nob Hill. After she had freed herself from a heavy canopied bedstead, her only thoughts were of the performance that afternoon. Again and again she tried to telephone the Metropolitan management, but finally she gave up, deciding that the performance must surely have been canceled.[30]

Fortunately, all of the musicians escaped the disaster without injury. The Metropolitan itself, however, suffered a tremendous financial loss in sets, properties, costumes, and musical instruments. The remainder of the tour had to be abandoned, and thousands of dollars in advance ticket sales had to be returned.[31]

For nearly thirty years after the great holocaust of 1906, San Francisco was without an adequate opera house. The Tivoli was rebuilt, but it was not of the proportions necessary to fulfill the city's musical needs. The Civic Auditorium was soon constructed, but this "huge stadium-like building [was] more suited to food shows and political rallies than opera."[32]

And yet San Francisco continued to have opera, primarily brought in by various companies on tour. In 1913 Ruggiero Leon-

cavallo visited the new Tivoli, where he conducted several performances of his *Pagliacci*.[33] The Chicago Opera, with Garden,
Muratore, Ruffo, Muzio, and Schipa among its galaxy of artists,
visited the bay city several times, while in the fall of 1920, and
again in 1921, the Scotti Opera Company gave a series of performances with Geraldine Farrar as its featured attraction.[34] But, while
the San Franciscans were generally blessed with bountiful opportunities for experiencing the lyric theater, the city was almost totally
dependent upon the services of outsiders, a situation which, while
often culturally rewarding, had obvious limitations.

Then in 1921, the San Carlo Opera came to San Francisco, with
Gaetano Merola as one of its principal conductors. Merola, who had
studied at the Royal Conservatory in Naples, making his Metropolitan debut in 1899, had been introduced to the west coast in
1906, when he toured California as Nordica's pianist. In 1909 he returned to the bay area, this time as conductor of the touring Edwards International Grand Opera Company. From the beginning
Merola had been as attracted to the San Francisco locale as he was
puzzled by the city's lack of resident opera. After all, the city contained a growing, dynamic metropolitan area with a large opera-
loving population, particularly the large Italian population. Equally
important was the fact that San Francisco, with its operatic tradition
extending back to 1851, was no babe in arms, musically speaking.
Why then, asked Merola, did the city not support its own opera
company? Consequently, while the conductor was visiting the bay
area in 1921 with the San Carlo, he began checking into the possibilities of establishing such a company. Within a short time he was
convinced that the city had both the financial resources and the
musical background necessary for supporting its own operatic organization. The result was that when the San Carlo troupe left,
Merola stayed behind, determined to build in California an opera
company of the highest caliber.[35]

In June, 1922, the young conductor, to show what he could do,
staked a sizable sum of his own personal capital, plus that of some
close friends, on a series of opera performances staged *al fresco* in
the stadium of Stanford University in Palo Alto. While the chorus
and ballet for these productions were recruited locally, the lead
artists were professionals, imported for the occasion. Merola himself

conducted, the repertoire consisting of three tried operatic war horses—*Faust, I Pagliacci,* and *Carmen.*

The primary difficulty encountered by the Stanford project was not one of artistry, but rather a lack of cooperation from the weather. Although Palo Alto itself was generally favored by a clear, moonlit sky, up in San Francisco a heavy summer fog often discouraged many from making the thirty-mile trek to Stanford to sample Merola's lyric productions, thus seriously cutting into the box-office. Nevertheless, music-lovers from the southern end of the peninsula, where the skies were usually clear, turned out in large numbers.[36]

News of Merola's venture, however, spread rapidly throughout the bay area, and the general consensus was that, while producing a financial deficit, the enterprise, artistically, had been an emphatic success. During the next few months Merola's plan moved into high gear, as work was begun for actually establishing a permanent opera company in metropolitan San Francisco.

At noon on April 4, 1923, a meeting was held in the Italian Ballroom of the St. Francis Hotel for the purpose of organizing the San Francisco Opera Association. With Robert I. Bentley as president, the Association agreed to secure the underwriters necessary for Merola to launch his first San Francisco season. The plan which the Association devised for financing the city's opera was unique in that, instead of a few wealthy individuals contributing the amount needed, some 2,700 founding members donated fifty dollars each to create a revolving fund. Remarkably enough, this fund served as a guarantee for the company for over a decade.[37]

With the immediate financial problems out of the way, Merola began artistic negotiations. By September ten performances of eight operas were scheduled for the introductory season, to be presented in the Civic Auditorium. The San Francisco Symphony was contracted to serve in the pit, and a local chorus of 150 voices was being trained. More than 95 per cent of the company's personnel were local San Francisco residents, with all of the minor roles being sung by Californians. Only the principals were to be imported. Merola himself acted as the company's artistic director, while Armando Agnini, Merola's nephew, was stage director, having worked earlier with operatic groups in Boston, Montreal, and New York. The scenery for that first year was rented, while most of the props were borrowed from the homes of subscribers.[38]

Two days before the scheduled opening, a crew of seventy-five carpenters, fifty drapers, and twelve electricians went to work to convert the arena-like Civic Auditorium into an opera house, or something like one. Actually, a theater was created "inside" the cavernous auditorium. A sloping platform, which began at the orchestra and gradually rose to a height of ten feet, was built on the main floor to provide everyone an unobstructed view of the stage. Overhead an immense canopy was stretched to improve the acoustics, and the base of the balcony was lined with sheets of burlap. Twenty-eight boxes, each of which accommodated eight patrons, were built along the sides and back of the "indoor" theater to serve as a dress circle. A stage was constructed with runways leading directly to the dressing rooms of the performers.

As late as four o'clock on the afternoon of the opening production, the frantic work on the Auditorium continued. But by performance time all was completed. Within two days and $35,000 after the work began, the huge convention hall was converted into an "indoor" opera house, seating over 6,500 patrons.

At eight o'clock on the evening of Wednesday, September 26, 1923, the San Francisco Opera Association was christened with a performance of Puccini's *La Bohème*. Giovanni Martinelli was the Rudolfo, Queena Mario the Mimi. Gaetano Merola conducted. By curtain time every seat in the house was taken and excitement ran high. As the performance progressed, it became obvious that Merola's talents had not been overestimated. And when the reviews came out in the morning papers, the positive verdict was assured. Ray Brown, writing for the *Chronicle*, stated, "Not only were the merits of the production such as to justify the prediction of the artistic success of the undertaking as a whole, but the standard . . . was such that we have no cause for diminution of pride."[39] The only real disappointment came from the chorus, which somehow never quite achieved unity. But considering that there had not even been time for a dress rehearsal, all had gone remarkably well.

The following evening a performance of *Andrea Chenier* "deepened the conviction that the new organization [had] the best of chances for survival."[40] By the end of the season, Merola and his company had scored a most impressive number of artistic coups, and the project had received both local and national praise. When the financial records were examined, the underwriters were astonished to learn that the company not only did not need to call for additional funds, but that it actually had a balance of $1,800 in the bank.[41]

Seven of the eight operas given during this first season were Italian; the other, Gounod's *Romeo and Juliet*, was French. And during the next eight years, the standard Italian works continued to dominate. *Aïda* was most frequently given, produced seven times within the company's first nine seasons. The only novelties offered (such as Mascagni's *L'Amico Fritz*, Vittandini's *Anima Allegra*, and Giordano's *La Cena delle Beffe*) were works that had been given with reasonable success a season or so earlier at the Metropolitan. Met stars repeatedly dominated the roster, and by and large the productions looked like copies of those given in New York.

In 1931 the San Francisco Opera celebrated its eighth anniversary by opening the season with Henri Rabaud's rarely performed *Marouf*, a tale of the Arabian Nights. The production as a whole was rather refreshing, with the only major disappointment coming from a burro which singer Lodovico Oliviero led on stage. During rehearsals, whenever Oliviero opened his mouth to sing, the quadruped followed suit, letting forth a magnificent, full-voiced, though somewhat discordant, bray. The management finally became rather conditioned to the situation and eventually decided that, although the aria had been written as a solo, it had a certain distinctiveness about it when sung as a duet. Then on opening night, Señor Burro made his entrance, but refused to utter a sound, undoubtedly suffering from a seizure of stage fright.

During these eight years the company's chorus had improved remarkably, but there were problems connected with directing a local chorus comprised mainly of amateurs. Stage director Armando Agnini complained, "They all want to hear the stars. They peek through holes in the scenery, and when I need them I can't find them." Then smilingly the good-natured director suggested a possible solution to his difficulty: "I'll put paint on the bottom of their shoes so that I can trail them."[42]

Still, as the San Francisco Opera celebrated this eighth birthday, the company could look back proudly on a galaxy of artistic triumphs, in addition to a remarkable financial record. Sometimes the seasons had ended with a slight surplus in the budget, sometimes with a slight deficit. But the deficit was never so large that it could not be covered by the original revolving fund created by the fifty-dollar contribution made by each of the 2,700 founders. Within these eight years the company's artistic prestige had steadily increased, despite one very pronounced handicap. As had been obvious from the beginning, the hangar-like Civic Auditorium, where the operas were normally staged, was completely inadequate for the finely-balanced performances which the company aspired to produce. It was equally clear that before the company could progress much farther it must have an adequately equipped opera house in which to play.

The city's music-lovers had realized the need for such an opera house ever since the earthquake of 1906, when all of the major theaters of San Francisco were destroyed. For years there had been much talk and planning, but always the primary obstacle was one of finance, in this case a matter of two million dollars. Then in November, 1918, World War I came to an end, and shortly the hundreds of San Francisco veterans began returning home. One of these veterans, Major Charles Kendrick, came up with an extremely practical plan for making the opera house dream come true. The soldiers killed in the World War, Kendrick suggested, deserved to be commemorated with some sort of memorial. And yet, why not make this memorial something useful which could be enjoyed by the living? An opera house, dedicated to the war dead, would serve this double purpose and enlist the support of the American Legion besides.

After putting their heads together, the San Francisco city fathers decided that Kendrick's idea made sense, and a fund-raising drive was launched. Conference after conference was held. Committees were set up. The American Legion went into action. So did the local newspapers and civic-minded groups all over the bay area. After weeks of diligent work, a sum of $2,150,000 had been pledged to the War Memorial Fund, approximately the sum needed before construction could begin. The money was turned over to the regents of the University of California, who appointed a Board of Trustees to supervise the project's financial affairs.

Meanwhile serious complications had developed to alter plans for the War Memorial. A local storage company somehow managed to buy an entire block in the Civic Center area, where the proposed opera house was to be built. The storage company intended to construct a giant warehouse, which would do nothing to improve the architectural beauty of the Civic Center. And so again the city fathers went into a huddle, but came up with nothing that could be considered a satisfactory solution. The result was near panic.

But Major Kendrick again proved the man with the idea. Why, asked the major, did not the city authorities simply buy the block in question? Because, Kendrick was quickly informed, the city had no funds for such a purpose. Then, replied the veteran, he would ask the War Memorial Trustees to advance the money which was needed. Upon request, the Trustees agreed to loan the city a sum of $175,000. It was soon learned, however, that the price which the storage company wanted for the area was outrageous. After long and involved court proceedings, the city finally succeeded in purchasing the block at a price not too objectionable to either side.

But the opera house, intended to occupy one block, now had two. How could the extra space be used? Throughout 1923 this question was debated by officials. As the discussions continued, it became more and more apparent that the war veterans were something less than enthusiastic about the idea of an opera house. What they wanted was a building of their own. Consequently, the debates took on new depth, growing more heated as they progressed. Eventually, it was decided that the Memorial should include two buildings—an opera house and a separate veterans' building.

Nevertheless, in solving one problem, another, equally perplexing, had been created. Certainly it took no skilled mathematician to calculate that, if two like buildings were constructed, the cost of the project would be doubled. This obviously meant beating the well-picked bushes again for funds. However, after careful consideration a bond issue was proposed. An election was held, and the issue carried by an appreciable majority.

On Armistice Day, 1926, construction of the twin memorial buildings began, a building project which was to continue for the next six years. Year after year, San Francisco's opera-lovers kept an anxious eye turned toward the Civic Center to note the slow, but steady, progress on the new opera house. Then at last, in the fall of 1932, just in time for the San Francisco Opera's tenth season, work on the buildings was completed. After nine years of patient waiting and putting up with makeshift facilities, the opera company was to have an ideal home for its productions, one more magnificent than even Merola himself had dared imagine. No longer was San Francisco's opera to be plagued by inadequate housing, for the imposing War Memorial Opera House which now stood at the corner of Grove and Van Ness Streets was immediately acclaimed one of the finest and most fully equipped in the world.[43]

With the completion of the War Memorial Opera House, the nation's first municipally-owned opera house, the San Francisco Opera entered the second phase of its history. Now, with a legitimate home for its productions, the company had unlimited possibilities for artistic growth and development. The years of infancy were over; those of maturation and adulthood lay ahead. Consequently, as the company moved into the new opera house, armed with the vigor of adolescence, its artistic potential was boundless. There was nothing now to stand in the way of the city's operatic growth, nothing to prevent the San Francisco Opera from producing lyric drama of the highest quality, nothing to hinder the organization from challenging even the high artistic standards of the Metropolitan itself.

San Francisco's
Operatic Nugget

As San Francisco's opera-lovers swarmed into the War Memorial Opera House on October 15, 1932, they were astonished to find that nothing short of a miracle had been wrought in their city. The beauty and elegance which met their eyes as they walked through those glass doors for the first time was almost breath-taking. One's attention was immediately drawn to the classic stone columns which surrounded the foyer and towered up to the high, chandeliered ceiling. In the near future—after prohibition—the basement would be converted into a spacious cocktail bar, where, chatting with friends, one might pleasantly await the warning signal.

Inside the theater itself, three tiers rose above the orchestra—a grand tier, a dress circle, and a balcony. The interior design of the house was "sparse with classic economy."[1] The walls were broken by sets of lofty arches, with gold and white decorations. "A ceiling of solid blue, illuminated by hidden lights, clasped to its bosom the bright star-like jewel of a great chandelier."[2] Each of the 3,250 seats was upholstered in a deep rose velvet, and the carpets were dark red and gold.

The stage, measuring 134 feet wide, 84 feet deep, and 140 feet high, was one of the most completely equipped in the world. It included a gorgeous gold brocade curtain, four elevators, five rows of traps, and facilities for producing such visual effects as smoke and fog. The lighting system, consisting of 88 lamps with a power of 88,000 kilowatts, contained a switchboard which permitted setting ten scenes ahead of time. The floor of the orchestra pit could be mechanically raised or lowered, making it possible for members of the orchestra to take their places at the basement level and then be lifted to the first floor.[3]

The total cost of the War Memorial, including both the Opera House and the twin Veteran's Building, was approximately $6,125,-000. Figured into this amount was the cost of the court between the two buildings and all the necessary furniture, draperies, carpets, seats, and lighting fixtures.[4]

The first work presented in the new theater was Puccini's *Tosca*, with Claudia Muzio in the title role. As the gold curtain went up on that inaugural production, Marsden Argall, a young San Francisco bass in the role of Angelotti, sang the first words uttered from the War Memorial Opera House stage. Appropriately enough, they were "*Ah! finalmente*." Certainly for a city that had been waiting a quarter century for this magnificent edifice, Angelotti's exclamation had special meaning. The first act of this opening production was broadcast by NBC all over the United States and by transcontinental hookup to Italy, the first nationwide broadcast of grand opera to originate from the west coast.[5]

The next morning the newspapers were filled with glowing reports of the new opera house. Annie Laurie, writing for the *San Francisco Examiner*, expressed the sentiments of most of the city's music-lovers: "It's come true at last, the dream of dreams—a magnificent Opera House for San Francisco, an Opera House that belongs to you and me and all the neighbors, and to every man and woman on the street, and every quiet little woman clearing away the breakfast dishes this very minute!"[6]

During the next twenty years Merola and company gave some excellent performances in the new Opera House. Lovely Lily Pons, the current sensation at the Metropolitan, showed up later in 1932 for a much-lauded *Lucia di Lammermoor*. When Pons went mad, the critics raved. "The greatest art of song is not dead," proclaimed the *Examiner*'s Alexander Fried. "It lives in Lily Pons."[7]

Opening week, 1935, brought a complete cycle of Wagner's *Ring*, by far the company's most ambitious undertaking up to that time. Some $80,000, in depression-type money, was spent to bring in such first-rate Wagnerians as Lauritz Melchior and Kirsten Flagstad. Another $40,000 was invested in scenery and props, including a horrible, life-like dragon and a special cloud machine which projected photographs of real clouds on a backdrop.[8]

Lotte Lehmann and Risë Stevens teamed for a remarkable *Der Rosenkavalier* in 1940, and three years later Sir Thomas Beecham came to town to conduct *Carmen* and *Don Giovanni*. Ezio Pinza proved the sensation of the 1945 season with his masterful interpretation of Moussorgsky's *Boris Godunov*. While *Boris* stands out as one of the finest presentations in the company's history, soprano Lucine Amara, then a young member of the San Francisco chorus, recalls that the production did contain a couple of amusing behind-the-scenes events which the audience, fortunately, never saw. During the snow scene, for instance, the chorus was going about its duties, singing mightily, when someone happened to notice a foreign figure on stage. In a moment the whole company had noticed him, and everyone was trying desperately to keep from laughing. The mysterious one, it seems, was none other than chorus master Kurt Herbert Adler, dressed in a Russian hat and cloak, who had come on stage to warn his singers of cues.

On another occasion in that same scene, the chorus momentarily panicked when Dmitri, the pretender to the Russian throne, came riding on stage on a galloping horse. The horse at that particular moment chose to rear, with the result that the cast was thrown into turmoil. After the initial shock, the singers anxiously looked to the prompter, expecting from him the cue that would restore some sort of order. However, the prompter—obviously an easterner —was nowhere to be seen. Apparently, he had gotten a gopher's eye view of those raised hoofs and had decided to dig in a little deeper.[9]

An examination of Merola's scrapbook would reveal a whole gallery of great vocal characterizations presented on the Opera House stage, among them Tibbett's Rigoletto, Lawrence's Sieglinde, Albanese's Violetta, Flagstad's Isolde, Rethberg's Countess, Bori's Magda, Milanov's Leonora, Warren's Amonasro, Moore's Fiora, Melchior's Tristan, Sayao's Juliet, Traubel's Brunnhilde, and Kirsten's Louise—performances that have passed into the realm of legend.

But the company gave its share of bad performances too. One notorious disaster was a 1940 production of *Carmen* with Marjorie

Lawrence. Although Mme. Lawrence was a truly capital singer on her own vocal ground, she was definitely no Carmen. Alfred Frankenstein, of the *San Francisco Chronicle*, noted in his review that "her characterization was a rather curious compound of brutality and effusiveness."[10]

Then during the 1943 season the management pulled out a production of Puccini's horse-opera *The Girl of the Golden West* and prepared it in an English translation, starring Florence Kirk as Minnie and Frederick Jagel as Dick Johnson. On the night the opera was presented chaos broke out in War Memorial. Frankenstein reported, "They hissed the villain last night at the Opry House as he twirled his black mustache and cried, 'Ya must and shall be mine, me proud and haughty beauty,' or words to that effect."[11] The critic himself was fairly tolerant of the production, but most of the audience found it a ludicrous fiasco and literally laughed the opera off the stage. The English translation only intensified the triteness of the somewhat laughable pseudo-western libretto. To make matters worse, Miss Kirk towered a head taller than her romantic counter-part, Mr. Jagel. Consequently, while the artists and management fidgeted uncomfortably, the audience enjoyed the best horse-laugh in years. A scheduled second performance of the work was canceled.[12]

And there were productions which went well enough once, but grew thin with repetition. Delibes' *Lakmé*, staged over and over for Lily Pons, is a case in point. The day after the opera's first 1946 performance, a letter appeared in the *Chronicle*, an open letter to Mme. Pons, written by Alfred Frankenstein. "I love you," the letter read. "My wife loves you. Everybody in San Francisco and the wife of everybody in San Francisco loves you like anything." But, the letter continued, "We want you to learn another role to replace that of Lakmé. As the years go by, Delibes' feeble, vapid score grows more and more insufferable."[13]

The company's sets served as a general weakness during the thirties and forties, and costumes were little better. Frankenstein quipped after a production of *Don Giovanni* that the interiors conveyed "the idea that Don Giovanni lived in a North Beach night club."[14] In a 1949 staging of *Samson and Delilah*, the critic found Delilah's abode in Act II to look rather like Tarzan's tree hut, while the temple scene "looked like something left over after **D. W. Griffith** had finished *Intolerance* in 1916."[15]

Yet overshadowing any other weakness was the San Francisco Opera's constant dependence upon the Metropolitan for both its artists and repertoire. Nearly all of the operas the west coast company chose to stage had been performed a short time earlier by the Met, often with the same singers, and most of the principals were Metropolitan artists who came to the bay area for a kind of warm-up session a few weeks before launching into their New York seasons.

In short, the San Francisco organization was too prone to let the Metropolitan do its thinking for it, content for the most part to duplicate whatever offering the Met had found successful. To critics like Alfred Frankenstein this situation was most unfortunate. Frankenstein repeatedly bemoaned the company's lack of creativity and yearned for the day when it could "cut itself loose from the Metropolitan except insofar as connection with the Eastern opera house [might] be artistically desirable, [thus creating] a truly American company drawing as it [might] choose upon the entire world for its repertoire and its personnel."[16]

Frankenstein went on to add that the company would do well also to diverge from the beaten path of the old operatic favorites. "The first performance of an opera by an American or European composer would do more than a galaxy of Flagstads for the prestige of the San Francisco Opera Company outside its own bailiwick." By the same token the organization desperately needed to become more daring in its methods of production, branching out from the standard stagings it was so inclined to copy. Here, Frankenstein concluded, the box-office played too large a role, both in determining the repertoire and the production techniques used. New works and new stagings were rarely seen, simply because they boosted the cost of production too high. Not only was there the original cost of the physical production to consider, but the expense of additional rehearsals for new operas and novel stagings must also be taken into account. As long as the company remained so preoccupied with finances, Frankenstein held, "the slow and careful work required by new operas or new approaches to old ones [was] out of the question, and the business of staging opera [was] reduced to standardized patterns, applicable with a minimum of time to any and all stages and companies."[17]

The basic question, then, facing Merola's company during the late thirties and early forties was whether the organization should become more independent and original or should sacrifice originality in order to keep the budget as small as possible. Which was more important, artistic advancement or a budget which was relatively easy to balance? To Merola's mind there could be only one answer. The public must be given the repertoire it knew and wanted, and the cost of operation must be kept at a minimum. And after all, even with a standard repertoire and conventional sets this was no easy task. Even when every effort was made to trim expenditures, staging opera remained an expensive game indeed. For example, the cost of the orchestra alone was prohibitive, totaling some $13,000 a week in 1938, as compared with the $6,000 a week required by the symphony during its season. For every hour the orchestra rehearsed, $300 more were needed. In addition, opera entails the expense of the singers, the ballet, the wardrobe people, the stage director and his staff, the lighting crew, and the stagehands. Even with a close eye on the budget and a rigid bookkeeping system, the deficit for the 1938 season had totaled $88,757.[18]

Merola thought that since the minimum price of opera was so great, costly experimentation was out of the question. Besides, the public generally preferred the standard works and established singers. Why, reasoned Merola, go against the wishes of the public by producing unusual operas with unknown artists, especially when such ventures were extremely costly for the underwriters? Consequently, the director stuck to the operatic straight and narrow, even though prophetic critics maintained that the company's artistic reputation would suffer. Therefore, throughout the early forties the San Francisco Opera remained essentially a carbon copy of the Metropolitan, bound to artistic subordination, an imitator rather than a creator, by a financial strait jacket.

When the Second World War broke out in 1941, the company at first questioned whether or not it could continue to operate, but Merola finally became convinced that now more than ever entertainment of every form was needed to help ease the wartime tensions. Opera in San Francisco went on as usual, or almost as usual. The men declared a black-tie edict shortly after hostilities began, but even in this time of shortage the women seemed to find "some very fancy sackcloth among the ashes."[19]

Patriotism, of course, was very much in the air, and the company's production of Donizetti's *Daughter of the Regiment,* sung in French, not Italian, reflected it. On the nights the opera was given, the stage of the War Memorial was flanked on either side by the flags of the Allied Nations. In the finale, the banner of Free France, the cross of Lorraine, was used in place of the usual French tricolor. At the end of the performance Lily Pons, singing the role of Marie, burst forth into a rousing "Marseillaise," beckoning the audience to join her. As a result, patrons left the Opera House with such *esprit de corps* that one wonders why the ranks of the French underground movement were not flooded with California volunteers. The second of these *Daughter of the Regiment* performances was sponsored by a group calling themselves "France Forever."[20]

Prior to the first of these war seasons, the management had been rather concerned about the possible drop in attendance. Advance ticket sales were extremely slow and continued to be throughout the war. But over-the-counter sales went up as never before, with block-long lines of patrons forming every night before the box-office for tickets for that evening's performance. These were not times in which one could plan very far ahead, particularly the military personnel, who flocked to the Opera House in droves. Much to everyone's surprise the 1942 season actually closed with a profit, the first since the company's move into the new opera house.[21] And as the war in the Pacific centered more and more activity in San Francisco, the city's opera continued to grow. In 1944 the ticket sales exceeded that of any other season in the company's twenty-two-year history. Practically every performance was sold out.[22]

The end of the war marked the beginning of the San Francisco Opera's maturity, when the company began showing signs of breaking away from its dependence on the Metropolitan, at least in casting. Perhaps the pleas of Alfred Frankenstein and others had been heard at last, or perhaps the change came simply because there were now new singers available in Europe for the company to engage. With Europe's operatic renaissance after the war, a new group of brilliant young singers was developing who would shortly take the whole operatic world by storm. Then too, there were older European singers, still essentially unknown in the United States, who, with the end of the war, suddenly became available.

For whatever reason, San Francisco now began to tap some of these artists, singers who had not yet sung at the Metropolitan and who, to a great extent, were San Francisco discoveries. The 1948 season, for example, brought the American operatic debut of Tito Gobbi and the reappearance of Ebe Stignani in this country. Stignani had been universally acclaimed in Europe as one of the great mezzos of her day, had made her American operatic debut in San Francisco in 1938, but never sang at the Metropolitan. Her return to San Francisco was delayed by the war. Gobbi, a bright young baritone, became one of the most coveted stars at *La Scala* and Covent Garden, but he did not sing at the Met until 1956 and then only briefly.

On opening night, 1950, Merola presented both Renata Tebaldi and Mario Del Monaco in Verdi's *Aïda*. Both singers were making their American debuts. Local and national critics alike found the two young artists to have rich, lush voices and both to be quite well endowed physically. Mme. Tebaldi, although tall, was very attractive, and Del Monaco proved "one tenor who can more or less strip to the waist . . . [without destroying] his opera character by showing an unheroic paunch."[23] On hand for the performance was Rudolf Bing, general manager of the Metropolitan, who engaged Del Monaco to sing for him later that same season. Tebaldi made her Met debut five years later.

Besides introducing new stars, Merola became more prone in his later years to offer already-established singers in roles they had never done before. Lily Pons, for instance, sang her first *La Traviata* with the San Francisco Opera in 1951, one of the company's more controversial performances. Patrons, however, packed the Opera House to hear what the soprano could do with the taxing, dramatic Verdi role. On the evening of her first Violetta, the diva "was as jittery as a teenage debutante at her first ball."[24] When the curtain went up, no one was surprised to find that she handled the first act coloratura passages with ease. The surprises, however, began with Act II when Mme. Pons departed completely from her usual decorative approach and with rather remarkable success transformed herself into a full-fledged singing actress. Marjory Fisher, writing for *Musical America*, maintained, "For the first time in the twenty years I have been listening to her, I heard her sing a role full-voice. Gone were the gleaming little whisperings, murmurings, and half-lights. The impulses of passion informed her singing. She spent her voice abundantly, even recklessly, as she was carried along by the dramatic situations, and she never spared herself in the climaxes."[25] As always, the soprano was elegantly costumed; her four gorgeous *Traviata* gowns cost an estimated $20,000.

Yet while the San Francisco Opera had taken the offensive in the casting aspect of its battle for independence, it continued to be timid in its repertoire and production concepts, reluctant to deviate from either the "old favorites" or the scenic stereotypes it had relied on so long. Then in August 1953, Gaetano Merola died. He was conducting an outdoor concert when suddenly he doubled up and fell to the stage floor, having suffered a heart attack. He was dead by the time the doctors reached him.

Kurt Herbert Adler, the company's chorus master since 1943, was shortly appointed the new general director. Although Adler had the highest admiration for Merola personally, he had disagreed with him on many things, particularly on the company's basic conservatism. As the organization's head Adler was determined to be even more experimental in casting and to branch out in repertoire and stage techniques as well. Essentially his production philosophy revolved around four basic principles. First, outstanding artists should be imported from every corner of the operatic world. Second, young singers on the Pacific Coast should be given every feasible chance for professional development. Third, the repertoire must continually be freshened through the presentation of new works and the revival of seldom-heard pieces. Finally, the company's techniques of staging must be constantly revitalized in terms of the modern theater.[26]

The results of this new policy have been miraculous. The San Francisco Opera has transformed itself into one of the most dynamic opera companies in the world. "In some ways," *Time* magazine wrote in 1959, "San Francisco is now the finest opera company in the United States, often on a par with the Met in quality (if not in size), and consistently ahead of the Met in dash and daring."[27] Even Alfred Frankenstein has been made happy by the change: "The San Francisco Opera Company, as a performing aggregation, now has a profile, color, and character of its own."[28] The repertoire, once so limited, has been broadened to include the first American staging of such operas as Cherubini's *The Portuguese Inn*, Honegger's *Joan at the Stake*, Walton's *Troilus and Cressida*, Poulenc's *Dialogues of the Carmelites*, Orff's *Carmina Burana*, Richard Strauss' *Die Frau ohne Schatten*, and Shostakovich's *Lady Macbeth of Mtsensk*, not to mention the world premier of Dello Joio's *Blood Moon*. The appearance of new stars has become an annual event. Giulietta Simionato, Cesare Valletti, Inge Borkh, Elisabeth Schwarzkopf, Leonie Rysanek, Birgit Nilsson, Boris Christoff, Leontyne Price, Giuseppe Taddei, Gabriella Tucci, and Sándor Kónya are just a few of the big names who have made their American operatic debuts in San Francisco.

Likewise, in production methods the San Francisco Opera has become exceedingly progressive during the last decade. New concepts in staging and lighting are continually being introduced there, while the use of such devices as projected scenery has added real depth and dimension to the company's productions. A look at the sets for *Die Frau ohne Schatten* or those designed for *Carmen* in 1959 by Broadway's Howard Bay (of *Music Man* fame) will reveal how truly creative this company has become.

The year after Adler's appointment as director, the first of the San Francisco Opera Debut Auditions was held, in an attempt to discover and train talented young singers from the west coast area. Each year since then, some two hundred applicants have been auditioned by Adler and his staff, with about fifteen of the most promising being selected to participate in regular San Francisco Opera productions either as understudies or in *comprimario* roles.[29]

It is true that operating costs have gone up, partly as a result of the postwar inflation and partly as a result of the company's more dynamic approach to opera. In 1954 the organization launched its first public fund drive. The goal was $100,000. After several weeks of campaigning, over $116,000 had been contributed by civic-minded individuals and businesses.[30] By 1960 this goal had been increased to $150,000, but the amount is always raised. The Los Angeles tour, begun in 1937, has helped the company financially. The auditorium in Los Angeles seats in the neighborhood of 6,000 and is almost always filled. Since the operas staged there have usually been presented earlier in San Francisco, they require no extra rehearsal. Not only have these performances brought in additional dollars through the box-office, they have enabled the company to broaden its guar-antor-support into the Los Angeles area as well.[31]

Through the years the San Francisco public has generally matured to the point that audiences welcome the new and unheard operas. There has, of course, remained a conservative faction which would prefer to stick to the tried masterpieces, sung by veteran performers. Following the 1958 season, one which had seen the first American staging of Cherubini's *Medea* and the American premieres of Carl Orff's *The Wise Maiden* and *Carmina Burana*, this right-wing dis-content reached a highly vocal climax, crystallizing in a letter written and circulated among the opera guarantors by Chalmers Graham, a prominent San Francisco attorney and opera backer. Graham spared Kurt Herbert Adler nothing in his letter, denounc-ing the impresario's new-fangled notions in no uncertain terms. "I haven't found anybody," Graham exploded, "who wasn't disgusted with this last season, and who hasn't become increasingly disgusted with what has been going on for the past few years. . . . I think it is about time that Adler was fired and we got back to good old-fashioned opera even though they are repeats of what we have heard a dozen times." The attorney concluded that the company would do well to worry less about satisfying the critics and concen-trate more on pleasing the guarantors, for he said, "An awful lot of people are getting tired of paying the deficits with bum opera."[32]

For several weeks during the winter of 1958–59 the Opera House was the scene of a rather serious internal squabble. When the smoke of battle cleared, it was evident that the liberal forces had emerged victorious and that no change in policy would take place. As a matter of fact, the reactionary criticism actually seemed to solidify the majority of the San Francisco Opera backers more thoroughly than ever behind Adler's policies.[33]

And certainly the company has not deserted "old-fashioned" op-era, for the standard works still constitute by far the bulk of the repertoire. The 1958 season, the one which Graham had objected to so strenuously, offered *Tannhäuser*, *La Forza del Destino*, *Don Carlo*, *The Barber of Seville*, *Manon*, *La Bohème*, *The Marriage of Figaro*, and *Il Trovatore*, none of which were exactly radical in-novations. Even the conservative faction had to admit that the *Trovatore* was magnificent, particularly Leontyne Price's Leonora. When Price finished singing her great aria at the beginning of the last act, conductor Georges Sebastian himself threw down his baton and led the applause.[34] Most of the other standard works were also smash hits.

Certainly it would be difficult to overestimate the contribution Gaetano Merola made to America's musical life when he planted the San Francisco Opera on the west coast. Nurtured by Merola's loving hand, the company weathered first the nation's worst depression and secondly the world's most devastating war. In the meantime, the director had successfully led the campaign for the building of the War Memorial Opera House, one of the three finest opera houses in the country.

But while Merola had a founder's daring, he also possessed a pragmatist's conservatism, belonging to "an old-fashioned and honorable school of impresarios, which had its source in Italy's nineteenth century opera houses."[35] Although Merola himself showed signs of becoming slightly more progressive in his last years, under Kurt Herbert Adler the San Francisco Opera quickly became a dynamic, creative organism, giving life to a host of new operas and polishing up old ones. Whereas for the first three decades of its history, the San Francisco Opera was, for the most part, merely a western expression of the Metropolitan, with Adler as head, the organization had become an independent integer, standing on its own artistic feet, and adding a significant new dimension to the American operatic picture in the process. The days of the San Francisco Opera's contenting itself with imitating others are gone. Although its season is short (in 1963 slightly over six weeks), the company now possesses an artistic dynamism, a youth, and a creative vitality which even the Metropolitan is hard-pressed to equal.

A Texas Success

If one asks the average Southwesterner a question concerning the arts, he may well receive a blank stare. However, if the question happens to be addressed to a Dallasite, the stare will probably not be quite so blank, and one might even get an answer. For in Dallas it is not particularly unusual to find someone who knows that Pablo Picasso is not a Cuban revolutionary leader, that *Bohème* is not a pill, and that a reference to Madame Tebaldi is not something one hides from the children.

Dallas, in fact, has been recognized for years—except in Houston, of course—as the "culture center of the Southwest." It was here that the noted Margo Jones Theater operated, presenting theater-in-the-round, including the premiere performances of Tennessee Williams' *Summer and Smoke* and Jerome Lawrence's *Inherit the Wind*. It was here that in December, 1959, the Dallas Theater Center, designed by Frank Lloyd Wright, opened, with Paul Baker as director. It was also here that Mary Martin in October, 1947, launched her successful road-show production of Irving Berlin's *Annie Get Your Gun* and that William Warfield and Leontyne Price in the summer of 1952 first appeared in the production of Gershwin's *Porgy and Bess* which the State Department later sent to Moscow. Every summer in Dallas (since 1941) the State Fair Musicals are presented, offering the best of Broadway's musical comedy and resulting in one of the best twelve-week box-office grosses in the nation. The city boasts a notable symphony orchestra, a magnificent art museum, and one of the most elaborate, and certainly most attractive, public libraries in the country.

Dallas heard its first opera with orchestra on February 12, 1875, when *Martha* was given at Field's Theater. The city heard a number of touring companies in the latter part of the century, including Emma Abbott's troupe and the Boston Ideals. The Metropolitan's first visit to Dallas came in April, 1905, when Wagner's *Parsifal* was presented with Andreas Dippel in the title role and Olive Fremstad as Kundry. The work was staged in the new Dallas Opera House at Main and St. Paul Streets. The Met had arranged for the performance itself, paying Will A. Watkin, a local music dealer, a fee of $500 to handle the details. The ticket prices ranged from ten to three dollars a seat, with three dollars also charged for the privilege of standing through the five-hour opera. Fortunately for the standees, there was an hour and a half intermission for dinner at the close of the first act.

The prices charged by the Metropolitan in 1905, interestingly enough, are not unlike those now charged locally during the company's spring tour. Apparently, however, the many obstacles involved in bringing opera to Texas were too much for the New York company, for with the conclusion of *Parsifal*, the Met packed up its scenery, gathered in its box-office receipts, and departed from the city, not to return for the next thirty-four years.[1]

In those intervening years a number of touring companies paid visits to Dallas, varying considerably in quality and frequency of stops. Small itinerant troupes, like the Henry Savage Company, presented all the opera that Dallas was privileged to hear for nearly a decade. Then, early in 1913, the most impressive of these operatic visitors made its first appearance in the Texas city—the young, ambitious Chicago Opera Company. Almost immediately after Dallasites heard that the Chicagoans were interested in making a tour of the Southwest, the city's chamber of commerce appointed an opera committee to negotiate with the company. This committee soon became known familiarly as the E.L. Club, for its successive chairmen were Elmer L. Scott, Edgar L. Pike, Edgar L. Flippen, and Eli L. Sanger.

With a guarantee of $12,500 a performance for the Chicago Opera, the 1913 season got under way.[2] One of the greatest sensations that year was a *Lucia di Lammermoor* from Luisa Tetrazzini, who

Dallas Civic Opera's *Daughter of the Regiment*

Dallas Civic Opera's
Alcina

Remains of the Tivoli
Opera House, San Francisco

San Francisco Opera's 1963 production of Rossini's *The Barber of Seville*

received the strange and, fortunately, passing audience demonstration known as the "Chautauqua Salute." "This bizarre mass gesture is, or was, achieved by the audience rising to its feet and everyone, men and women alike, lifting their handkerchiefs high over their heads and agitating them violently."[3] What a sight it must have been. A more aesthetic spectacle, however, came with a performance of Massenet's *Thaïs*, starring the incomparable Mary Garden. And there was Mario Sammarco as Tonio and a *Die Walküre* with Charles Whitehill. All in all, it was quite a season from the artistic standpoint; nor had the box-office fared badly, for every performance had virtually filled the 4,300-seat Fair Park Coliseum, a glorified livestock arena containing a stage at one end.

A return visit by the Chicago organization in 1914 proved less successful, largely because two of the leading artists announced for the tour, Mary Garden and Maggie Teyte, were ill and could not appear. After that season the visits from the Chicago company became more sporadic, with several years often passing between Texas appearances.

In 1915, and again in 1916, Max Rabinoff's Boston National Company visited Dallas, one year teamed with Anna Pavlova's ballet group. Fortune Gallo's San Carlo Opera Company soon began making yearly stops, playing either at the Opera House or the Coliseum, without any guarantee at all. In 1918 Chicago returned, as it did again for the next two years. Antonio Scotti presented his group in 1919 and 1920, but met with financial disaster.

In 1923 the newly reorganized Chicago Civic Opera came to Texas, introducing to Dallas such artists as Edith Mason and Feodor Chaliapin. The next year the company returned, playing now in a downtown vaudeville house, the Majestic, as the old Coliseum was no longer available and the new Fair Park Auditorium was still in the planning stages.[4] This 1924 season marked the last appearance in the city of soprano Mary Garden, with results that were none too happy.

Garden had chosen to sing Richard Strauss' *Salomé*, the opera that, largely because of its controversial "Dance of the Seven Veils," had created such a scandal in Chicago. Now Dallas was to have a chance to judge for itself the merits of the Strauss music and be shocked, if it would, by the daring, seductive dance. These, of course, were the days before radio or long-playing records, and audiences were not as aware then of the newer and less-familiar works as they are today. The Dallas Grand Opera Committee, realizing this, felt that some effort should be made to bolster the attendance for the Strauss à la Garden production. Eventually, a plan was devised for bringing in a "music evangel" from New York, a man who had recently gained considerable fame in the East for stimulating the interest of the general public in classical music.

The operatic drummer arrived and eagerly began his campaign of salesmanship, speaking at schools, churches, luncheon clubs, and, in short, to any group of twenty people he could gather together. The gist of his bill-of-sale took two general directions. At the schools and churches, the evangel bore down heavily on the Biblical theme of the opera, while at the luncheon clubs, he dwelt at length on the "strip tease aspects of the dance of the seven veils and painted it with such carefully chosen words that the veils seemed to fall away one by one and it became apparent the opera had to be seen to be appreciated."[5]

When the night of the much-heralded performance finally rolled around, the house was sold out, and the audience sat eagerly expecting either the greatest inspirational message since Billy Sunday or the most sensational display of feminine flesh this side of the *Folies Bergère*. Both camps were soon to know gross disappointment.

What the evangel had neglected to mention was that the opera consists of only one act, lasting a scant hour and forty minutes, and that the music is of a strange, and to the untutored ear, discordant nature. Since the Chicago company had another engagement two nights later in Los Angeles, it was anxious to fulfill its Dallas contract and move on as quickly as possible to points west. Consequently, as the clock struck eight, the orchestra sounded a few alarming chords, and the curtain went up. Mme. Garden made her entrance, and all went reasonably well until that lauded, and supposedly shocking, "Dance of the Seven Veils."

Despite all Mary Garden's talent and stagemanship, it could never be said that she was a dancer, and it seemed now that in Salomé's sensual exhibition, the soprano's forty-seven years had finally caught up with her. "Even to eyes susceptible to her usual magic she became a middle-aged woman awkwardly waving a few pieces of tulle."[6] Needless to say, those Dallas gentlemen who had finally eluded the wife for an evening "with the boys" were sorely disappointed, art or no art.

In addition, many Dallasites found the Strauss music to have a "rasping, unmelodic quality,"[7] not to mention that several thousand people had spent up to ten dollars a seat for a performance which they expected to last all evening. Here it was a bare 9:40 on a Saturday night with half of the Dallas social circle, dressed to the teeth, out in the street with nothing to do. As the years passed, and as *Salomé's* greatness as an opera became more clearly established, "there are those who look back on the performance with fancied pleasure, but at 10 o'clock on the night of March 1, 1924, satisfied customers would have been hard to find."[8]

In 1925 the new auditorium at Fair Park (later renamed the State Fair Music Hall) was completed, ready to welcome any operatic troupe which might pass its way. Chicago did return in 1927, and again in 1929, but with the depression even the Chicago Civic Opera collapsed, and Dallas saw little opera for the next decade.

For years Dallas had sought to find a way of luring the Metropolitan over to Texas. The city had long been envious of Atlanta, at that time the only Met stop in the South. Surely, the Dallas opera-lovers thought, there must be some way of inducing the New York company to extend its tour farther west. Herbert Marcus, then chairman of the Grand Opera Committee, and Arthur Kramer, president of the Dallas Symphony, began making it a point to drop by the Metropolitan offices once or twice a year, every time that either happened to be in New York City. On each visit plans were discussed for including Dallas in the Met's spring tour, but the management was always reluctant and politely cool toward the notion. This went on for nearly a decade.[9]

On one of these routine visits to the Metropolitan in January, 1939, Arthur Kramer was informed as he entered manager Edward Johnson's office that the company was planning a three-day visit to New Orleans during the coming April and the management was looking for a city in that general area to fill out the week. Would Dallas be interested in putting up a $65,000 guarantee for four Metropolitan performances?

Kramer immediately got on the telephone and informed the Dallas Chamber of Commerce of his stroke of good fortune. But to his surprise and dismay, he found that the chamber was reluctant to put up such a huge guarantee. In fact, he ended his long-distance conversation with nothing more than a flat refusal from the Dallas end. After ten years of diligent work Kramer was not willing to let opportunity slip through his fingers so easily. After diplomatically asking the Metropolitan management for a few days to complete arrangements, he struck off for Texas, determined to take matters into his own hands.

The enterprising Texan had no more than arrived in Dallas, when he was again on the telephone, calling firms and individuals who he felt would be interested in seeing the Met come to Dallas, interested enough to serve as a guarantor. Within a few hours Kramer had his $65,000 and more.[10]

And so, in April, 1939, the Met made its first call on Dallas in thirty-four years. Grace Moore opened the season in Massenet's *Manon* and closed it two days later as Mimi in *La Bohème*. Since that time, the Metropolitan has visited Dallas annually, with the exception of the wartime years, 1943–45, and the 1960–61 season, when a disagreement arose over the length of the stay. During these visits the Texas city has been privileged to view some truly magnificent performances and to hear most of the Met's roster of stars—Tibbett, Pons, Pinza, Milanov, Albanese, Tucker, Stevens, Traubel, Peerce, Steber, Tebaldi, Warren, Price, Bergonzi, Moffo, Merrill, and many others.

Since the Metropolitan comes to Dallas in April, at the end of the season, the laborious rehearsal hours are essentially over, and the members of the company have a chance to relax and enjoy themselves. Following the first performance of each season, a grand opera ball is held, where many of the singers and townspeople renew their acquaintances and generally have a gay time.

For nearly twenty years this spring festival presented by the Metropolitan was enough to satisfy the operatic tastes of the prosperous Texas community. As the years passed, however, the city grew, not only in population, but in cultural awareness as well. By the 1950's Dallas was in full possession of those prerequisites for the birth of resident opera, including a dynamic society, a thriving metropolitan area, a culturally aware public, and—certainly not to be overlooked—money.

In March, 1957, the Dallas Civic Opera was formed, actually no more than a paper corporation at first. Lawrence V. Kelly, who had just lost out in Chicago as a result of the internal squabble within the ranks of the Chicago Lyric Theatre, was invited to come to Dallas as the general manager of the new company. Kelly, then only twenty-nine years old, accepted the invitation and began working to get the project ready for a fall launching. Henry S. Miller, Jr., a local realtor and civic leader, who was chosen president of the company, singlehandedly raised a sum of $25,000 as a deficit fund, for a deficit very definitely figured into the plan.[11]

Next the dynamic Kelly set off for Europe to search for talent and production ideas. By the end of his tour of the European opera houses he had decided on Rossini's comic *L'Italiana in Algeri* as his first Dallas production. It was an odd vehicle for the debut of a new company—unfamiliar in this country, highly stylized, and demanding "a chorus that could sing Italian like natives."[12] But Kelly staked his life on this production, determined to show Dallas what could be done if the talent were right. The project was bulldozed through on determination, intestinal fortitude, and very little else, operating all the while on the financial shoestring so familiar in operatic circles. A conscious effort was made to attract attention to the enterprise through publicity, and with the help of a sympathetic press, this part of the plan was realized without serious difficulty.

Meanwhile, Nicola Rescigno, former artistic director of the Chicago Lyric Theatre, was selected as the musical director of the new Dallas company, and Broadway's Jean Rosenthal, also lighting director for the New York City Ballet and production director for the Shakespeare Festival at Stratford, Connecticut, became Kelly's production manager. Franco Zeffirelli, the brilliant young Italian stage director and designer who later made such a hit with his Old Vic production of *Romeo and Juliet*, was chosen to serve in these capacities in Dallas. Contracted also was the Dallas Symphony, which with the opera season added would have its season extended several weeks. A resident chorus was formed, and the many hours of training and rehearsing began.

Lawrence Kelly brought to Dallas two big assets. First, he was determined to show the operatic world what he could do on his own now that Carol Fox was in control of the Lyric Opera of Chicago. Second, he had an agreement from soprano Maria Callas that she would sing for him during his first Dallas season if a suitable production could be provided.

However, by the time the company's final organizational problems had been ironed out and Kelly got around to drawing up his
season, Callas was already committed to other opera engagements.
It was therefore agreed that the diva, rather than appearing in
production, would sing a benefit concert with the Dallas Symphony
to launch the artistic activities of the Dallas Civic Opera.

And so the season was set. Callas would begin the vocal fireworks
on November 21, with her concert, and *L'Italiana in Algeri* would
play for two performances on November 22 and 24. Until almost
the last minute the christening of the new company seemed more an
event of national rather than local interest, and for Texas that is
saying a lot.[13] Many Dallasites were more than a little skeptical that
Callas would even show up. After all, not three months before, she
had canceled her San Francisco appearances, claiming illness. Would
the notorious soprano really make it to Dallas?

But to the surprise of many, the diva arrived a full week before
the concert was scheduled. She rehearsed, attended social functions,
and was most cordial to everyone concerned. In the process La
Callas added a great deal of glamor to the Dallas opening and did
more than her share to turn the eyes of the operatic world on the
Texas city.

Nevertheless, on the night of the soprano's concert, despite the
fact that 3,126 people were in the audience,[14] the huge State Fair
Music Hall was almost a quarter empty, with many patrons still
dubious that they would ever hear Callas. But as Lawrence Kelly
had known all along, these fears were groundless. Callas showed up,
"shimmering and glowing in a Venetian-gold gown with diamonds
glittering at her ears." One had to look twice to make sure that it
was not Dietrich herself. Behind the diva was "a black-bordered set
with a sky-blue backdrop, creating the effect of an immense shadow
box."[15] Madame had committed herself to do five operatic *aria-
scenas*, any one of them a taxing feat in itself. All week she had
tried to cut the program down to three, but Kelly stood firm. And
five it was.[16]

Callas began with an aria from Mozart's *The Abduction from the
Seraglio*, which was "carefully but none too artfully negotiated."[17]
Yet by the end of this first selection the diva had the audience in
the palm of her hand. Then she moved into that area upon which
she had built her career—Bellini, Donizetti, and early Verdi. In two

arias from Bellini's *I Puritani,* including its challenging "Mad Scene," the diva hit her vocal stride, "rippling down her famed arpeggios, her tone pure and vibrant."[18] Concluding the first half of the program was an exciting "Letter Scene" from Verdi's *Macbeth,* which was articulated with "notable musical line and intensity."[19]

After the intermission, she rendered the magnificent *scena* from *La Traviata* which includes "*Ah! Fors e Lui*" and "*Sempre Libera,*" acting it out "to the point where the celebrated number . . . plunged deep into mood and character. Miss Callas sang it well and with no compromise between operatic purpose and mere display."[20] Then as the Dallas Symphony gave a reading of the overture to Verdi's *Vespri Siciliani,* the diva changed into a black lace sheath, set off by a blazing diamond necklace which added visual impact to the sombre mood of her last *scena,* the finale from Donizetti's *Anna Bolena.* In this scene Anne, who is about to be beheaded by her flirtatious ex-spouse, Henry the Eighth, alternates between lunacy and semi-sanity. On the last magnificent phrase—"Only my blood is lacking to finish the crime, and this will be shed!"—Callas "took a single step forward, so dramatic that people all but jumped. She raised a commanding hand over her head, then threw her arms wide and sent that last full note straight up through the roof."[21]

The critics agreed that the concert had been magnificent, but differed as to which particular aria was the zenith. John Rosenfield of the *Dallas Morning News* felt that the soprano "Verdied best,"[22] while Dorothea Bourne, writing for *Theatre Arts,* concluded that she hit her peak in the *Anna Bolena* scene.[23] Callas had thrilled not only vocally, but also registered "a dramatic and emotional point with the slug of an unerring sledge hammer."[24]

And yet, Dallas was still not convinced that resident opera was actually being born here on the north Texas plains. Yes, Callas had been great, but what of the company itself? Could it really produce opera? And after all, who was this "Italian girl in Algiers" anyway? As the curtain went up on the evening of the company's debut, the State Fair Music Hall was half empty, and skepticism again penetrated the air. Never had such doubts been to less avail, for that production of *L'Italiana in Algeri,* given with the "dream" circumstances which Lawrence Kelly and Carol Fox had earlier envisioned for the Lyric Theatre of Chicago, was soon to make operatic history.

The guiding ideal of the Dallas Civic Opera has always been "integrated opera," where every aspect of the production is finely worked out and then skillfully woven into the whole, with no effect more or less significant. Every medium of theatrical expression must be blended so that each lends itself to the total impact of the whole. The company's production of *L'Italiana* came as near seeing this ideal realized as one may reasonably expect it ever to be. The sets for the Rossini romp were designed by Franco Zeffirelli, who also served as stage director. Jean Rosenthal's lighting proved a creative achievement virtually unprecedented in the history of theater in the Southwest. Bathed in Miss Rosenthal's light, the Zeffirelli sets actually seemed to come to life. And then there was a cast consisting of Giulietta Simionato, Giuseppe Taddei, Nicola Monti, and Paolo Montarsolo, the latter two making their American debuts.[25]

By the time the first act was over, even the most dubious member of that opening night audience had come to appreciate the fact that Dallas had a live resident opera company on its hands. The local press had nothing but praise for the production, but national critics were even more enthusiastic, bestowing more flowers upon the Dallas company than the Texas plains had known in many a day. *Musical Courier* reported that the Dallas Civic Opera "gave bewitching and well-integrated performances of Rossini's *L'Italiana in Algeri* and in so doing set standards of singing, acting, playing, and stage design that any company in the world would have difficulty in matching."[26] *Theatre Arts* held that Lawrence Kelly in two nights "had put Dallas on the country's opera map,"[27] while *Newsweek* went a step farther by stating, "For a couple of nights running . . . Dallas, Texas, was the operatic capital of the United States."[28] Without a doubt, Dallas had joined the ranks of San Francisco and Chicago as one of the leading opera companies of the American West, a cultural oasis in a geographical desert.

The introductory season was no more than over when Lawrence Kelly began thinking in terms of 1958. The beginning had been magnificent, but it was merely a beginning. There was much to be done if the infant company were to live up to the high standards it had set for itself. And so the work began again, work which for Kelly included another trip to Europe. By summer the fall season was shaping up, promising to be as exciting as anything the city had ever known in its long, illustrious cultural history. Maria Callas agreed to return, this time in two productions. Unlike the year before, Dallasites now knew what their resident company was capable of, and excitement mounted as the season grew near, with financial contributions, opera guild membership, and advance ticket sales exceeding the management's wildest anticipations. Nor was the excitement limited to Dallas, for some 4,000 people from outside the city ordered tickets, coming from as far away as New York, California, Alaska, Cuba, and Mexico.[29]

When opening night arrived, the Music Hall was filled to capacity. The opera was Verdi's *La Traviata*, a rather ordinary event, one might say, in operatic circles. But this was not just another *Traviata;* this was integrated music-drama in the purest sense. On stage as the lady of the camellias was Maria Callas, creating in Violetta a character of real depth, for Callas brought to the role not only vocal power, but a spectacular acting ability. Zeffirelli designed the production, slanting the staging toward the Dumas novel, *Camille*, rather than toward the later stage play. Unique here was the presentation of the story as a series of flashbacks. While the orchestra played the opening prelude, Violetta was found dying in her bedroom, pondering the events leading up to her fatal illness, beginning with the party at which she met her beloved Alfredo. Rapid transition in scenes was achieved through the use of scrim sets, which enabled Violetta in Act I to retreat to her bedroom to have her consumptive seizure rather than having to drive her friends out of the salon, as is more traditional. The Zeffirelli sets contained "a gentle, gaslit quality and never once sought after operatic grandeur, not even in Flora's house—an episode spliced into Act II."[30] The whole production was geared toward artistic realism, with Callas even wearing unbecoming, contemporary (1852) hairstyles to add to the total effect.

The *Traviata* was not all vocal perfection—even Callas was less than a vocal paragon—but the full impact of the opera was tremendous, the prima donna holding "her audience in a kind of hushed trance" throughout the performance.[31] At the conclusion of the work, the packed house gave the diva and her fellow workers a jubilant standing ovation, heretofore a rare event in this Texas city.

On November 4, Rossini's *L'Italiana in Algeri* was presented again, now introducing in her American debut the young Spanish mezzo-soprano Teresa Berganza as Isabella. Berganza proved "complete mistress of the stage,"[32] displaying a sumptuous voice, a real gift for comedy, and a comely and petite appearance. To many this mounting of *L'Italiana* even surpassed the one staged the year before, and this one performance actually outdrew the two given in 1957, illustrating the increase in the company's reputation.

Immediately after the completion of the two performances of *Traviata*, Maria Callas began rehearsing a production which was not only the pinnacle of the Dallas season, but one that was to become an international sensation. This was the now-famous Dallas Civic Opera production of Cherubini's *Medea*, staged in Dallas for only the second time in the United States, San Francisco having mounted it for the first time two months earlier. Alexis Minotis of the Greek National Theater was the stage director for this production, bringing "refreshing new concepts to the trite and tired traditions of operatic stage movement."[33] Through the combined efforts of Kelly, Minotis, and Callas, it was decided to take the opera out of the eighteenth century setting conceived by Cherubini and restore the action to the fifth century B.C., the time of Euripides' play. The results are now legendary in the annals of opera.

For a full week before the first performance, Callas, who always strives for perfection, rehearsed the difficult Minotis stage movements, carefully ironing out the finest details. After the success of *Traviata*, excitement among the city's opera-goers, including a horde of folks not ordinarily in that select category, had reached fever pitch. Then, on the day that *Medea* opened, just hours before curtain-time, Rudolf Bing of the Metropolitan wired Mme. Callas that her contract with the New York company had been canceled because of apparently irreconcilable viewpoints concerning the roles she would sing there later that season. It seems that Callas felt she could not sing two *Traviatas* between two performances of Verdi's *Macbeth*, claiming that the roles were too diverse to be sung intermittently, the first requiring a coloratura voice, the second demanding heavy, dramatic vocal powers. Bing called this temperament, with the result that the soprano was fired.[34] To Dallas, however, its prima donna had been dealt a total injustice, and emotionalism hit a new high. For twenty-four hours La Callas dominated front-page headlines in both local newspapers. After all Dallas now had Callas when the Metropolitan did not, and this seemed to make her a sort of adopted daughter.

On Thursday evening, November 6, 1958, with the State Fair Music Hall filled to capacity, tense anticipation could be sensed in every corner of the house. Finally Maestro Rescigno appeared in the pit, and the orchestra began a reading of the *Medea* overture. When the curtain went up, the audience discovered a magnificent set, depicting the entrance of the palace of King Creon, designed in a classical Greek style by John Tsarouchis, with Glauce, Creon's daughter, and her handmaidens superbly attired in costumes imported from Athens. For half an act the throng sat in anxious anticipation, waiting for Callas. At last as the citizens of Corinth stood in terror, a guard brought word that a mysterious veiled woman waited outside the city's gates; the pulse of the audience quickened. In another moment—from out of nowhere, it seemed—the diva appeared, her face half-covered with a heavy veil, only her blazing eyes peering out at the citizenry assembled before Creon's palace. Immediately, the Music Hall was filled with an ovation that was unprecedented. Before the soprano had been on stage five minutes, the Dallasites sensed that here was one of the greatest—if not the greatest—operatic performances the city had ever seen. Vocally, Callas had never been better, while her acting was worthy of Euripides' original play, producing the full measure of terror and pity aimed at by the dramatist.[35] As the audience sat mesmerized, Callas as Medea poured out her wrath on the faithless Jason, her eyes burning with jealous hate. Then, as the house sat motionless, she was the pleading mother, desperately begging Jason to return to her. But with rejection, she became the vengeful tigress, determined to strike where it would hurt Jason most.

At the end of Act II, Medea, watching the wedding procession of Jason and Glauce from her place of hiding, could restrain her anger no longer. Like a demon possessed, she ran to the center of the stage, grabbed the torch out of the ceremonial fire, and swiftly mounted the staircase toward the back of the stage, determined in her vengeance. The enthusiasm of the Dallas audience was unparalleled.

As the last act opened, a temple was discovered with steps covering all but a small portion of the stage. In the background dark clouds were speeding by, creating an atmosphere of imminent doom.

For almost an entire act Callas held the stage—first as one tormented with indecision, then as the loving mother, and finally as a desperate fiend, blinded by jealousy and rage, even determined to slay her own children in order to strike out at Jason. In the finale the stage was dimly lighted, except for one prominent ray to the side. Medea, working herself up to the point of committing that last dastardly deed, stood on the temple steps, Callas singing as gloriously as she ever had in her life, each phrase expertly colored. With the need for facial expressions, the soprano manipulated herself into that sole beam of light in order to impart to the audience the full impact of the dramatic situation. Finally, she wrenched the knife from her belt, flew up the steps to the temple, her long cape flowing behind her, singing magnificently all the while.

By the final curtain the frenzy of the audience was not far behind that of the action on stage. When Callas, Jon Vickers (Jason), and Teresa Berganza (Neris, Medea's maid) appeared for their curtain call, the house almost spontaneously rose to its feet, with *bravos* and applause filling the air. Time and again, the crowd demanded a solo bow from Callas, but the diva insisted that her fellow artists share the honors with her. Only when Vickers and Berganza faked an entrance, only to withdraw hastily to the wings, leaving Callas alone before the footlights, did the audience have its way. At that moment the fiery soprano with the legendary temperament looked more like a demure schoolgirl who had just performed well in the senior play than an international opera star with the musical world at her feet, for there she stood before the cheering throng, apparently touched by the honor being paid her, a faint, shy smile on her face, dragging a huge bouquet of long-stemmed roses behind her.

At the conclusion of the season Dallas was told that it was not only on the opera map, but was now definitely one of the leading lyric capitals of the world. As the *Chicago American* put it, "Opera, ideally, is a fusion of theatric and musical elements into a stylized whole able to move and exalt all who witness it. It is Dallas' enviable legacy to have an opera that fulfills the ideal as nearly as any establishment in the world, Vienna and La Scala included."[36] But actually Dallas needed no one to point out its operatic virtues, for by now civic pride had swollen to a zenith. And the success had not all been artistic, for the five performances given that season brought more than 20,000 patrons and over $100,000 into the box-office till, causing local pride to be matched by civic amazement.[37]

Six months later, Lawrence Kelly announced that he had negotiated an exchange agreement, the first international exchange in the history of opera, with London's Covent Garden. According to the arrangement, Dallas' *Medea*, complete with Maria Callas and Alexis Minotis, would be presented in London, while the Royal Opera Company's physical production of Donizetti's *Lucia di Lammermoor* would be used in Dallas. The *Lucia* mounting, designed by Zeffirelli, had received rave notices from the European press, comparable to those which *Medea* had gotten in this country. Kelly felt that here was an opportunity to display American production techniques in Europe, and at the same time a chance for American audiences to glimpse the European style of opera. Then too, there was a very real financial factor involved; both companies stood to save thousands of dollars as a result of the exchange, and yet the seasons of both would be greatly enhanced.

On a Saturday morning in May 1959, a line of people began forming outside the Royal Opera House in London. All through the weekend it continued to grow, despite the sweltering heat. Finally, on Tuesday the line began to disappear as tickets went on sale for the first London staging of Cherubini's *Medea* in eighty-nine years. Three hours after the box office opened, every seat in the house was sold. A month later, just before curtain time, seats normally priced at $5.60 were selling for $98 on the scalpers' market. "When a purposeful posse from Dallas came yipping into town but found itself seatless, Ambassador John Hay Whitney patriotically handed over his own four seats, and black marketeers supplied the rest at oil-well prices."[38]

On the night of the opening performance, the London audience was warm and enthusiastic, demanding twelve curtain calls from Callas and her fellow artists. The press also rendered a sincere round of critical *bravos* for both the Dallas production and the performers. Actually, it seemed that each of the five performances of the opera in London was better than the one before it.[39]

Any doubts still harbored concerning the reputation of the Dallas Civic Opera abroad were now dispelled. Most assuredly, the commotion in Dallas the past season had not been just a case of civic pride. True, the Texas city had taken enormous pride in its opera, but a sample of the company's talents had now been judged by an impartial audience. The verdict was positive.

Three months later, Covent Garden's production of *Lucia di Lammermoor* arrived in Dallas, packed in 164 bales weighing in excess of 50,000 pounds and including some 200 costumes.[40] The opera had been chosen to launch the 1959 Dallas season.

As November dawned, Maria Callas, who had just experienced a rift in her marital relations with Italian industrialist Giovanni Battista Meneghini, was scheduled to sing three roles in Dallas—Lucia, Rosina, and a repeat of Medea. There were problems involved, however, for the diva's separation hearing was to come up in Italy right in the middle of the Dallas season. No one, including Callas apparently, knew whether she would be able to sing more than the opening role.

On Thursday, October 29, a week before the season's opening, Mme. Callas was due to arrive in Dallas, following a concert engagement in Kansas City. But when the plane landed at Dallas' Love Field, reporters found that the nearest thing to Callas on board was her secretary and French poodle. Madame, it seems, had gone to Europe to try to get her legal hearing postponed.[41]

The tension and suspense throughout the city's operatic circle became almost unbearable as rehearsals began without the prima donna. Would the soprano really come this year, or was this to result in another of those much-discussed Callas scandals? Three nights before the opening, a full dress rehearsal was called, but without Callas. The work went on, however, with stage director Zeffirelli in open shirt and loosened tie walking through the diva's role and Maestro Rescigno moaning her vocalism. But at 5 A.M. the next day, in flew Callas, ready to begin rehearsals the next evening. The question of her hearing was still unsettled.

On Friday, November 6, all was ready for the launching of the new season—or almost ready, at least. Callas' costumes had gone astray somewhere between London and Dallas. Consequently, on opening night frenzied substitutions had to be made. One costume was borrowed from a chorister, and a new gown for Act III was still being sewn when Act II began. On stage things went better than anyone had a right to expect.[42]

The Zeffirelli sets and costumes added an air of realism to the production, with scrims placed over the front of the outdoor scenes to suggest the Scottish fog. One would-be critic in the audience quipped that the use of these scrims was nothing to get excited about, for back home in Ardmore, Oklahoma, they achieved the same effect by simply allowing the audience to smoke. It is doubtful that the Oklahoma gentleman ever saw anything in Ardmore to match those Covent Garden sets. "Each was a tableau . . . of beauty—a battlement, a sombre park, a meditative Enrico Ashton gazing into a fireplace, the castle's great hall with its spiral stairway and wall of leaded windows, and the gloomy Ravenswood cemetery"[43]—all of which did much to transplant the Italian libretto and the Italian music to the somber Scottish locale of the Sir Walter Scott novel on which the opera is based.

Still unsettled was the problem of Callas' legal separation. It had become apparent by the last performance of *Lucia* that the diva would not be able to participate in the forthcoming *Barber of Seville*, for these performances directly conflicted with her court hearing in Italy. Hence, immediately after her standing ovation on Sunday afternoon, Madame boarded a plane for Europe. The question for Dallas now was would she be back for *Medea* two weeks later. The crisis was intensified by the fact that sopranos who sing *Medea* are a rare vocal species. If Callas should vacate the role, a replacement might not easily be found. And so the suspense continued, with Dallas rushing out on its front porch every morning to pick up the newspaper, eager to read the next installment of the true-to-life musical serial.

While this anxious waiting continued, *The Barber of Seville* was given its two performances, with *La Scala*'s Eugenia Ratti substituting as Rosina. The Figaro was handsome Ettore Bastianini, who skipped, pranced, and spoofed his way to a complete triumph, even delighting the audience by stealing the prompter's score during the final curtain call.

The sets for *Barber* were designed by the contemporary Italian abstractionist Bice Brichetto. "Few opera houses the world over," wrote *Musical Courier*'s Serge Saxe, "can boast such lavish and provocatively beautiful scenery."[44] New for Dallas was the use of a raked stage in this production. Here the stage floor is slanted so as to throw the action forward, making the drama more intimate. Since most of the cast was unaccustomed to walking on an angle of ten degrees, the raked stage was set up in a spare building in

Dallas' Fair Park so that the chorus could begin practice sessions on it several weeks in advance.

All in all, *The Barber of Seville* proved a highly significant production, going a long way to undermine the snide nickname "Callas Civic Opera" which had been applied to the Kelly organization on several previous occasions. The company had stood on its own, without the Callas name and talents, and had come through extremely well, a healthy sign for the future.

Finally, for the 1959 season, there were two performances of *Medea*. On Saturday, November 14, it was announced that Callas' legal separation was complete, but it was still not known whether the singer would be back in Dallas for her scheduled performances on November 19 and 21. For nearly two days the Dallas management nervously awaited word from its prima donna. But a few hours before dawn on Monday, November 16, Lawrence Kelly was awakened by a long-distance call from Callas in Milan, telling him that she would be able to sing for him the following Thursday. A city of opera-lovers and one very tired impresario breathed a long sigh of relief.

And so the previous year's giant was mounted again. Callas, despite her harrowing dash to Europe, returned in top vocal form. As with the year before, the last act of the Cherubini opera proved spellbinding, and Callas again thrilled her audience by mounting the towering staircase, knife in hand, to put an end to her two young sons. During the second performance the diva started a dramatic ascent up the temple stairs, only to be stopped short when her sweeping cloak caught on a nail, nearly pulling her over backwards. Showing incredible stage presence, she immediately improvised new stage movement, while she remained bound by the hooked cloak. Since at this point in the drama Medea is on the verge of the blind fury which causes her to slay her children, Madame's wild tugging at her ensnared garment was not out of character. Eventually, the diva was forced to rip the bottom piece of the cloak completely off in order to gain freedom. Then, without appearing flustered over her mishaps and singing gloriously all the while, she picked up the stray piece of cloak, folded it into a neat ball, and, as she poured out her jealous wrath vocally, heaved the delinquent cloth over to one side of the steps so that the chorus, which was about to appear, would not trip on it. Never has Medea been so considerate of her fellow humanity.

A year later the company staged its first season without Maria Callas, the diva having declined an offer to sing in Dallas in 1960. While things might be a little more relaxed, there was no doubt that without Callas, the company's box-office, if not its artistic, future was seriously endangered. Then too, could the company continue to arouse international interest without its vocal angel?

The answer has been affirmative. Where Maria Callas left off in 1959, Joan Sutherland took up in 1960. The Australian-born Sutherland had skyrocketed to fame as Lucia in the 1959 Covent Garden production, the one Dallas had borrowed. She came to Texas the next year for her United States debut in Handel's *Alcina*, which despite its 225 years had never before been staged in America. The production, borrowed from Venice's *La Fenice*, was designed by Zeffirelli as a masque being presented before a royal court, thus making the static action of the baroque drama more plausible. While the whole performance was superb, Sutherland emerged as the undisputed sensation. "Miss Sutherland," wrote the *Dallas News'* Rual Askew, "easily enthroned herself as a most remarkable prima donna . . . blessed with an incredibly flawless technique and vocal expressivity that is the finest of our time certainly and possibly as great as any in musical history. . . . Her trills alone are not to be believed in an age of flagrant technical cheating."[45]

Sutherland was also presented that season as Donna Anna in a star-studded production of Mozart's *Don Giovanni*. The young German baritone Eberhard Wächter sang the title role. Giuseppe Taddei was Leporello, Luigi Alva the Don Ottavio, Eugenia Ratti the Zerlina, John Reardon the Masetto, and Nicola Zaccaria the Commendatore. But to many the most brilliant portrayal came from Elisabeth Schwarzkopf as Donna Elvira. Beautifully made up and displaying masterful acting abilities, Schwarzkopf simply *was* Elvira, "a fetchingly nutty woman of superficial mannerisms but convincing desperation, huffing and giving off sparks like a 1928 vacuum cleaner."[46] Professional opera-goer Elsa Maxwell left the performance exclaiming, "It's really incredible—incredible—the greatest opera in the world in a little town like Dallas."[47]

Returning in 1961, Joan Sutherland remained the star attraction, but sang only one role—*Lucia di Lammermoor.* Then in 1962, the stellar focal point shifted to Mario Del Monaco, who portrayed Otello and Canio, both to mixed reviews. The next year, while it boasted no great central luminary, saw the American premiere of Monteverdi's *Incoronazione di Poppea,* Regina Resnik's Carmen, and a *Ballo in Maschera* with Antonietta Stella and Giuseppi di Stefano, neither of whom had sung in the United States in several seasons.

Continuing Kelly's policy of giving American audiences a chance to view European stagemanship, a 1960 production of Donizetti's *The Daughter of the Regiment* was air-lifted from Palermo's *Teatro Massimo,* thanks to a Neiman-Marcus donation. The next year brought a staging of *La Bohème* from Spoleto's Festival of Two Worlds. Singers heretofore unknown in this country have repeatedly been introduced. Luigi Alva made his American debut in *The Daughter of the Regiment,* and Denise Duval made hers in 1961 in *Thaïs,* the company's first French production. Ilva Ligabue, who had sung a few weeks earlier in Chicago, created such a stir in the 1961 *Bohème* that she was brought back the next season for *Otello* and *Suor Angelica.*

Guided by its ideal of "integrated opera," the Dallas seasons have consistently scored positive success both with the critics and at the box office. That is not to say that these Dallas seasons have made a profit, for the business of opera production is not a money-making operation. Nevertheless, the company's financial record has been remarkable on every account, with performances as frequently as not playing to capacity houses. Artistically, the organization's productions are already on a plane with those presented in Chicago, San Francisco, and New York. The seasons have remained short (only three weeks long), but quality has made up for brevity. Kelly's aim has been "to get opera out of the warehouse. He wants opera to look and sound as though it were being born afresh at each of his performances. Each work must evolve, on the stage, directly from the style, and musical and dramatic power within it."[48]

The Dallas Civic Opera has never been content with a routine production; neither has it been satisfied to copy production trends set by other leading opera houses. Most emphatically, Dallas has steered away from the habit of building its productions along lines established by the Metropolitan, as is so frequently the case with lesser American companies. The Dallas Opera prides itself as an innovator, unwilling to fall into the stagnancy which comes from employing only those techniques which have been enshrined as "tradition." As might be expected, not all of the company's efforts have been successful. A 1960 *Butterfly*, staged by Kizi Koyke and employing a number of Japanese Kabuki touches, never quite caught fire. When the management dreamed up teaming Jacques d'Amboise and a night-club "cooch" dancer in the *Thaïs* ballet, critics called it a nightmare. Nor did a modernization of Leoncavallo's *Pagliacci* go over particularly well. Still, this spirit of originality, plus the idea that each production must be an operatic rejuvenation, goes a long way toward explaining the artistic depth which the Dallas Civic Opera has attained in its brief history.

Another strong point in Dallas' favor is its fresh repertoire. Fearing the esthetic hazards that result from the constant repetition of the "old favorites," the Dallas management has enlivened its offering by presenting the first *L'Italiana in Algeri* in the United States in nearly forty years, the second American staging of *Medea*, as well as *Alcina* and *Incoronazione di Poppea* in their American premieres.

Only rarely does Dallas look to the Metropolitan for its artists, instead preferring to turn to the opera houses of Europe for its principals, where fresh talent—artists relatively unknown in this country—may be found. Not that the Dallas company is hostile to the Metropolitan, for it definitely is not. The feeling simply is that the Southwest gets a chance to view the Metropolitan's production methods and hear the Met's artists every spring when the New York company visits Dallas on tour. Why imitate in the fall what was seen earlier in the spring? Why not instead add another dimension to the operatic diet of the region? Why should the Dallas Civic Opera be content to copy when it possesses the resources and know-how to innovate?

Summer Festivals Along the Divide

Every summer when the nation's schools have stacked away books for another year, thousands of eager tourists squeeze into the family automobile and head for the West. What a few weeks before had been a quiet, peaceful mountain community suddenly becomes thronged with visitors. While this vacationing multitude is primarily concerned with the more common pursuits of sightseeing and souvenir hunting, their excursions often lead them to strange and astonishing endeavors. Caught up in a festive, carefree atmosphere, the fun-seekers may find themselves engaged in activities they would never think of doing back home. One might be found camping out—in the wilderness, with no restaurant or grocery in two, maybe three, miles. Likewise, one who normally does not care for such things at all might possibly be discovered at the opera house.

Actually, summer opera festivals, as in Europe, have become quite popular in this country, especially in the West. Two projects stand out as particularly significant—the Central City Opera House Association and the more recent Santa Fe Opera Company. Both not only attract large audiences, but also play an important role artistically in the nation's musical life. While these companies are probably most outstanding for their training of young American singers, the productions themselves cannot be overlooked. Both organizations have consistently given fine performances, which, while not on a plane with those of San Francisco, Chicago, or Dallas, often contain an intimate quality the larger companies could never attain.

Central City: Youthful Sound of the Past

On May 6, 1859, a Georgia prospector, John Gregory by name, struck gold at "Gregory's Diggings" between the present towns of Black Hawk and Central City, Colorado, some thirty-odd miles west of Denver. When news of the strike spread, a flood of lusty, brawling gold-seekers came pouring into the mountain wilderness virtually overnight. The area shortly became known as "the richest square mile on earth," and is said to have attracted over 15,000 prospectors. Central City sprang up as the principal base of supply, soon becoming a thriving mining community.[1]

Before long, however, placer mining played out in the area, and the large-scale work of removing ore from solid rock began. Consequently, the independent prospector moved on, and a group of more permanent workers, mostly Welsh and Cornish, was brought into the valley. These newcomers loved their music, enough so that in 1860 they built a log theater where plays and later light operas were presented. This was the Montana Theater, where for three months out of the year some sort of musical or dramatic performance was given every night. Such diverse works as *She Stoops to Conquer, Mazeppa, Ten Nights in a Bar Room, A Trip Across the Ocean,* and *A Texas Steer* were staged with huge success.[2]

The city's first experience with grand opera came in December, 1864. The Gruenwalds, principal singers of Thomas Maguire's Opera Company in San Francisco, arrived in Denver on their way to an engagement in New York. However, because of heavy snows, roads to the east had become impassable, and it was necessary for the singers to remain in Colorado until the lanes could be cleared. Upon request by the management of a local theater, the Gruenwalds decided to give a concert right there in Denver. The press waxed enthusiastic at the proposal, and on the designated evening the theater was filled to capacity. The singers rendered selections from Bellini and Donizetti and performed a comic duet in German, but the reaction of the audience was sharply divided. Some liked the performance; others definitely did not. Probably the latter were in a majority.

Meanwhile, the people of Central City read the press notices announcing the singers' engagement and shortly invited the Gruenwalds to give a recital in the Montana Theater. The couple, still unable to get through to New York, accepted and were received most graciously by the little mining community, certainly far more enthusiastically than they had been by the "elite" and "fashion" of Denver.[3]

A decade later Central City was ravaged by a fire which stopped just short of the Teller House, the town's leading hotel. The beloved Montana was completely consumed. Soon a new theater, the Belvedere, took its place, offering minstrel shows, circuses, and amateur dramatic and musical productions.[4] In 1876, however, the citizens of Central staged their own production of *The Bohemian Girl* with such success, both artistic and financial, that they were determined to build a truly fine opera house.

In the spring of 1878, five years before the opening of the Metropolitan, the present Central City Opera House was completed at a cost of $18,000, financed by popular subscription. The theater was built of native stone with walls four feet thick. The interior, measuring fifty-five by 115 feet, was of simple design, with a seating capacity of 742. At the time it was built the opera house rented for forty dollars a night. When it came time for the theater's opening, the musical and dramatic factions of the town clashed. Finally, it was decided to have two dedication performances, one on March 4 for the musicians, another on March 5 for the actors.[5]

Soon the opera house became known as "the finest theater west of 'The River.' " For a time the management offered nine unbroken months of music and drama, and during the next several years such luminaries as Salvini, Bernhardt, Ristori, Joseph Jefferson, Maggie Mitchell, Rose Coghlin, and Edwin Booth made the uncomfortable trek up the canyon either by narrow-gauge railroad or bruising stagecoach to appear on the Opera House stage.[6]

Financially, the theater proved considerably less successful. Most of the men who put up the money for it were never even paid the interest on their investment.[7] Soon the boom days passed, and the bonanza kings retired to the larger cities. Central City became a virtual ghost town. The homes on the surrounding hillsides fell into decay. "The abandoned mines became yawning throats and brilliant orange dumps among the aspens and pines—all to the delight of the artist and romantic sightseer in search of color and ghost town legends."[8]

By 1910 the Opera House too had become a symbol of the past, abandoned except for shadows, cobwebs, and rats. Occasionally, in the summer a handful of tourists would make their way into the town, where "old-timers" delighted in telling them thrilling tales of the past. To visit the old Opera House, particularly, was to enter a bygone era. "The outside world was forgotten; it seemed as though . . . [one] were trespassing on sacred ground. A visitor could see but little in the darkness—the roof had caved in somewhat, the walls were black, the ceiling was water-stained and obliterated and partly fallen, too."[9] But it could not be denied that there was a real fascination about the place.

In the intervening years the Opera House had become the property of Peter McFarlane, one of the original builders, and then later of their heirs, Mr. and Mrs. Frederick McFarlane. In 1931 the Mc-Farlanes presented the theater to the University of Denver, throwing the school's officials into a quandary as to what to do with it. Eventually, it was suggested that the Opera House be turned into a memorial to the Colorado pioneers, and a committee headed by Anne Evans, daughter of the second territorial governor of Colorado, and Ida Kruse McFarlane, a local educator and lover of drama, was set up to supervise the project.

Within the next year the old theater was restored and redecorated. The frescoes were cleaned and retouched, the crystal chandeliers rehung. Wooden kitchen chairs were purchased and painted a mellow red. The cane seats were knocked out, and leather substituted. On the back of each chair was carved the name of some famous person—Horace Greeley, Sarah Bernhardt, Edwin Booth, Jim Bridger, Kit Carson, William F. Cody, Adelina Patti, Zebulon Pike —all supposedly having something to do with Colorado's pioneer history. The chairs were then sold to residents of Denver for $100 each.[10]

On July 16, 1932, Central City's Opera House was dedicated a second time. More than ten thousand people lined the streets of the little town for the occasion, most of them dressed in "western" garb.

There were ore-digging contests, fire runs, and Faro. The old town lived again! Launching the artistic activities at the Opera House was Lillian Gish in a production of Dumas' *Camille*. The play, directed by Robert Edmund Jones, was a smash hit, not only with those quasi-cowboys and miners out in the streets, but with local drama critics as well.[11]

The whole festival in fact was such a success that other buildings in the town were soon restored, and accommodations were made for the thousands of visitors who were now to pour into Central each summer. The Opera House, however, remained the center of all the activity, presenting during the next seven years an interesting array of drama and light opera. Gladys Swarthout came in 1933 for *The Merry Widow*, followed the next year by Walter Huston as Shakespeare's *Othello*. *The Gondoliers*, *A Doll's House*, *Ruy Blas*, and *The Yeoman of the Guard* were given during succeeding summers, all with great success.[12]

Then in 1940 the Opera House management staged twenty-five performances of Smetana's *The Bartered Bride*, its first real opera, with a cast headed by Colorado's own Josephine Antoine, Metropolitan soprano. The ticket prices ranged from $2 to $2.50,[13] and attendance was phenomenal. In fact the opera was received with such enthusiasm that it was decided to attempt somewhat heavier operas the next summer.

The following year two operas were presented on alternate nights, Rossini's *The Barber of Seville* and Gluck's *Orpheus and Eurydice*, both sung in English. The productions used primarily Metropolitan artists (John Brownlee was Figaro; Anna Kaskas sang Orpheus), and both were staged by the Met's Herbert Graf.[14] All twenty-five performances played to capacity houses, and over 20,-000 people were turned away at the box office. For the first time scalpers appeared in the streets of Central City. Even self-professed non-opera-goers like columnist Ernie Pyle found themselves impressed by what they saw. "By nature," wrote Pyle, "I have no affinity for opera; it does not move me as other things do. But maybe because of the setting, or the imagination, or the tempo of the whole day—the opera [*The Barber of Seville*] to me was superb."[15]

But 1941 also brought the Japanese bombing of Pearl Harbor, forcing the United States to turn its resources to the serious business of war. Because of the rationing of gasoline and the scarcity of tires, the nation's tourist traffic was cut to a minimum. Consequently, during the four years of war no summer festival was held, and again the Opera House knew darkness.

With the close of the war, opera returned to the little mountain city, and the atmosphere surrounding the operas was more festive than ever. Folk dances were held during the day, while the saloons did as roaring a business as they ever did during the gold-rush days. The law even looked the other way while various wheels of chance spun.[16] Each opera performance was announced by the traditional town crier. Ladies, dressed in grandma's bustles and hoop skirts, and gentlemen, sporting sideburns and whiskers, rode up the steep hill to the Opera House in a fringe-top surrey. Eureka Street became crowded with sight-seers standing on the plank sidewalks to view the festivities. And after the opening night opera (Mozart's *The Abduction from the Seraglio*, with Eleanor Steber), a gala ball was held in the Teller House ballroom.[17]

From virtually every standpoint, the 1947 season was one of the finest in Central City's history. The festival was opened that year with Beethoven's *Fidelio*, a work which proved particularly well-suited to the confines of the small theater. The production, starring Regina Resnik, was well sung and acted, and the scenery and costumes were expertly conceived. The one damaging ingredient was the English translation (containing such lines as, "Heavens, Heavens what is this I hear?"), which the local press denounced as "nothing short of corny."[18]

The alternate opera that year was Flotow's *Martha*, featuring Frances Greer in the role of Lady Harriet and Leopold Simoneau as Lionel. Late in the season, Miss Greer suddenly came down with laryngitis, and the management had a moment of uneasiness. It was eventually learned that soprano Marguerite Piazza was vacationing in the city. A hasty search through the town found the singer eating a late breakfast. When asked if she would take over for the indisposed Frances Greer that evening, Miss Piazza confessed that she had not sung a note of *Martha* in two years. No matter, the management was desperate. And so, cleverly concealing the score in her hand, Piazza undertook the performance without so much as a rehearsal. She, of course, knew no stage movements whatever. "I lost six pounds," said tenor Leopold Simoneau, "trying to find out where

Miss Piazza would be on stage and getting there to sing my lines. But she was wonderful."[19] Judging from the hearty ovation, the audience thought so too.

The total receipts that summer grossed $112,500, by far the largest yet. Still the management was left with a $40,000 deficit. Both of the leads, Regina Resnik and Frances Greer, helped out the accounting department by performing for token amounts.[20]

The following season, however, was less fortunate at the box office. Both operas, Offenbach's *The Tales of Hoffmann* and Mozart's *Cosi Fan Tutte*, received rave reviews from the critics, but only mild applause from the public.[21] Consequently, the next year financial considerations necessitated a temporary shift to one light opera and a sophisticated burlesque. The operetta was Johann Strauss' *Die Fledermaus*, with Regina Resnik. The burlesque was Mae West's classic vehicle, *Diamond Lil*. On the first day of ticket sales over 9,000 orders came in.[22] And the enthusiasm was well deserved. Resnik's Rosalinde was deemed a "glowing interpretation,"[23] and the fifty-seven-year-old Mae West, looking twenty years younger, proved that she was still capable of tossing off a "It's not the men in my life, but the life in my men that counts" with her inimitable spark.

In 1950 with its financial standing improved, the Opera House Association returned to grand opera, and with the exception of 1955, when the whole season was devoted to Gilbert and Sullivan, Central City has presented opera every year since. The company's perennial success has been little short of astounding. *Don Pasquale*, presented in 1951, was one of the Opera House's biggest hits, repeated the following year by popular demand. Menotti's *Amelia Goes to the Ball*, given in 1951 with its setting shifted from Milan to Central City, Colorado, was another triumph. So was the 1953 *Carmen* with Mildred Miller and Lucine Amara, which alternated with Nicolai's *The Merry Wives of Windsor*. The following season brought a highly polished production of Richard Strauss' *Ariadne auf Naxos*, presented in Central City just five years after its American premiere at the New York City Center.

In 1956 the Opera House Association celebrated its twenty-fifth anniversary by staging the world premiere of Douglas Moore's *The Ballad of Baby Doe*, featuring Dolores Wilson in the title role. The opera, set in the Denver area, was so successful that three extra performances had to be added. These too were sold out. The *Rocky Mountain News* called Moore's score "magnificent."[24] Later the work was staged at the New York City Center, on NBC television, at Santa Fe, and was repeated by Central City in 1959, then starring Laurel Hurley.

In the spring of 1960 the management of the Opera House surprised the operatic world by announcing its plans to produce *Aïda*, one of the grandest of all lyric spectacles. Because of the theater's small stage, it had always been assumed that spectacles were out as far as Central City was concerned. But *Aïda* was staged that summer, winning considerable critical acclaim. Scenic designer Robert O'Hearn, using simple principles of perspective, gave height, depth, and width to the sets without sacrificing surface space. In the "Triumphal Scene" over ninety people were gathered on the stage.[25] Also presented that season was a charming mounting of Donizetti's *Lucia di Lammermoor*. In the intimate little theater Lucia's "Mad Scene" became a touching, dramatic display, as well as a vocal showstopper.[26]

The 1962 season brought to the Opera House a work particularly suited to the Central City Festival, Puccini's *The Girl of the Golden West*. Again the intimacy of the house made scenes like the second act poker game most effective. Less successful, largely because the English translation seemed out of keeping with the mood of the opera, was the 1963 *Trovatore*, although Lucine Amara's singing of Leonora was said to be "like dark velvet."[27] The world premiere of Ward's *Lady from Colorado* in 1964 saw a return to a local theme.

Certainly the intimacy of its productions has been one of the outstanding features of the Central City Opera House, an advantage which could never be obtained by companies operating in theaters seating 3,000 or more. The smallness of the house also makes opera in English more feasible, for here not a word of the text is lost (which probably was the trouble with *Trovatore*, since its libretto is literally too silly for words). For good or bad—and usually for good—the audience contact in the Opera House is almost perfect.

Although the Central City Festival is primarily geared to the tourist trade and contains many aspects which are highly romanticized and totally bizarre, the Opera House Association makes every effort to keep its productions on as high a plane as possible. The scenery and costumes are consistently well executed, and the productions are thoroughly rehearsed, first in New York and later in Colorado. Young energetic singers are chosen for the leads, many of them not yet ready to sing major roles in a massive house like the Metropolitan, but perfectly capable of singing in the petite Central City Opera House. Undoubtedly, the Association renders one of its greatest services in the experience it offers young, upcoming artists. A Cornell MacNeil can sing *Rigoletto* in Central City in 1957 and, with similar experience elsewhere, is ready to perform the same role at the Metropolitan two years later. Or take the case of Laurel Hurley, who, having sung at the New York City Center, was brought to Central in 1951 to do a minor, one-aria role and to understudy four larger parts. When the management heard Hurley's voice, they were so impressed that they saw to it that she got to sing both Juliet and Galatea before the season was over.[28] Three years later the soprano was graduated from the City Center to the Metropolitan.

In addition to giving young singers experience, the Central City Opera House Association provides the Denver area with a seasonal opportunity to view grand opera, an opportunity which the city is offered but rarely. For Denver's music-lovers and social set, the opening of the Central City Festival is an event of paramount importance, something that is anticipated all year long. Then, too, many of the tourists who come to Central find themselves first attracted to the Opera House because of all the activity and color that surrounds it. Once in the old theater, more that one patron has discovered that the show on stage is not half bad. Although the number of overnight converts to the opera cult is few, it is not unknown for one who formerly would get no closer to opera than an occasional aria on television to sit through a trial performance, only to find himself willing to try it again.

Sante Fe: Mature Sound of the Future

Another western city which sees an annual influx of summer tourist traffic is Santa Fe, New Mexico. An enchanting city, located high in the mountains, Santa Fe has a colorful history going back to 1610 and is blessed with a mild, pleasant night climate—all of which combines to form an atmosphere of near universal appeal. Consequently, thousands of tourists flock to the city each summer, many returning year after year.

Since 1940 one of these annual visitors has been John Crosby, a wealthy New Yorker, who first came to New Mexico to attend the Los Alamos Ranch School. But like so many others, he promptly became so enamored with the area that he has spent a part of the year there ever since. Eventually, the Crosby family even bought a ranch just outside Santa Fe as a sort of permanent summer retreat.

In the meantime John Crosby graduated from Yale with a major in music and went on to postgraduate work at Columbia. Later he studied conducting with Pierre Monteux. Opera had always held a particular fascination for this talented musician. In 1954 Crosby hit upon the idea of forming an opera company—to be located, of course, near his beloved Santa Fe. "I always wanted to work in opera, and I always wanted to live at least part of the year in the Southwest," he recalls. "Somehow the two things just had to go together."[29]

And so the energetic Crosby began talking to local businessmen to find out what kind of financial support his proposed company might expect. He pointed out to them that with the annual tourist trade, coupled with the local interest in opera, the project, if planned for the summer months, had the best possible chances of success. Most of the people Crosby talked with were both enthusiastic and generous. The Santa Fe Opera Company was founded with Crosby as musical director, and by fall of 1956 the ground had been broken for the organization's new outdoor theater.

Crosby and his guarantors agreed that it would be a shame to present their opera in the confines of the traditional theater. Santa Fe's natural scenery and its cool, starlit summer nights were perfect for outdoor opera. And what better place was there to build an outdoor theater than on the Crosby ranch, approximately a five-mile drive to the north of the city?

By the summer of 1957 the theater was completed, shortly to be pronounced by *Time* magazine "one of the handsomest operatic settings in the Western Hemisphere."[30] Built on a piñon-studded mountainside at a cost of about $250,000, the structure seats a capacity of 755 and is designed to acoustical perfection. The wings of the stage are projected out to embrace the first few rows of the audience, while the roof, virtually a flying polygon, is canted slightly upward. The whole stage is constructed of redwood, and the only color used in the theater's decoration is an occasional sky blue trim. A system of sliding panels at the rear of the stage may be adjusted to the demands of each opera or left open to afford the audience a view of the Jemez Mountains. A pool of water between the orchestra and the audience reflects the action on stage, serves to aid the acoustics, and adds an extra touch of beauty to the interior. Surrounding the theater are gardens of white and yellow snap-dragons and petunias, and in front is an attractive fountain which not only beautifies, but also eliminates possible noises from the highway at the foot of the hill. "There is a sense, in the clean lines and clear colors of the whole place, of belonging to this old land of limitless distances and vast skies."[31]

On July 3, 1957, the Santa Fe Opera was christened with a production of *Madama Butterfly*, sung in English, with Maria Ferriero in the title role and Regina Sarfaty as Suzuki. John Crosby conducted. The performance was sensational, displaying "a homogenous blending of wonderful vocal and dramatic talent, fine musicianship on the part of the orchestra, thoughtful and highly effective staging and lighting, excellent costuming, and an obviously excellent taste for quality on the part of the entire company."[32] At the close of the opera the capacity audience gave the performers a shouting, standing ovation.

Two evenings later, the company unveiled a staging of *Cosi Fan Tutte*, again with great success. "There is nothing except praise that can be written of this production," wrote Alfred Morang for *Musical America*. "It was splendid in every way."[33] Then came a *Barber of Seville* which boasted several unusual features. First, the work was staged in its original two acts, rather than the customary three. Also, Rosina was sung by a mezzo, Mary McMurray, instead of the more common coloratura soprano. And finally, stage director Bill Butler devised a pantomime which was acted out by the whole cast during the playing of the overture.

On August 4, the company presented an interesting double bill, Pergolesi's *La Serva Padrona* and the world premiere of Marvin David Levy's *The Tower*, a one-act *opéra bouffe*. But the undisputed peak of that first Santa Fe season was a magnificent mounting of Igor Stravinsky's *The Rake's Progress*. Robert Craft, long-time associate of Maestro Stravinsky, conducted, and the composer himself supervised. The production was superb in every respect. Again a standing ovation was in order, with Stravinsky, who had been sitting in the audience, shouted to the stage to receive his share of acclaim.[34]

The only real disappointment that year was a staging of Strauss' *Ariadne auf Naxos*. Here the singers, according to Constance Mellen, "seemed tentative in their approach, and the musical pace set by conductor Vernon Hammond was listless."[35]

By the end of this eight-week season, however, the Santa Fe Opera "had joined the ranks of important festivals and broken all records for speed in establishing a tradition."[36] The young singers, coming mainly from the Metropolitan, the Chicago Lyric, and the New York City Center, spent most of their time together, living at the Crosby ranch, and this continuous proximity was clearly reflected in the quality of their work. Selected with an eye to physical attractiveness, the performers displayed not only beautiful voices, but real dramatic ability as well. The orchestra, forty strong, came from all over the United States. The stagings of all the operas were of superior caliber, often quite unique. For *Madama Butterfly*, for instance, the stage itself became Cio-Cio-San's house, with the sliding panels to the rear serving as the doors of the house. The costumes were consistently well designed and executed.

Every performance had played to a near-capacity audience, with about 40 per cent of the patrons coming from Santa Fe, 30 per cent from Albuquerque and Los Alamos, 10 per cent from other parts of New Mexico, and 20 per cent from out of state. Nevertheless, at the end of the season there was the usual operatic deficit. The company's business manager, Frank Magee, says that if the theater were filled to capacity for every performance, the ticket sales would cover only about half the cost of production. Since the maximum intake for one performance is $3,300, this would put production cost on an average of $6,600 a performance. The resulting deficit is made up by local underwriters and by contributions made by tourists from all over the nation—people who have seen a sample of the company's work and are interested in helping out.[37]

This first season pretty well set the pattern for those to follow, with the repertoire consistently bold. The 1958 season, for example, brought the world premiere of Carlisle Floyd's *Wuthering Heights*, a work commissioned by the Santa Fe Opera, and the first professional staging in this country of *Capriccio*, Richard Strauss' last opera. In addition, Rossini's rarely-performed *Cenerentola* played to standing ovations. The following year found the group tackling Donizetti's *Anna Bolena*, giving the first United States staging of that opera in over a hundred years, and Marc Blitzstein's contemporary *Regina*. A 1960 *Gianni Schicchi* marked the operatic debut of actor Jose Ferrer, who turned out a rather good performance. Moore's *The Ballad of Baby Doe* and Hindemith's *Neues vom Tage* were both given in 1961, followed the next season by Honegger's *Joan at the Stake*. In 1963 the company won critical bravos the world over for its American premiere performance of Alban Berg's *Lulu*, one of the company's finest presentations. It was repeated in 1964, the same year the company gave Strauss' *Daphne* its first American staging.

However, Sante Fe is probably most noted for its Stravinsky performances, particularly *The Rake's Progress*. After supervising a performance of this opera in 1960, Stravinsky declared, "Other companies don't know how to do *The Rake*. They should come to Santa Fe to learn how to do it."[38] But while *The Rake* may be Santa Fe at its best, the company has been highly acclaimed for its other Stravinsky offerings as well. *Oedipus Rex*, given first in 1960, was conducted by the Maestro himself. Although *Oedipus* was sung in Latin, Pulitzer Prize winner Paul Horgan, chairman of the Santa Fe Opera board, read e.e. cummings' English narrative of the work. The performance saw not one, but two standing ovations—one when Maestro Stravinsky entered the pit; the other at the opera's conclusion. Then, to celebrate the composer's eightieth anniversary in 1962, the company did six of his works: *The Rake's Progress*, *Oedipus*, *Persephone*, *Mavra*, *Le Rossignol*, and *Renard*.

But Santa Fe presents its share of operatic staples, too. *Carmen*, *Bohème*, *Tosca*, *Traviata*, *Der Rosenkavalier*, and *Fledermaus* have all been given, and Mozart is a constant favorite. Practically all of the operas are sung in English translation, although the 1962 *Le Rossignol* was given in Russian with good effect.

Occasionally the company has trouble with the weather; it usually counts on two rained-out performances a season. Once in a while a norther blows in, and everyone has to give up glamour for heavy

San Francisco Opera's 1957
production of Poulenc's
The Carmelites

San Francisco Opera's 1963
production of Richard Strauss'
Capriccio

Santa Fe Opera Theater

War Memorial Opera House, San Francisco

coats and blankets. Strangely enough, the operas seem to look none the worse for the weather.

Within its brief history the Santa Fe Opera has made rapid progress toward entrenching itself permanently into New Mexico's artistic and social life, winning its share of national acclaim in the process. And certainly the project has merited applause, particularly for its fresh approach to opera. Not only are the singers young and energetic, but new stage techniques have become a trademark of the company. And the repertoire has been incredible by anybody's standards. John Crosby feels that one reason for his company's rapid acclaim has been "the fact that we've always tried to add a good strong dash of the unusual to the regular operatic fare." By and large the whole endeavor, including the theater itself, has flaunted tradition, and consequently, the innovations in repertoire and staging have simply been a consistent part of the over-all plan. "Even though we think the Opera is pretty well established," says John Crosby, "it will always be an experiment."[39]

As in the case of Central City, opera here can be presented successfully in English largely because of the intimacy of the theater. Unlike Central City, Santa Fe does not as a rule contract its singers for just one specific role. The Santa Fe Opera is a resident company in the truest sense. An artist may sing the lead in one opera and a relatively small role in another, making for a casting evenness which the "star system" all too frequently misses.

The Santa Fe Opera has not only brought the lyric drama to an area blessed with few such opportunities, but its experimentalism and artistic dynamism, coupled with the experience and training it gives budding young artists, have made a real contribution to the American operatic picture. At the same time, with such productions as *The Rake's Progress, Capriccio, Oedipus Rex,* and *Lulu,* the company has earned itself a significant place among the nation's foremost operatic enterprises.

Chapter Nine ⬦⟨⬦⟨⬦⟨⬦⟨⬦⟨⬦⟨⬦⟨⬦⟨⬦⟨⬦⟨⬦⟨⬦⟨⬦⟨⬦⟨⬦⟨⬦⟨⬦⟨⬦

The Finale

During the prosperous years since the close of World War II, a virtual renaissance has taken place in the production of opera, paralleling a general boom in culture. People line up for opera tickets just as they do to glimpse the *Mona Lisa* or the *Pietà*. One can now buy original oils at Sears Roebuck on time payment, and the housewife can pick up a disc of Verdi arias at the grocery, probably at a discount, when she buys her meat and vegetables. With the advent of FM, more good music can be heard on radio than ever before, and record sales are at an all-time high. In 1946 there were only twenty-eight resident opera companies in the United States, giving a total of 527 performances that season.[1] A decade later operatic performances here had swollen to 3,217 a year, an average of nine per day.[2] And the number has increased every year since. Not only have the major companies expanded their offering, but a host of lesser organizations have sprung up, generally presenting from two to six productions a season.

To sketch the history of each of the smaller western opera companies would be repetitious and pointless, but the example of the San Antonio Opera Festival should illustrate some of their basic characteristics. San Antonio is unique in only two ways: The opera is presented there within the framework of the Symphony Society, rather than by an independent opera company; and the Symphony has had incredible success with its operas at the box office, incurring a deficit only once in its twenty-year history. In operatic circles this is a feat almost impossible to duplicate. But artistically, San Antonio's offering is fairly typical of the seasons staged by a number of smaller professional groups now operating in the American West.

It was in 1944, during the San Antonio Symphony's sixth season, that conductor Max Reiter, a refugee from Nazi Germany, formulated his idea for extending his season by adding an opera festival at the end. The purpose was two-fold: to bring opera to an area that had seen relatively little and to increase the orchestra's contracting powers, helping Reiter attract high-caliber musicians.

The venture was launched on Tuesday, February 20, 1945, with a production of *La Bohème* starring Grace Moore. Two nights later *Cavalleria Rusticana* and *Pagliacci* were presented on a double bill. *Bohème* was repeated on Saturday, followed by a Sunday matinee of *Cavalleria* and *Pagliacci*.[3] From the very beginning San Antonians took an intense pride in their opera, and with reason, the critics assured them. Besides, the local citizenry had had more than a casual hand in the productions. The one-hundred-voice chorus and the ballet had been locally recruited, and some of the solo roles had even been taken by San Antonio singers. Since there was no place to rent stage properties in the city, homes and hotel lobbies were denuded for the cause. All in all, it was quite a civic enterprise.[4]

During the next five years Max Reiter presented highly credible opera, dominated by the popular, "bread and butter" repertoire: *Carmen* with Stevens, *Traviata* with Albanese, *Aïda* with Roman, *Rigoletto* with Warren, *Trovatore* with Baum, and so on. *Tannhäuser*, the first Wagner, was given in 1948, followed by a 1949 *Lohengrin* and a 1950 *Tristan und Isolde*. Beginning in 1949 the custom of giving all of the season in a single, crowded week was dropped in favor of spreading the operas out over two successive weekends. Four works would be staged each year, each given a single performance. The two Sunday performances would be matinees. It was felt that this change would enable more people, especially those from out of town, to enjoy the full season and at the same time permit more extensive rehearsal of each production.

Then in December 1950, Max Reiter died. As there was no time to select a permanent replacement, Jonel Perlea was brought in as guest conductor of the 1951 Festival. A new scenic designer was introduced that year, too. He was Peter Wolf of Dallas, a product of the Yale School of Drama. Since then, Wolf's talents have become one of the real assets of the operas, and rare is the occasion when his imaginative sets fail to win enthusiastic applause.

After much deliberation Victor Alessandro, formerly musical director of the Oklahoma City Symphony, was finally chosen as Reiter's successor. Alessandro was a native Texan, born in Waco and reared in Houston, who had received a music degree from the Eastman School of Music at the University of Rochester, followed by postgraduate studies in Europe. He had gone to Oklahoma City when he was only twenty-two and within three years had built the orchestra there into a highly respectable organization.[5] Although Alessandro was not experienced in the field of opera, members of the Symphony Society felt that the young musician had potential. As a result, he became the Symphony's new musical director.

Through the years, San Antonio has gradually become more venturesome with its repertoire than it once was, although the standard works still predominate. During Alessandro's first season there, Smetana's *The Bartered Bride* was offered, followed the next year by Mozart's *Don Giovanni*. George London was the Don in that production, and a fine figure he cut, too. "When he appeared in white velvet the audience gasped as if Victor Mature had arrived in a breach-clout."[6] But Dorothy Kirsten balanced things for the ladies two years later when she sang *Manon*, wearing gowns that must have cost as much as the rest of the production. *Turandot* made its first Southwestern appearance in San Antonio in 1956, and a fifty-four-year-old Lily Pons sang *Lakmé* in 1958, looking not a day over thirty.

One of San Antonio's most ambitious undertakings was a staging of Verdi's *Nabucco* in 1960, a year before its Metropolitan premiere. The work demanded and received more rehearsal time than any other opera in the city's history, for only two of the singers had performed their roles previously. Considering the magnitude of the production, it came off quite well. The chorus was in unusually good form, particularly in the "Hebrew's Chorus." The sets were properly spectacular, although the shattering of the pagan idol in the last act was slightly premature, startling both the audience and the singers.

Ranking close to the top of the Symphony's presentations was a performance of Richard Strauss' *Elektra* in 1961, starring Astrid

Varnay. Well-rehearsed and beautifully executed, the opera proved as thrilling an experience as San Antonio's opera-goers had ever witnessed. More than one critic said it was the finest thing ever done there. But this year the Festival lost money, forcing a brief return in 1962 to a season made up entirely of sure-fire box-office hits: *Bohème, Carmen, Lucia,* and *Trovatore.* A year later, with financial standing and confidence restored, the Symphony resumed a more balanced lyric diet, including a production of Rimski-Korsakov's *Coq d'Or.* Two fairly novel works were mounted in 1964, Montemezzi's *L'Amore dei Tre Re* and Gounod's *Romeo and Juliet.*

Considerable though San Antonio's artistic success has been, its financial standing has been even more amazing. As a rule the ticket sale has numbered between 20–25,000 a season. Even when San Antonio does poorly at the box office, it is phenomenal by normal standards. John Rosenfield, the noted Dallas critic, once commented that "a crowd of merely 4,000 to 4,500 for a San Antonio Opera Festival performance brings out the alibi brigade of the Symphony Society."[7] In 1961, the one time the operas went in the red, the deficit was less than $1,000. Yet, strange as it may seem to outsiders, this was enough to cause San Antonio to become quite conservative the next season, determined to make financial amends. What is the explanation for this unprecedented box-office record? Two things contribute: One is that the orchestra salaries are already taken care of by the regular salary budget, so the orchestra's services are not charged against the Opera Festival; the second is that the Municipal Auditorium, where the operas are staged, seats nearly six thousand people. Any capacity house—and San Antonio has had many—produces over $25,000.[8]

But with the exception of this financial wizardry, San Antonio's opera is not unlike that given by a number of other ambitious western cities. As a rule, these smaller groups try to import name artists, primarily stars from the Metropolitan and the New York City Center, for the leads, while local singers take the minor roles. Frequently, the company will spend a lion's share of its funds on one star attraction, preferably a glamorous prima donna who will have big box-office appeal, leaving the rest of the production to shift for itself. Dorothy Kirsten, for example, may be brought in for *Tosca,* only to find herself singing opposite a vocally insecure and histrionically adolescent tenor. Combine this with a chorus that is struggling with both Puccini and Italian, stage direction that is token at best, and lighting only slightly superior to that of the local high school extravaganza, and the result is a production lacking any semblance of unity or cohesion. No matter how gloriously Kirsten may be singing that evening, she alone cannot save a performance that is ragged in most other respects.

Not always is the offering this bleak. Tulsa Opera, Inc., for instance, has assembled some magnificent casts and has been quite successful at integrating its productions. In March, 1958, Roberta Peters teamed with Giuseppi Campora and Giuseppi Valdengo for a noteworthy *Lucia di Lammermoor,* and a year later *Il Trovatore* was mounted with Elinor Ross, Jussi Bjoerling, Leonard Warren, Jean Madeira, and Nicola Moscona producing a fine ensemble.

The repertoire of all these smaller companies is, of course, heavily weighted in favor of the standard favorites. *La Bohème, Madama Butterfly, La Traviata, Rigoletto,* and *Carmen* are about as common as election year. But, as in the case of San Antonio, novelties are given. In 1954 the Fort Worth Opera Association presented Brenda Lewis in Strauss' *Salomé* with great success. The Houston Grand Opera staged *Cenerentola* in 1957, *Elektra* in 1958, *Turandot* in 1960, and *Il Tabarro* in 1963. And Aspen, Colorado, home of another significant summer festival, in 1962 gave a rare performance of Bizet's *The Pearl Fishers.*

While most of these groups prefer to offer their opera in the original language, others, like the Kansas City Lyric Theater and the Fort Worth Opera Association, have had extremely good luck with opera in English. Generally, the local symphony is employed for the opera season, although a special conductor is usually brought in for the occasion. Scenery and costumes are normally rented. For example, Fort Worth, Tulsa, and Shreveport, along with San Antonio, acquire most of their sets from Dallas' Peter Wolf Associates.

Sometimes these companies choose to concentrate their seasons within a short period of time. The Kansas City Lyric Theater, for instance, stages its twenty or so performances all during the month of October. A more common practice, however, is to scatter the productions over several months. Tulsa and Shreveport both give two operas a year, one in the fall, the other in the spring. Portland,

Oregon, stages three operas annually, one in November, another in February, and the third in May.

Of primary concern to each of these companies is the education of young people in the understanding and appreciation of the lyric drama. Illustrative is the program worked out by Tulsa Opera, Inc. Every year since 1956 a student matinee has been presented by the company free of charge. The schools help prepare the children for the opera in advance, discussing the work and playing recorded portions of it in music classes. These matinees have become so popular that each year hundreds of requests for tickets have to be turned down. Also for the past several years the Tulsa company has awarded two $300 scholarships to promising young singers in that area.

These lesser companies are frequently restricted in repertoire and weak in production unity, but they are to be commended for bringing the lyric drama to cities that otherwise would hear none. Despite their weaknesses, these groups do a remarkable job of enriching the cultural life of the area they serve. Invariably, they operate under sharp financial limitations, forcing rehearsals to a minimum, and yet their productions are usually adequate and occasionally even rise to artistic heights. Considering the budget on which they operate and the brevity of their seasons, no more could reasonably be expected.

Certainly the success of these smaller operatic groups has both stimulated and is a product of the postwar cultural boom. But the role that these organizations play in developing a taste for opera cannot be overestimated, no more than that of radio and long-playing records. And it goes without saying that the major companies, rather than competing with each other in the classical sense, actually tend to stimulate one another. A San Francisco opera-goer will undoubtedly want to visit the Metropolitan on his trips to New York, while more than one New York working girl, reared in the shadow of the Metropolitan, has planned her vacation to coincide with the season on the west coast. Recently the country's four major opera companies negotiated agreements whereby sets and costumes are now exchanged, a more tangible stimulation. The Metropolitan's 1961–62 season opened with Puccini's *The Girl of the Golden West*, the sets of which were borrowed from the Chicago Lyric. Chicago's

1963 season found three physical productions on loan from the Met: *Tannhäuser, Nabucco,* and *Don Pasquale.* Dallas borrowed a *Lucia* from San Francisco in 1961 in exchange for the Zeffirelli *Don Giovanni* which San Francisco used the following year. And Chicago and San Francisco have exchanged occasional productions. The result has been a reduction of costs without loss of artistry, enabling these companies to develop other areas of production.

There can be little doubt that opera's future looks brighter than ever before. The prosperity of the times and advancements in transportation and communication have combined to make the operatic world one sprawling community. In the midst of this rebirth the American West, traditionally the most culturally barren section of the country, has blossomed into a region fraught with lyric vitality. San Francisco, Chicago, and Dallas are internationally recognized opera capitals. While the Metropolitan may still be the recognized guardian of the nation's operatic treasury, its western siblings possess a freshness and artistic dynamism which has become increasingly apparent. The West, once a vast cultural wasteland, has recently grown into a giant kaleidoscope, teeming with musical possibilities, the richness of whose hues seems constantly to be deepening.

NOTES

Chapter One

[1] André Lafargue, "Opera in New Orleans in Days of Yore," *Louisiana Historical Quarterly*, XXIX (July 1946), 662–63; Lafargue, "Past Glories of Opera in New Orleans," Part I, *Opera News*, X (November 19, 1945), 10–11.

[2] Nellie Warner Price, "Le Spectacle de la Rue St. Pierre," *Louisiana Historical Quarterly*, I (January 8, 1918), 218–19.

[3] Harry Brunswick Loeb, "The Opera in New Orleans," *Publications of the Louisiana Historical Society*, IX (1916), 30; Loeb, "The Story of Music in America—New Orleans," *Musical America*, LXVII (November 1, 1947), 7.

[4] Price, "Le Spectacle," 217.

[5] Quoted in O. G. Sonneck, *Early Opera in America* (New York: G. Schirmer, 1915), 181.

[6] Loeb, "Opera in New Orleans," 30; Ann M. Lingg, "Great Opera Houses—New Orleans," *Opera News*, XXV (December 10, 1960), 22.

[7] Lafargue, "Opera in New Orleans in Days of Yore," 633; Loeb, "Story of Music in America—New Orleans," 7.

[8] Price, "Le Spectacle," 220.

[9] Loeb, "Opera in New Orleans," 31.

[10] *Ibid.*, 32; David Barrow Fischer, "The Story of New Orleans's Rise as a Music Center," *Musical America*, XIX (March 14, 1914), 3.

[11] Lafargue, "Opera in New Orleans in Days of Yore," 664.

[12] Lingg, "Great Opera Houses—New Orleans," 22.

[13] Lafargue, "Opera in New Orleans in Days of Yore," 665.

[14] Harnett T. Kane, *Queen New Orleans* (New York: William Morrow and Company, 1949), 245. Copyright 1949 by Harnett T. Kane.

[15] Lafargue, "Opera in New Orleans in Days of Yore," 666.

[16] *New Orleans Daily Picayune*, November 8, 1838.

[17] Kane, *Queen New Orleans*, 243.

[18] Daniel Gregory Mason (editor), *The Art of Music* (New York: National Society of Music, 1915), IV, 164.

[19] *L'Abeille* (New Orleans), February 16, 1828.

[20] Albert L. Voss, "'Norma' in New Orleans," in the program for the 1959 production of *Norma*, New Orleans Opera House Association (February 1959), 11.

[21] *El Correo Atlantico* (New Orleans), February 29, 1836.

[22] *New Orleans Daily Picayune*, April 30, 1839.

[23] *Ibid.*, November 7, 1838.

[24] *Ibid.*, November 8, 1838.

[25] Lyle Saxon, *Fabulous New Orleans* (New York: Century Company, 1928), 282–83.

[26] Kane, *Queen New Orleans*, 243–44.

27 *New Orleans Daily Picayune,* December 30, 1841.

28 *Ibid.,* March 24, 1846.

29 Edward A. Parsons, *A History of Opera in New Orleans: A Sketch* (New Orleans: New Orleans Opera House Association, 1959), 5–6.

30 *New Orleans Weekly Picayune,* February 17, 1851.

31 *New Orleans Daily Picayune,* November 4, 1853.

32 *Ibid.,* November 15, 1853.

33 *Ibid.,* February 27, 1854.

34 *Ibid.*

35 *Ibid.*

36 *Ibid.,* April 12, 1857; Fischer, "Story of New Orleans's Rise as a Music Center," 3.

37 Loeb, "Opera in New Orleans," 33; Kane, *Queen New Orleans,* 248.

38 *New Orleans Daily Picayune,* December 3, 1859; Kane, *Queen New Orleans,* 248–49; Lafargue, "Past Glories of New Orleans Opera," Part II, *Opera News,* X (November 26, 1945), 11.

39 Loeb, "Opera in New Orleans," 36.

Chapter Two

1 *New Orleans Daily Crescent,* December 3, 1859.

2 *Ibid.*

3 Lafargue, "Past Glories of New Orleans Opera," Part II, 11–12.

4 *New Orleans Daily Picayune,* November 23, 1860.

5 Kane, *Queen New Orleans,* 249–50.

6 *New Orleans Daily Picayune,* December 20, 1860.

7 *Ibid.*

8 *Ibid.,* December 29, 1860, and December 31, 1860.

9 *Ibid.,* January 3, 1861.

10 *Ibid.,* February 8, 1861.

11 *Ibid.,* March 4, 1861.

12 Loeb, "Opera in New Orleans," 35; *New Orleans Daily Picayune,* October 7, 1866.

13 *New Orleans Daily Picayune,* October 9, 1866.

14 *Ibid.,* November 23, 1866, and January 12, 1867.

15 Lafargue, "Opera in New Orleans in Days of Yore," 670.

16 Kane, *Queen New Orleans,* 240.

17 Lafargue, "Opera in New Orleans in Days of Yore," 670.

18 *Ibid.,* 672.

19 Lafargue, "Past Glories of New Orleans Opera," Part II, 11.

20 Eliza Ripley, *Social Life in Old New Orleans* (New York: D. Appleton and Company, 1912), 65–67.

21 Lafargue, "Opera in New Orleans in Days of Yore," 671.

22 Federal Writers' Project, *New Orleans City Guide* (Boston: Houghton Mifflin Company, 1952), 139.

23 Kane, *Queen New Orleans,* 239.

24 *Ibid.*

25 *Ibid.*

26 Ripley, *Social Life in Old New Orleans*, 69.
27 James Henry Mapleson, *The Mapleson Memoirs* (London: Remington and Company, 1888), 101–02.
28 *New Orleans Times-Democrat*, February 1, 1885.
29 Loeb, "Opera in New Orleans," 36.
30 *New Orleans Times-Democrat*, February 13, 1892, January 23, 1890, and January 4, 1893.
31 *Ibid.*, January 13, 1899.
32 *Ibid.*
33 *Ibid.*, January 25, 1900, and January 26, 1900.
34 *Ibid.*, February 1, 1901.
35 *Ibid.*, January 26, 1905.
36 Kane, *Queen New Orleans*, 256–57.
37 *New Orleans Times-Democrat*, January 4, 1913.
38 *Ibid.*, January 27, 1912.
39 Loeb, "Opera in New Orleans," 37.
40 *Ibid.*; Saxon, *Fabulous New Orleans*, 283; Kane, *Queen New Orleans*, 257–58.
41 Loeb, "Story of Music in America—New Orleans," 32.
42 Lafargue, "Past Glories of New Orleans Opera," Part II, 13.
43 Loeb, "Story of Music in America—New Orleans," 32.
44 *New Orleans Times-Picayune*, December 5, 1919; Kane, *Queen New Orleans*, 258.
45 Kane, *Queen New Orleans*, 258.
46 *New Orleans Times-Picayune*, December 5, 1919.
47 "New Orleans Opera Burns," *Musical America*, XXXI (December 6, 1919), 2; Lafargue, "Past Glories of New Orleans Opera," Part II, 13.
48 Lafargue, "Opera in New Orleans in Days of Yore," 674.
49 *Ibid.*, 669.
50 Saxon, *Fabulous New Orleans*, 283.
51 Lafargue, "Opera in New Orleans in Days of Yore," 676.
52 Marshall W. Sterns, *The Story of Jazz* (New York: Oxford University Press, 1956), 73.
53 Lafargue, "Opera in New Orleans in Days of Yore," 667; Lafargue, "Past Glories of New Orleans Opera," Part II, 13.
54 Walter Herbert, "Opera in New Orleans Today," *Opera News*, X (November 5, 1945), 21; Interview with Gus G. Jaquet (General Manager of the New Orleans Opera House Association), New Orleans, June 8, 1960.
55 *New Orleans Times-Picayune*, October 31, 1943.
56 *Ibid.*, November 14, 1943.
57 *Ibid.*, March 18, 1949.
58 "New 'Livewire' Saves New Orleans Opera," *Variety*, CCVI (March 20, 1957), 73.
59 Interview with Gus G. Jaquet, New Orleans, June 8, 1960.
60 *Opera News*, XXII (November 11, 1957), 2.
61 Interview with Gus G. Jaquet, New Orleans, June 8, 1960.
62 *New Orleans Times-Picayune*, November 9, 1945.
63 *Ibid.*, October 23, 1953.
64 Interview with Gus G. Jaquet, New Orleans, June 8, 1960.
65 Lafargue, "Past Glories of New Orleans Opera," Part II, 13.

Chapter Three

[1] Cecil Smith, "The Story of Music in America–Chicago," *Musical America,* LXVII (April 10, 1947), 6; Karleton Hackett, *The Beginnings of Grand Opera in Chicago* (Chicago: Laurentian Publishers, 1913), 16–17.

[2] Hackett, *Beginnings of Grand Opera in Chicago,* 20–21.

[3] *Ibid.,* 39–40; Smith, "Story of Music in America–Chicago," 6.

[4] Hackett, *Beginnings of Grand Opera in Chicago,* 43–45.

[5] Smith, "Story of Music in America–Chicago," 6.

[6] George P. Upton, *Musical Memories* (Chicago: A. C. McClurg and Company, 1908), 235–36.

[7] *Chicago Tribune,* April 17, 1865, and April 21, 1865.

[8] *Ibid.,* June 13, 1865.

[9] Bessie Louise Pierce, *A History of Chicago* (New York: Alfred A. Knopf, 1940), II, 424, 433.

[10] Upton, *Musical Memories,* 153.

[11] Edward C. Moore, *Forty Years of Opera in Chicago* (New York: Horace Liveright, 1930), 4–6.

[12] *Ibid.,* 5, 9; Smith, "Story of Music in America–Chicago," 6; Luigi Arditi, *My Reminiscences* (New York: Dodd, Mead and Company, 1896), 239.

[13] Moore, *Forty Years,* 6–11.

[14] *Chicago Tribune,* January 1, 1890.

[15] Moore, *Forty Years,* 15.

[16] Smith, "Story of Music in America–Chicago," 7.

[17] Agnes G. Murphy, *Melba: A Biography* (New York: Doubleday and Company, Inc., 1909), 87. Permission to quote granted by Doubleday and Company, Inc.

[18] Vincent Sheean, *First and Last Love* (New York: Random House, 1956), 36–37.

[19] Quaintance Eaton, *Opera Caravan: Adventures of the Metropolitan on Tour,* 1883–1956 (New York: Farrar, Straus and Company, 1957), 72.

[20] *Ibid.,* 248, 256–57; Smith, "Story of Music in America–Chicago," 7.

[21] Moore, *Forty Years,* 51–58.

[22] *Ibid.,* 60.

[23] *Chicago Tribune,* November 6, 1910.

[24] Sheean, *First and Last Love,* 40–41.

[25] Moore, *Forty Years,* 65.

[26] *Chicago Tribune,* November 26, 1910.

[27] Mary Garden and Louis Biancolli, *Mary Garden's Story* (New York: Simon and Schuster, 1951), 124.

[28] Moore, *Forty Years,* 71–76.

[29] *Ibid.,* 77–83.

[30] *Ibid.,* 85–86.

[31] *Ibid.,* 90.

[32] *Ibid.,* 91–92.

[33] *Ibid.,* 95–96.

[34] Garden and Biancolli, *Mary Garden's Story,* 236.

[35] Moore, *Forty Years,* 93.

[36] *Ibid.*, 109.

[37] *Ibid.*, 115.

[38] "Philadelphia Opera Problem Unsolved," *Musical America,* XIX (November 8, 1913), 1.

[39] Moore, *Forty Years,* 123, 126.

[40] Maurice Rosenfeld, " 'Don Quichotte' the Novelty of Chicago's Opening Week," *Musical America,* XIX (December 6, 1913), 30; Rosenfeld, "Novelty in Chicago's Opera Week," *Musical America,* XIX (December 13, 1913), 32.

[41] Moore, *Forty Years,* 131.

[42] *Ibid.,* 139; "No Chicago or Boston Opera," *Musical Courier,* LXIX (September 2, 1914), 20.

[43] Moore, *Forty Years,* 143–45.

[44] Rosenfeld, "More Americans Make Debuts in Chicago's Opera," *Musical America,* XXIII (December 4, 1915), 1.

[45] Moore, *Forty Years,* 160–65; Rosenfeld, "Chicago's Opera Has Momentous Inaugural Week," *Musical America,* XXV (November 25, 1916), 1.

[46] Moore, *Forty Years,* 156.

[47] C. E. Le Massena, *Galli-Curci's Life of Song* (New York: Paebar Company, 1945), 118–19; Sheean, *First and Last Love,* 46.

[48] Le Massena, *Galli-Curci's Life of Song,* 109–10; Moore, *Forty Years,* 156; Adella Prentiss Hughes, *Music Is My Life* (Cleveland: World Publishing Company, 1947), 225.

[49] Farnsworth Wright, "Chicago Opera Company Chorus Goes on Strike," *Musical America,* XXV (December 16, 1916), 1; Rosenfeld, "Chicago Opera Chorus Returns to Work," *Musical America,* XXV (December 23, 1916), 43.

[50] Wright, "Chicago Assured of Five Years More of Grand Opera," *Musical America,* XXV (December 23, 1916), 1.

[51] Wright, "Chicago's Opera Season Launched in Brilliant Style," *Musical America,* XXVII (November 24, 1917), 1.

[52] *Ibid.,* 3.

[53] Wright, "Chicago Marvels at Galli-Curci's 'Rosina,' " *Musical America,* XXVII (December 29, 1917), 6.

[54] Moore, *Forty Years,* 171–73.

[55] *Ibid.,* 187–88.

[56] *Ibid.,* 190.

[57] "Campanini Dead; Chicago Mourns Loss of Great Impresario," *Musical Courier,* LXXIX (December 25, 1919), 5.

[58] Garden and Biancolli, *Mary Garden's Story,* 169.

[59] *Chicago Daily Tribune,* January 15, 1921.

[60] "McCormick Pledges Chicago Two Years More of Opera," *Musical America,* XXXI (January 24, 1920), 31.

[61] *Chicago Daily Tribune,* November 18, 1920.

[62] *Ibid.*

[63] *Ibid.,* January 6, 1921; Wright, " 'Lohengrin' Is Manna to Eager Chicagoans," *Musical America,* XXXIII (January 1, 1921), 19.

[64] *Chicago Daily Tribune,* December 20, 1920.

[65] *Ibid.,* January 7, 1921.

[66] *Ibid.,* January 14, 1921, and January 15, 1921.

[67] Wright, " 'An American Company' Is Mary Garden's Watchword," *Musical America,* XXXIII (January 22, 1921), 3; Moore, *Forty Years,* 219.

[68] Moore, *Forty Years,* 219–20.

[69] Garden and Biancolli, *Mary Garden's Story,* 170–71.

[70] René Devries, "Spangler Out as Manager of Chicago Opera," *Musical Courier,* LXXXIII (November 24, 1921), 55; Moore, *Forty Years,* 225.

[71] Devries, "Spangler Out as Manager of Chicago Opera," 55.

[72] Emil Raymond, "Hear Fine Cast in 'Samson' as Chicagoans Open Eleventh Season," *Musical America,* XXXV (November 19, 1921), 1, 6; Moore, *Forty Years,* 231.

[73] Arthur E. Knight, "Edith Mason," *The Record Collector,* X (September 1955), 81–82.

[74] Devries, " 'The Love for Three Oranges,' Produced at Last in Chicago," *Musical Courier,* LXXXIV (January 5, 1922), 6.

[75] Raymond, "Mary Garden Brings Dramatic Gifts to 'Salome,' " *Musical America,* XXV (January 5, 1922), 6.

[76] Devries, "Mary Garden Scores Greatest Triumph of Her Career in Revival of 'Salome,' " *Musical Courier,* LXXXIV (January 5, 1922), 6.

[77] Raymond, "Mary Garden Brings Dramatic Gifts to 'Salome,' " 27.

[78] Garden and Biancolli, *Mary Garden's Story,* 212–13.

[79] "Mme. Gadski Brings Suit Against Chicago Opera Claiming $500,000 Damages," *Musical Courier,* LXXXIV (February 9, 1922), 5.

[80] Raymond, "Gadski Barred by Chicago Executive, Schipa to Quit, D'Alvarez Is Paid Off as Storm Clouds Gather Over Opera," *Musical America,* XXV (December 10, 1921), 1.

[81] "Mary Garden Resigns as General Director of the Chicago Opera Association," *Musical Courier,* LXXXIV (April 27, 1922), 5.

[82] Interview with Edith Mason, Chicago, November 26, 1960.

[83] "Mary Garden Resigns as General Director of the Chicago Opera Association," 5.

[84] Moore, *Forty Years,* 239.

[85] Sheean, *First and Last Love,* 62–63.

[86] Garden and Biancolli, *Mary Garden's Story,* 178–79.

Chapter Four

[1] Devries, "Chicago Opera Association Reorganized with Samuel Insull as Its New Head," *Musical Courier,* LXXXIV (January 19, 1922), 5; Moore, *Forty Years,* 240–41.

[2] Moore, *Forty Years,* 251–52.

[3] *Ibid.,* 259.

[4] Wright, "Emotions of Role Seize Muzio in Opera," *Musical America,* XXXIX (December 29, 1923), 5.

[5] Wright, " 'Cleopatre' and 'Konigskinder' Restored to Repertoire of Chicago Civic Opera," *Musical America,* XXXIX (January 5, 1924), 28.

[6] Devries, "Garden and Vanni-Marcoux in Monna Vanna," *Musical Courier,* XCV (December 15, 1927), 5, 41.

[7] Le Massena, *Galli-Curci's Life of Song,* 186.

[8] *Ibid.,* 187–89.

[9] Devries, "La Gioconda Opens Chicago Opera Season," *Musical Courier,* LXXXIX (November 13, 1924), 5.

[10] Eugene Stinson, "Harling's 'Light from St. Agnes' Thrills Chicago," *Musi-*

cal America, XLIII (January 2, 1926), 1; Devries, "World Premiere of W. Franke Harling's Opera, 'A Light from St. Agnes,' Arouses Chicago Audience to Great Enthusiasm," *Musical Courier,* XCI (December 31, 1925), 5.

11 Moore, *Forty Years,* 285.

12 *Ibid.,* 325.

13 *Ibid.,* 334.

14 *Ibid.,* 340–45; "Chicago Opera House Sold to Insurance Firm," *Musical America,* LXCIII (December 1, 1948), 4.

15 Devries, "Chicago Civic Opera Opens Season with 'Aida' in Its New Twenty Million Dollar Home," *Musical Courier,* XCIX (November 9, 1929), 26; "Art and Science Combine to Make New Home of Chicago Civic Opera a Marvel of Ingenuity," *Musical America,* XLIX (October 25, 1929), 38.

16 Devries, "Chicago Civic Opera Opens Season with 'Aida' in Its New Twenty Million Dollar Home," 26.

17 Moore, *Forty Years,* 347, 351.

18 Lotte Lehmann, *Midway in My Song* (New York: Merrill Company, 1938), 186.

19 *Ibid.,* 182, 186.

20 Interview with Lawrence V. Kelly, Dallas, August 25, 1959.

21 Devries, "Forest's 'Camille' Given World Premiere in Chicago," *Musical Courier,* CI (December 20, 1930), 5, 12.

22 Garden and Biancolli, *Mary Garden's Story,* 239.

23 Albert Goldberg, " 'Camille' Heard in Premiere by Chicago Forces," *Musical America,* L (December 25, 1930), 3.

24 Goldberg, "Brilliant Chicago Opera Fortnight Brings Debuts of Eight Artists," *Musical America,* LI (November 25, 1931), 3.

25 *Chicago Daily Tribune,* November 1, 1933.

26 Goldberg, "Chicago Views 'La Fiamma' as Superior Opera," *Musical America,* LV (December 25, 1935), 7.

27 "Chicago's Worst," *Time,* XXVI (December 16, 1935), 51.

28 Smith, "Story of Music in America—Chicago," 7, 22.

29 Goldberg, "Chicago Welcomes Newcomers to City Opera," *Musical America,* LVI (December 10, 1936), 3, 6.

30 Elsa Borowski, "Chicago's Operatic Traditions Live in Record 1946–47 Season," *Musical Courier,* CXXXIV (October 1946), 7.

31 "Weber Resigns Chicago Opera Post," *Musical America,* LXI (August 1941), 3.

32 *Chicago Sun,* December 12, 1941.

33 *Musical America,* LXIII (December 10, 1943), 3.

34 "Chicago Opera House Sold to Insurance Firm," *Musical America,* LXVIII (December 1948), 4.

35 Borowski, "Chicago's Operatic Traditions Live in Record 1946–47 Season," 6.

36 *Chicago Sun,* November 12, 1944.

37 Claudia Cassidy, "Highlights of the Chicago Opera Season," *Opera News,* IX (November 20, 1944), 9.

38 *Chicago Tribune,* November 12, 1944.

39 Borowski, "Chicago Operatic Ovations," *Musical Courier,* CXXXIV (November 1, 1946), 20.

40 William Leonard, "Musical Questions in Chicago," *Musical America,* LXIX (January 15, 1949), 13.

[41] Cassidy, "Chicago's Lyric—Scorched But Soaring," *Theatre Arts,* XLI (January 1957), 77.

[42] Interview with Carol Fox, Chicago, November 25, 1960.

[43] Cassidy, "Lyric Chicago . . . Opera Ascendant," *Theatre Arts,* XL (January 1956), 84.

[44] Interview with Carol Fox, Chicago, November 25, 1960; Emily Coleman, "Callas and Company for Chicago," *Theatre Arts,* XXXIX (January 1955), 69.

[45] Cassidy, "Lyric Chicago . . . Opera Ascendant," 78.

[46] *Ibid.;* Interview with Carol Fox, Chicago, November 25, 1960.

[47] Interview with Lawrence Kelly, Dallas, August 25, 1959.

[48] Cassidy, "Lyric Chicago . . . Opera Ascendant," 78.

[49] *Ibid.;* Coleman, "Callas and Company for Chicago," 68.

[50] Coleman, "Callas and Company for Chicago," 68–69.

[51] *Chicago Tribune,* November 2, 1954.

[52] Ronald Eyer, "Brilliant Debut Marks Chicago Inaugural," *Musical America,* LXXIV (November 15, 1954), 3.

[53] Dosha Dowdy and René Devries, 'The National Scene—Chicago," *Musical Courier,* CL (December 1, 1954), 28.

[54] *Chicago Tribune,* November 16, 1954.

[55] Interview with Edith Mason, Chicago, November 26, 1960.

[56] *Chicago American,* November 7, 1954.

[57] *Chicago Sun-Times,* November 4, 1954.

[58] Cassidy, "Lyric Chicago . . . Opera Ascendant," 84.

[59] "Spotlight on Chicago," *Musical America,* LXXIV (November 15, 1954), 4.

[60] George Jellinek, *Callas: Portrait of a Prima Donna* (New York: Ziff-Davis Publishing Company, 1960), 126.

[61] Howard Talley, "Crescendo of Enthusiasm Greets Chicago Opera," *Musical America,* LXXV (December 1, 1955), 7.

[62] Jellinek, *Callas,* 140–41.

[63] *Time,* XLV (January 10, 1955), 59.

[64] Interview with Carol Fox, Chicago, November 25, 1960.

[65] "Spotlight on Chicago," 4.

[66] Interview with Lawrence Kelly, Dallas, August 25, 1959; Interview with Carol Fox, Chicago, November 25, 1960.

[67] Talley, "Dispute Threatens Future of Chicago Lyric Theatre," *Musical America,* LXXVI (April 1956), 5; "Musical Chairs," *Musical America,* LXXVI (October 1956), 4.

Chapter Five

[1] Alexander Fried, "The Story of Music in America—San Francisco," *Musical America,* LXVII (September 1947), 6.

[2] Works Progress Administration, *History of Opera in San Francisco* (San Francisco: San Francisco Theater Research Council, 1939), Part I, 10; Edmond M. Gagey, *The San Francisco Stage: A History* (New York: Columbia University Press, 1950), 32.

[3] Works Progress Administration, *Opera in San Francisco,* Part I, 1.

[4] *Ibid.,* 10–11, 86.

[5] *Ibid.*, 19; Gagey, *San Francisco Stage*, 32.

[6] Works Progress Administration, *Opera in San Francisco*, Part I, 12; George R. MacMinn, *The Theater of the Golden Era in California* (Caldwell, Idaho: Caxton Printers, 1941), 403.

[7] Quoted in MacMinn, *Theater of the Golden Era in California*, 404.

[8] *Ibid.*, 405–06.

[9] Gagey, *San Francisco Stage*, 92.

[10] Works Progress Administration, *Opera in San Francisco*, Part I, 7, 12.

[11] *Ibid.*, 10.

[12] MacMinn, *Theater of the Golden Era in California*, 402.

[13] Mason, *Art of Music*, IV, 158–60.

[14] Oscar Thompson, *The American Singer: A Hundred Years of Success in Opera* (New York: Dial Press, 1937), 39.

[15] Gagey, *San Francisco Stage*, 32.

[16] *Ibid.*, 126; Mason, *Art of Music*, IV, 158–60.

[17] Gagey, *San Francisco Stage*, 126.

[18] Works Progress Administration, *Opera in San Francisco*, Part I, 84–85, 99.

[19] Works Progress Administration, *History of Music in San Francisco* (San Francisco: San Francisco Theater Research Council, 1939), IV, 118–19; Mapleson, *Memoirs*, 50–52.

[20] Works Progress Administration, *Music in San Francisco*, IV, 119; Herman Klein, *The Reign of Patti* (New York: Century Company, 1920), 208–09.

[21] *San Francisco Bulletin*, March 23, 1884.

[22] *Ibid.*, April 20, 1898.

[23] Henry C. Lahee, *Grand Opera in America* (Boston: L. C. Page and Company, 1902), 272–73.

[24] Murphy, *Melba*, 135–36.

[25] Works Progress Administration, *Opera in San Francisco*, Part II, 1.

[26] *Ibid.*, Part I, 110.

[27] Fried, "Story of Music in America—San Francisco," 6.

[28] Eaton, *Opera Caravan*, 114–15.

[29] Pierre V. R. Key, *Enrico Caruso: A Biography* (Boston: Little Brown and Company, 1922), 229.

[30] Eaton, *Opera Caravan*, 116.

[31] Key, *Enrico Caruso*, 229.

[32] Works Progress Administration, *Opera in San Francisco*, Part I, 104, 112.

[33] *Ibid.*, 112.

[34] Fried, "Story of Music in America—San Francisco," 7.

[35] *Ibid.*, 6; Works Progress Administration, *Opera in San Francisco*, Part II, 45.

[36] Works Progress Administration, *Opera in San Francisco*, Part II, 45; Marjory M. Fisher, "San Francisco Opera House—Its 25th Birthday," *Musical America*, LXXVII (September 1957), 8.

[37] Fisher, "San Francisco Opera House—Its 25th Birthday," 8; *San Francisco Chronicle*, October 16, 1932; Esther Bentley Powell, "Silver Anniversary at the Golden Gate," *Opera News*, XII (October 6, 1947), 9–10.

[38] *San Francisco Chronicle*, September 16, 1947, and March 29, 1960; *San Francisco Grand Opera* (San Francisco: San Francisco Opera Association, n.d.), n.p.

[39] *San Francisco Chronicle*, September 27, 1923.

[40] *Ibid.*, September 28, 1923.

41 Fisher, "San Francisco Opera House—Its 25th Birthday," 8.
42 *San Francisco Chronicle,* September 13, 1931.
43 Works Progress Administration, *Opera in San Francisco,* Part II, 77–83.

Chapter Six

1 *San Francisco Chronicle,* October 16, 1932.
2 *Ibid.*
3 Fisher, "San Francisco Opera House—Its 25th Birthday," 9; Works Progress Administration, *Opera in San Francisco,* Part II, 84.
4 San Francisco Opera Association, *Program,* October 15, 1932, 17.
5 Fisher, "San Francisco Opera House—Its 25th Birthday," 9; Works Progress Administration, *Opera in San Francisco,* Part II, 85.
6 *San Francisco Examiner,* October 15, 1932.
7 *Ibid.,* October 18, 1932.
8 "San Francisco's *Ring,*" *Time,* XXVI (November 4, 1935), 48.
9 Interview with Lucine Amara, San Francisco, September 15, 1960.
10 *San Francisco Chronicle,* October 26, 1940.
11 *Ibid.,* October 16, 1943.
12 Interview with Herbert Scholder (Publicity Director of the San Francisco Opera Company), San Francisco, September 23, 1960.
13 *San Francisco Chronicle,* October 3, 1946.
14 *Ibid.,* October 29, 1943.
15 *Ibid.,* October 20, 1949.
16 *Ibid.,* October 30, 1938.
17 *Ibid.*
18 *Ibid.,* August 4, 1946.
19 *Ibid.,* September 30, 1944.
20 *Ibid.,* October 17, 1942, and October 23, 1942.
21 "San Francisco Opera Season Shows Profit," *Musical America,* LXII (December 25, 1942), 4; Fisher, "San Francisco," *Musical America,* LXIII (February 10, 1943), 234.
22 Fried, "San Francisco Opera Thrives in Wartime," *Opera News,* IX (October 2, 1944), 10.
23 *San Francisco Examiner,* September 27, 1950.
24 *Ibid.,* October 7, 1951.
25 Fisher, "Opera in San Francisco," *Musical America,* LXXI (November 1, 1951), 24.
26 Frankenstein, "San Francisco's Place in the Sun," *Theatre Arts,* XLII (January 1958), 57.
27 "San Francisco Smash," *Time,* LXX (October 28, 1957), 54.
28 Frankenstein, "San Francisco's Place in the Sun," 57.
29 "Artists and Management," *Musical America,* LXXVII (August 1957), 27.
30 Fisher, "National Report," *Musical America,* LXXVI (May 1956), 11.
31 Interview with Alfred Frankenstein, San Francisco, September 19, 1960.
32 *San Francisco Chronicle,* December 30, 1958.
33 Interview with Herbert Scholder, San Francisco, September 23, 1960.

34 *San Francisco Chronicle*, September 28, 1958.
35 *New York Times*, October 16, 1955. © 1955 by The New York Times Company. Reprinted by permission.

Chapter Seven

1 John William Rogers, *The Lusty Texans of Dallas* (New York: E. P. Dutton and Company, 1951), 239–40.
2 John Rosenfield, "Texas Joins the Parade in the Story of Music in America," *Musical America*, LXVIII (March 15, 1948), 50.
3 Rogers, *Lusty Texans of Dallas*, 240.
4 Rosenfield, "Texas Joins the Parade," 50.
5 Rogers, *Lusty Texans of Dallas*, 241.
6 *Ibid.*
7 *Ibid.*
8 *Ibid.*, 241–42.
9 Rosenfield, "Texas Joins the Parade," 50.
10 Rogers, *Lusty Texans of Dallas*, 242–43.
11 Interview with Lawrence Kelly, Dallas, August 25, 1959; Rosenfield, "The Southwest Scene," *Theatre Arts*, XLII (January 1958), 63.
12 Dorothea Bourne, "Debut in Dallas," *Theatre Arts*, XLII (February 1959), 88.
13 *Ibid.*, 79.
14 *Dallas Morning News*, November 23, 1957.
15 "Callas in Dallas," *Time*, LXX (December 2, 1957), 71.
16 *Ibid.*; *Dallas Morning News*, November 23, 1957.
17 Bourne, "Debut in Dallas," 79.
18 "Callas in Dallas," 72.
19 *Dallas Morning News*, November 23, 1957.
20 *Ibid.*
21 "Callas in Dallas," 72.
22 *Dallas Morning News*, November 23, 1957.
23 Bourne, "Debut in Dallas," 79.
24 *Dallas Morning News*, November 23, 1957.
25 "Dallas Civic Opera to Present Callas," *Musical America*, LXXVII (October 1957), 14.
26 Jack Frederick Kilpatrick, "The National Scene—Dallas," *Musical Courier*, CLVII (January 1, 1958), 27.
27 Bourne, "Debut in Dallas," 88.
28 "The Sumptuous in Texas," *Newsweek*, L (December 2, 1957), 72.
29 Henry S. Miller, Jr., "Dallas Civic Opera Company," in the program for the 1958 season, Dallas Civic Opera Company, 1958, 1.
30 Rosenfield, "Contrasts in Dallas," *Opera News*, XXIII (December 8, 1958), 12–13.
31 "Love Affair in Dallas," *Time*, LXXII (November 17, 1958), 54.
32 George C. Leslie, "Callas Hailed as Violetta and Medea in Dallas Opera," *Musical America*, LXXVIII (December 1, 1958), 3.

33 *Dallas Times Herald,* November 7, 1958.
34 "Cast Out," *Time,* LXXII (November 17, 1958), 53.
35 *Dallas Times Herald,* November 7, 1958.
36 *Chicago American,* November 9, 1958.
37 Kilpatrick, "The National Scene—Dallas," *Musical America,* CLVIII (December 1958), 29.
38 "Callas at Covent Garden," *Time,* LXXIII (June 29, 1959), 43.
39 *Ibid.*
40 *Dallas Morning News,* September 2, 1959.
41 *Ibid.,* October 30, 1959.
42 Katherine Griffith, "Callas from the Chorus," *Opera News,* XXIV (January 16, 1960), 12.
43 *Dallas Morning News,* November 7, 1959.
44 Serge Saxe, "Callas Again Stirs Dallas," *Musical Courier,* CIX (December 1959), 5.
45 *Dallas Morning News,* November 18, 1960.
46 John W. Freeman, "Opera on Records," *Opera News,* XXV (January 14, 1961), 35.
47 *Dallas Morning News,* November 22, 1960.
48 *New York Herald Tribune,* November 22, 1959.

Chapter Eight

1 Caroline Bancroft, *Gulch of Gold: The History of Central City, Colorado* (Denver: Sage Books, 1958), 30–36.
2 *Ibid.,* 164; Charles Bayly, Jr., "The Opera House at Central City," *Theatre Arts Monthly,* XVI (March 1932), 206–07.
3 Melvin Schoberlin, *From Candles to Footlights* (Denver: Old West Publishing Company, 1941), 134–36.
4 Bancroft, *Gulch of Gold,* 266; Bayly, "The Opera House at Central City," 207.
5 Schoberlin, *From Candles to Footlights,* 258–59.
6 *Central City Opera House Association* (pamphlet issued by the Central City Opera House Association), 14.
7 Schoberlin, *From Candles to Footlights,* 259.
8 *Central City Opera House Association,* 15.
9 Schoberlin, *From Candles to Footlights,* 260.
10 *Ibid.;* Vera Cravath Gibbs, "Central City Souvenirs," *Opera News,* VI (October 6, 1941), 13.
11 Schoberlin, *From Candles to Footlights,* 260.
12 *Central City Opera House Association,* 15–21.
13 *Rocky Mountain News,* June 8, 1940.
14 Gibbs, "Central City Souvenirs," 12–13.
15 *Rocky Mountain News,* July 14, 1941.
16 *Pueblo Chieftain,* July 8, 1946.
17 Charles F. Collisson and Stewart Manville, "Central City Opera," *Opera News,* XII (October 6, 1947), 18–19.
18 *Rocky Mountain News,* July 6, 1947.
19 *Ibid.,* July 23, 1947.

[20] *Ibid.*, August 5, 1947.

[21] *Denver Post*, July 4, 1948.

[22] *Rocky Mountain News*, July 12, 1949.

[23] *Ibid.*, July 3, 1949.

[24] *Ibid.*, July 8, 1956.

[25] *Ibid.*, June 26, 1960.

[26] Emily Brady Rogers, "Contrasting Tragedies," *Musical America*, LXXX (September 1960), 13–14.

[27] Allen Young, "Central City Festival," *Musical America*, LXXXIII (August 1963), 5.

[28] Alex Murphree, "Central City—Mining for Youth," *Opera News*, XVI (October 29, 1951), 10–11.

[29] Frank Magee, Jr., "Opera and the Royal City," *New Mexico*, XXXVIII (June 1960), 8, 11.

[30] "Opera on the Ranch," *Time*, LXX (July 15, 1957), 49.

[31] Magee, "Opera and the Royal City," 11.

[32] *Santa Fe New Mexican*, July 5, 1957.

[33] Alfred Morang, "Santa Fe Launches Opera Festival," *Musical America*, LXXVII (August 1957), 21.

[34] *Santa Fe New Mexican*, July 19, 1957.

[35] Constance Mellen, "A Passion in the Desert," *Opera News*, XXII (October 28, 1957), 7.

[36] *Ibid.*

[37] Interview with Frank Magee, Santa Fe, September 6, 1960.

[38] *Ibid.*

[39] Magee, "Opera and the Royal City," 11, 38.

Chapter Nine

[1] Francis D. Perkins, "Criticism—A Half Century of Opera," *Musical America*, LXVIII (February 1948), 23.

[2] "Opera Conference Meets in New York," *Musical America*, LXXVI (April 1956), 3.

[3] *San Antonio Express*, February 21, 1945, and February 23, 1945.

[4] Statement by Pauline Reiter, as quoted in Coleman, "Surveying the National Production Scene," *Theatre Arts*, XL (August 1956), 87.

[5] *San Antonio Symphony* (a pamphlet giving biographical sketches of members of the San Antonio Symphony), 1959.

[6] *Dallas Morning News*, February 9, 1953.

[7] *Ibid.*

[8] Letter from Clinton E. Norton (Manager of the Symphony Society of San Antonio), August 2, 1960.

INDEX

A

Abbey, Henry, 40
Abbott, Emma, 114
Abduction from the Seraglio, The,
120, 139
Academy of Music, 38, 83
Adams, Milward, 40
Adelphi Theater, 85
Adler, Dankmar, 39
Adler, Kurt Herbert, 103, 109, 110,
111, 112
Adriana Lecouvreur, 81
Agnini, Armando, 95, 97
Aïda, 41, 43–44, 48, 59, 66, 78, 97,
103, 108, 141, 149
Aimée Opera Company, 88
Albanese, Licia, 103, 118, 149
Albuquerque, 145
Alcina, 131, 133
Alessandro, Victor, 150
Alfano, Franco, 62
Alhaiza brothers, 19
Alva, Luigi, 131, 132
Alvary, Lorenzo, 75
Amara, Lucine, 103, 140, 141
Amboise, Jacques d', 133
Amelia Goes to the Ball, 140
American Legion, 98
American Theater, 85
Amico Fritz, L', 97
Amore dei Tre Re, L', 33, 57, 103, 151
Andrea Chenier, 49, 62, 96
Anima Allegra, L', 97
Anna Bolena, 9, 121, 146
Annie Get Your Gun, 113
Anti-Cigarette League, 47
Antoine, Josephine, 138
Aphrodite, 54
Ardmore, Oklahoma, 129
Argall, Marsden, 102
Ariadne auf Naxos, 140, 145
Aspen, Colorado, 152
Astor family, 83
Athenaeum, 29

Athens, 125
Atlanta, 117
Auditorium (Chicago), 39–42, 43–65,
66

B

Bachman, Arthur, 93
Bagarozy, Edward, 78–79
Baker, Paul, 113
Balfe, Michael, 38
Ballad of Baby Doe, The, 140–141,
146
Ballo in Maschera, Un, 88, 132
Barber of Seville, The, 8, 9, 11, 18,
41, 46, 50, 51, 77, 90–91, 111, 128,
129–130, 138, 144
Barili, Clotilda, 86
Barnum, P. T., 10, 86
Bartered Bride, The, 138, 150
Bartlett, Michael, 72
Bastianini, Ettore, 81, 129
Baum, Kurt, 149
Bay, Howard, 110
Beautiful Galatea, The, 142
Beecham, Sir Thomas, 103
Beethoven, Ludwig van, 38, 139
Bella Union, 88
Belle Assise, La, 11
Bellini, Vincenzo, 8, 23, 37, 76, 78,
85, 87, 120–121, 135
Belvedere Theater, 136
Bentley, Robert I., 95
Berg, Alban, 146
Berganza, Teresa, 124, 126
Bergonzi, Carlo, 80, 118
Berlin, Irving, 113
Bernhardt, Sarah, 136, 137
Berry, Walter, 81
Bianchi Opera Company, 88
Bing, Rudolf, 108, 124
Biscaccianti, Eliza, 85–86, 87–88
Bishop, Anna, 86
Bizet, Georges, 20, 32, 152
Bjoerling, Jussi, 152
Blackstone Hotel, 54, 55

Blitzstein, Marc, 146
Blood Moon, 110
Bohème, La, 25, 41, 45, 70, 77, 78, 96, 111, 113, 118, 132, 146, 149, 151, 152
Bohemian Girl, The, 38, 136
Boïto, Arrigo, 62, 81
Bolshevik revolution, 50
Booth, Edwin, 136, 137
Borghese, Mme., 9
Bori, Lucrezia, 103
Boris Godunov, 103
Borkh, Inge, 110
Borodin, Alexander, 81
Boston, 18, 95
Boston Ideals, 114
Boston National Company, 115
Boston Opera Company, 41
Boudousquie, Charles, 9, 13, 16–17, 18
Brambilla, Signora, 88
Brichetto, Bice, 129
Bridger, Jim, 137
Brienti, Eliza, 37
Brownlee, John, 138
Buffalo Bill's Wild West Show, 23–24
Bultman, Fred, 32–33
Butler, Benjamin F., 19
Butler, Bill, 144

C

Callas, Maria (Meneghini), 75, 76–77, 78–79, 119–121, 123–131
Calvé, Julia, 9, 16
Camille (Dumas), 123, 138
Camille (Forrest), 66–68
Campanini, Cleofonte, 43, 46, 47, 48, 49, 50, 51, 52–53, 60
Campora, Giuseppi, 152
Capriccio, 146, 147
Carmen, 20, 28, 31, 32, 46, 57, 77, 92, 93, 95, 103–104, 110, 132, 140, 146, 149, 151, 152
Carmina Burana, 110, 111
Carrier, M., 11
Carson, Kit, 137
Carteri, Rosanna, 77
Caruso, Enrico, 41, 45, 77, 92–93
Cassidy, Claudia, 73, 74, 75, 76
Cavalleria Rusticana, 92, 149
Cellini, Renato, 34
Cena delle Beffe, La, 97
Cendrillon, 46

Cenerentola, La, 33, 81, 146, 152
Central City, 135–142, 147
Central City Opera House, 136–142
Central City Opera House Association, 134–135, 137–142, 147
Chaliapin, Feodor, 62, 115
Charles VI, 11
Charpentier, Gustave, 44
Charley, M., 25
"Chautauqua Salute," 115
Cherubini, Luigi, 4, 110, 111, 124, 127, 130
Chestnut Theater, 8
Chicago, 36–82, 122, 132, 135, 154
Chicago Association of Commerce, 55
Chicago City Opera Company, 69–70
Chicago Civic Opera Company, 30, 60, 61–68, 115–117
Chicago Grand Opera, 69
Chicago Grand Opera Company, 43–48, 114–115
Chicago Music Foundation, 71
Chicago Opera Association, 49–59, 62, 94, 115
Chicago Opera Company, 70–73
Chicago-Philadelphia Grand Opera Company, 46
Chicago Theater (Rice's), 36–37
Christoff, Boris, 80, 81, 110
Cilea, Francesco, 81
Cincinnati Opera, 71
City Park Stadium (New Orleans), 31, 32
Civic Auditorium (San Francisco), 93, 95–98
Civic Center (San Francisco), 99
Civic Opera House (Chicago), 64, 65–82
Civic Theater (Chicago), 65
Civil War, 16–19
Cléopâtre, 62
Cleva, Fausto, 71–73
Cody, William F., 137
Coghlin, Rose, 136
Coq d'Or, Le, 151
Cosi Fan Tutte, 140, 144
Covent Garden, 92, 108, 127, 128, 129, 131
Craft, Robert, 144–145
Crespin, Régine, 80
Cristoforo Colombo, 48

Crosby, John, 143, 144, 145, 147
Crosby Opera House, 38
Crosby, Uranus H., 38
cummings, e. e., 146
Cushman, Charlotte, 11

D

Dallas, 47, 80, 113–133, 134, 154
Dallas Chamber of Commerce, 117–118
Dallas Civic Opera, 80, 118–133, 154
Dallas Grand Opera Committee, 114, 116, 117
Dallas Opera House, 114, 115
Dallas Symphony, 117, 119, 120, 121
Dallas Theater Center, 113
D'Alvarez, Marguerite, 56, 58
Damrosch, Walter, 41
Daphne, 146
Daughter of the Regiment, The, 87, 107, 132
Davis, John, 5, 6, 7
Davis, Pierre, 7, 9
Dawes, Charles G., 43, 49, 51, 61
Debussy, Claude, 44
Delibes, Leo, 104
Dello Joio, Norman, 110
Del Monaco, Mario, 81, 108, 132
Denver, 135, 136, 137, 140, 142
Destinn, Emmy, 41
Deux Journées, Les, 4
Dialogues of the Carmelites, 110
Diamond Lil, 140
Dinorah, 18, 41, 51, 63
Dippel, Andreas, 43, 47, 114
Di Stefano, Giuseppe, 75, 132
Dolci, Alessandro, 52
Doll's House, A, 138
Don Carlo, 111
Don Giovanni, 38, 75, 103, 104, 131, 150, 154
Donizetti, Gaetano, 9, 11, 17, 23, 38, 77, 81, 87, 88, 107, 120–121, 127, 132, 135, 141, 146
Don Pasquale, 88, 140, 154
Don Quichotte, 27, 48
Dua, Octave, 50
Dubois, Theodore, 40
Dufau, Jenny, 46
Dufrère, Desiré, 50
Dumas, Alexandre, 123, 138
Durand, Rosalie, 37

Duval, Denise, 132
Dux, Claire, 56

E

Eames, Emma, 93
Eastman School of Music, 150
Eckert, Carl Antonin Florian, 39
Eddy, Nelson, 72
Edwards International Grand Opera Company, 94
Elektra, 150–151, 152
Erlanger, Camille, 54
Ernani, 85
Escalais, M., 26
Esmeralda, La, 9
Euripides, 124, 125
Evans, Anne, 137
Evening Star, 19

F

Fair Park Auditorium, 115, 117
Fair Park Coliseum, 115
Falcon, The, 10
Falstaff, 81
Farrar, Geraldine, 41, 45, 49, 94
Farrell, Eileen, 80
Farwell, Arthur, 45
Fausses Consultations, Les, 4
Faust, 21, 23, 32, 38, 54, 73, 88, 91, 95
Favorita, La, 11, 81
Fedora, 81
Fenice, La, 131
Ferrer, Jose, 146
Ferriero, Maria, 144
Festival of Two Worlds, 132
Fevrier, Henri, 63
Fiamma, La, 69
Fidelio, 38, 139
Field's Theater, 114
Flagstad, Kirsten, 69, 103, 105
Fledermaus, Die, 140, 146
Fleury-Joly, Mme., 9
Flippin, Edgar L., 114
Flotow, Friedrich von, 18, 23, 139
Floyd, Carlisle, 33, 145
Folie, D'une, 4
Folies Bergère, 116
Ford Foundation, 34
Forrest, Hamilton, 66–68
Fort Dearborn, 36

Fort Sumter, 18
Fort Worth Opera Association, 34, 152
Forza del Destino, La, 38, 80–81, 111
Fox, Carol, 73–76, 77, 79–80, 119, 121
Franchetti, Alberto, 48
Frankenstein, Alfred, 104, 105, 107, 109
Frau ohne Schatten, Die, 110
Freischütz, Der, 86
Fremstad, Olive, 41, 92, 93, 114
French Opera House, 13, 14, 15–22, 24–25, 26–29, 30, 31, 33, 35

G

Gadski, Johanna, 58
Galli-Curci, Amelita, 49–50, 51, 52, 59, 63, 70
Gallier, James Jr., 13
Gallo, Fortune, 71, 74, 115
Garden, Mary, 30, 41, 42, 44–45, 46–47, 49, 52, 53, 54–59, 61, 62–63, 66–68, 81, 94, 115–117
Gatti-Casazza, Giulio, 41
Gauthier, M., 25
Gaveaux, Pierre, 3
General Finance Corporation, 71
Gershwin, George, 113
Ghioni and Susini Italian Opera Company, 19
Giannini, Victorio, 77, 81
Gianni Schicchi, 146
Gilbert and Sullivan, 91, 140
Gioconda, La, 41, 63–64
Giordano, Umberto, 49, 81, 97
Girl of the Golden West, The, 45, 104, 141, 153
Gish, Lillian, 138
Gluck, Christoph Willibald, 7, 138
Gobbi, Tito, 75, 77, 80, 81, 108
Gondoliers, The, 138
Götterdämmerung, Die, 50
Gounod, Charles, 20, 24, 25, 40, 64, 72, 73, 88, 97, 151
Graf, Herbert, 138
Graham, Chalmers, 111
Grand Opera House, 88, 92
Grau, Maurice, 38, 40, 41
Great Depression, 68–69, 102, 112, 117
Greater New Orleans Opera Foundation, 33
Greek National Theater, 124
Greeley, Horace, 137

Greer, Frances, 139, 140
Gregory, John, 135
Grétry, André Ernest Modeste, 7
Griffith, D. W., 105
Grisélidis, 49
Gruenwalds, 135–136

H

Hackett, Charles, 64
Halévy, Jacques, 11
Hammerstein, Oscar, 42–43, 44
Hammond, Vernon, 145
Handel, George Frederick, 131
Handy, W. C., 30
Harding, Warren G., 54
Harling, W. Franke, 64
Harrison, Benjamin, 39
Harvest, 81
Herbert, Victor, 46–47, 91
Herbert, Walter, 31, 34
Her Majesty's Opera Company, 22–24
Hérodiade, 24
Hérold, Louis Joseph, 90
Herz, Henri, 84–85
Hindemith, Paul, 146
Hodson, Georgia, 37
"Home, Sweet Home," 39, 41, 51, 65, 89, 91
Honegger, Arthur, 62, 110, 146
Horgan, Paul, 146
Houston, 113
Houston Grand Opera, 34, 152
Huguenots, Les, 8, 9, 11, 28, 33, 40
Humperdinck, Engelbert, 49
Hurley, Laurel, 141, 142
Huston, Walter, 138

I

Incoronazione di Poppea, L', 132, 133
Inherit the Wind, 113
Insull, Samuel, 61, 62, 63, 64, 65, 67, 68, 69, 71, 74, 75, 76
Intolerance, 105
Irby, William Ratcliffe, 27
Isabeau, 51
Italiana in Algeri, L', 119, 120, 121–122, 123–124, 133
Italian Company of the Grand Theatre of Mexico, 19
Italian Grand Opera Company, 38, 40–41
Italian Opera Troupe, 37, 86

J

Jackson, Andrew, 1, 7
Jackson Square, 10, 28
Jacquerie, 53
Jagel, Frederick, 104
Janácek, Leos, 81
Jazz, 29–30, 64
Jefferson, Joseph, 136
Jemez Mountains, 144
Jenny Lind Theater, 85
Jenufa, 81
Jewels of the Madonna, The, 53
Joan at the Stake, 110, 146
Johnson, Edward, 54, 117
Johnson, Herbert, 53
Jones, Robert Edmund, 138
Jongleur de Notre Dame, Le, 30, 46, 57
Jordan, Irene, 75
Judith, 62

K

Kansas City, 128
Kansas City Lyric Theater, 152
Kaskas, Anna, 138
Kelly, Lawrence, 73–76, 77, 78, 79–80, 118–120, 121, 122, 124, 127, 130, 132
Kendrick, Charles, 98–99
Kirk, Florence, 104
Kirsten, Dorothy, 103, 150, 151–152
Königskinder, Die, 49, 50
Konya, Sándor, 110
Koyke, Kizi, 133
Kramer, Arthur, 117–118

L

Lady from Colorado, 141
Lady Macbeth of Mtsensk, 110
Lafayette, Marquis de, 7
Lakmé, 46, 63, 104, 150
Lalo, Edouard, 24
"Last Rose of Summer, The," 51
Law and Order League, 45
Lawrence, Jerome, 113
Lawrence, Marjorie, 103–104
Leahy, "Doc," 92
Lehmann, Lotte, 66, 69, 73, 103
Leoncavallo, Ruggiero, 48, 54, 90, 93–94, 133
Levy, Marvin David, 144
Lewis, Brenda, 152
Ligabue, Ilva, 80, 132
Light from St. Agnes, A, 64

Lincoln, Abraham, 18, 38, 65
Lind, Jenny, 10–11, 35
Linda di Chamounix, 23
Loeb, Harry B., 27
loges grillées, 5–6
Lohengrin, 41, 54, 149
London, 127–128
London, George, 150
Longone, Paul, 69–70
Los Alamos, 145
Los Alamos Ranch School, 143
Los Angeles, 47, 110–111, 116
Loubat, Walter L., 31
Louise, 44, 57, 103
Love Field, 128
Love of Three Oranges, The, 57
Lucia di Lammermoor, 9, 11, 17, 23, 37, 46, 50, 77, 102, 114–115, 127, 128–129, 131, 132, 141, 151, 152, 154
Lucrezia Borgia, 38
Ludwig, Christa, 81
Lulu, 146, 147
Lyric Opera of Chicago, 65, 80–82, 145, 153–154
Lyric Theatre of Chicago, 74–80, 119, 121

M

Macbeth (Verdi), 121, 124
McCormick, Edith Rockefeller, 53, 55, 59, 61
McCormick, Harold F., 43, 48, 49, 51, 53, 54, 55, 59, 60, 61, 62
MacDonald, Jeanette, 72–73
McFarlane, Frederick, 137
McFarlane, Ida Kruse, 137
McFarlane, Peter, 137
McMurray, Mary, 144
MacNeil, Cornell, 81, 142
McVicker's Theater, 38
Madama Butterfly, 41, 45, 56–57, 78–79, 133, 144, 145, 152
Madeira, Jean, 152
Magee, Frank, 145
Maguire, Thomas, 86–87, 88, 135
Majestic Theater, 115
Manhattan Opera Company, 42, 43, 44
Manhattan Opera House, 42, 43, 44
Manon, 50, 111, 118, 150
Mapleson, James Henry, 22–23, 88–89
Marcus, Herbert, 117
Margo Jones Theater, 113

Marinuzzi, Gino, 53, 54
Mario, Queena, 96
Marouf, 97
Marriage of Figaro, The, 81, 93, 103, 111
"Marseillaise," 107
Marshall, Charles, 59, 66
Martha, 18, 23, 38, 114, 139–140
Martin, Mary, 113
Martinelli, Giovanni, 69, 96
Martyrs, Les, 9, 10
Mascagni, Pietro, 51, 92, 97
Mason, Edith, 56–57, 59, 64, 69, 76, 77, 115
Massenet, Jules, 24, 27, 30, 33, 44, 45, 48, 49, 62, 81, 115, 118
Mature, Victor, 150
Mavra, 146
Maxwell, Elsa, 131
Mayhoff, Maria, 32
Mazeppa, 135
Medea, 111, 124–127, 128, 129, 130–131, 133
Mefistofele, 62, 81
Méhul, Étienne Henri, 3, 4, 7
Melba, Nellie, 41, 45, 90–91
Melchior, Lauritz, 69, 103
Meneghini, Giovanni Battista, 79, 128
Menotti, Gian-Carlo, 140
Merola, Gaetano, 83, 84, 94–95, 96, 100, 102, 103, 106, 108, 109, 112
Merrill, Robert, 118
Merry Widow, The, 138
Merry Wives of Windsor, The, 140
Metropolitan Life Insurance Company, 65
Metropolitan Opera Company, 1, 25, 30, 33, 41, 42, 43, 56, 60, 66, 68, 69, 71, 72, 74, 75, 77, 80, 81, 82, 83, 92–93, 94, 97, 100, 102, 105, 106, 107, 108, 109, 112, 114, 117–118, 124–125, 132, 133, 136, 138, 142, 145, 150, 151, 153, 154
Metropolitan Theater (San Francisco), 86
Meyerbeer, Giacomo, 8, 9, 11, 18, 19, 28, 51
Mignon, 20
Mikado, The, 44
Milanov, Zinka, 103, 118
Miller, Henry S. Jr., 119
Miller, Mildred, 140

Milwaukee, 37
Minotis, Alexis, 124, 127
Miró, Estevan, 1
Mitchell, Maggie, 136
Moffo, Anna, 80, 81, 118
Mona Lisa, 148
Monna Vanna, 54, 57, 63
Montana Theater, 135, 136
Montarsolo, Paolo, 122
Montemezzi, Italo, 33, 151
Monteux, Pierre, 143
Monteverdi, Claudio, 132
Monti, Nicola, 122
Montreal, 95
Moore, Douglas, 140–141, 146
Moore, Grace, 69, 103, 118, 149
Morton, Levi P., 40
Moscona, Nicola, 152
Moussorgsky, Modeste, 103
Mozart, Wolfgang Amadeus, 7, 33, 75, 93, 120, 131, 139, 140, 146, 150
Municipal Auditorium (New Orleans), 31, 32
Municipal Auditorium (San Antonio), 151
Muratore, Lucian, 54, 56, 58, 94
Music Man, The, 110
Muzio, Claudia, 62, 94, 102

N

Nabucco, 81, 150, 154
National Broadcasting Company, 102, 141
Natoma, 46–47
Neiman-Marcus, 132
Nemeroff, Ada, 53
Neues vom Tage, 146
Nevada, Emma, 23–24
New Orleans, 1–35, 36, 60, 83, 88, 117
New Orleans English Opera Troupe, 37, 87
New Orleans Experimental Opera Theater, 34
New Orleans French Opera (Chicago tour), 41
New Orleans Opera House Association, 31–35
New York City, 1, 7, 8, 9, 18, 19, 42, 47, 50, 54, 59, 72, 74, 83, 92, 95, 97, 105, 117–118, 123, 124, 132, 133, 135, 136, 142, 153

New York City Ballet, 119
New York City Opera, 33, 140, 141, 142, 145, 151
Nicolai, Otto, 140
Nilsson, Birgit, 80, 110
Noblet, Gaston, 25
Nordica, Lillian, 40, 90, 94
Norma, 8, 11, 37, 38, 76, 85
Nougues, Jean, 27

O

Oedipus Rex, 146, 147
Offenbach, Jacques, 39, 88, 91, 140
O'Hearn, Robert, 141
Oklahoma City Symphony, 150
"Old Folks at Home," 91
Old Vic Company, 119
Oliviero, Lodovico, 97
Opéra-Comique, 44, 67
"Opera under the Stars," 31
Orff, Carl, 110, 111
Original Dixieland Jazz Band, 30
Orpheus and Eurydice, 138
Otello (Rossini), 11
Otello (Verdi), 40, 41, 81, 132
Othello (Shakespeare), 138

P

Pagliacci, I, 31, 45, 48, 90, 94, 95, 132, 133, 149
Palace Hotel, 92
Palermo, 132
Pardon of Ploërmel, The, 18, 41, 51
Parepa-Rosa, Euphrosyne, 88
Paris Opera House, 6
Parlange, Charles, 12–13, 14
Parley, Andreas, 53
Parsifal, 52, 114
Pataques, 5
Patti, Adelina, 16–18, 23–24, 35, 39–41, 65, 88–89, 90, 137
Patti, Amelia, 19, 37–38
Pavlova, Anna, 115
Pearl Fishers, The, 152
Peck, Ferdinand W., 39, 40, 41
Peerce, Jan, 118
Pelléas and Mélisande, 44, 57
Pellegrini Opera Troupe, 85
Pergolesi, Giovanni Battista, 144
Périchole, La, 88
Perlea, Jonel, 149
Persephone, 146

Peters, Roberta, 152
Petite Fille de la Grande Armée, La, 11
Pettigiani, Maria, 40
Philadelphia, 7, 8, 18, 34, 45–46
Piazza, Marguerite, 34, 139–140
Picasso, Pablo, 113
Picchi, Mirto, 76
Pietà, 148
Pike, Edgar L., 114
Pike, Zebulon, 137
Pinza, Ezio, 69, 103, 118
Pirata, Il, 8
Pisa, 63
Polacco, Giorgio, 51–52, 55, 59, 62, 63, 65, 68, 76
Poliuto, 9, 10
Ponchielli, Amilcare, 63
Pons, Lily, 69, 102, 104, 107, 108–109, 118, 150
Ponselle, Rosa, 8
Pontalba Apartments, 10, 13, 28
Porgy and Bess, 113
Portland, Oregon, 152–153
Portuguese Inn, The, 110
Pouilly, M., 13
Poulenc, Francis, 110
Prevost, Eugene, 9, 15
Price, Leontyne, 80, 81, 110, 111–112, 113, 118
Prince Igor, 81
Prince Tekeli, Le (Le Siège de Mantgatz), 3
Prokofiev, Serge, 57
Prophète, Le, 11
Puccini, Giacomo, 25, 26, 56, 70, 96, 102, 104, 141, 152, 153
Puritani, I, 23, 38, 78, 121
Pyle, Ernie, 138

Q

Quo Vadis, 27

R

Rabaud, Henri, 97
Rabinoff, Max, 115
Raisa, Rosa, 48, 49, 51, 52, 53, 54, 59, 63–64, 66, 69, 76
Rake's Progress, The, 144–145, 146, 147
Ratti, Eugenia, 129, 131
Ravinia Park, 56, 69

Reardon, John, 131
Redding, Joe, 47
Regina, 146
Reine, Alice and Tony, 24
Reine de Saba, La, 24–25
Reiter, Max, 149, 150
Renard, 146
Rescigno, Nicola, 73–76, 77, 79–80, 119, 125, 128
Resnik, Regina, 132, 139, 140
Respighi, Ottorino, 69
Resurrection, 62
Reszke, Jean de, 41
Rethberg, Elisabeth, 103
Reyer, Ernest Louis Étienne, 25
Rice, J. B., 36, 37
Richelieu Hotel, 40
Rigoletto, 18, 32, 46, 47, 49–50, 63, 90, 103, 142, 149, 152
Rimsky-Korsakov, Nicolas, 151
Ring des Nibelungen, Der, 49, 102–103
Ristori, 136
Robert le Diable, 11
Roi d'Ys, Le, 24
Roman, Stella, 149
Romeo and Juliet (Gounod), 20, 40, 41, 50, 63, 64, 72–73, 97, 103, 142, 151
Romeo and Juliet (Shakespeare), 119
Rondine, La, 103
Roosevelt, Theodore, 90
Rosenkavalier, Der, 69, 103, 146
Rosenthal, Jean, 119, 122
Ross, Elinor, 152
Rossignol, Le, 146
Rossi-Lemeni, Nicola, 75, 76, 81
Rossini, Gioacchino, 7, 8, 11, 15, 23, 33, 81, 87, 90–91, 119, 122, 123, 138, 146
Royal Opera Company, 127
Ruffo, Titta, 48, 49, 94
Ruy Blas, 138
Rysanek, Leonie, 80, 110

S

St. Francis Hotel, 95
"St. Louis Blues," 30
Saint-Saëns, Camille, 24, 56
Salammbô, 25
Salomé, 44–45, 51, 57–58, 62, 115–117, 152

Salvini, 136
Salzburg Opera Guild, 30
Sammarco, Mario, 115
Samson and Delilah, 24, 56, 58, 104–105
San Antonio, 148–151, 152
San Antonio Opera Festival, 148–151, 152
San Antonio Symphony, 148–151
San Carlo Opera Company, 30, 71, 94, 115
San Francisco, 83–112, 120, 122, 124, 132, 134, 135, 153, 154
San Francisco earthquake, 92–93, 98
San Francisco Opera Association, 83–84, 95–112, 154
San Francisco Opera Debut Auditions, 110
San Francisco Symphony, 31, 95
Sanger, Eli L., 114
Santa Fe, 142–147
Santa Fe Opera Company, 134–135, 141, 143–147
Santa Fe Opera Theater, 143–147
Santo Domingo, 2, 5
Santo Domingo rebellion (1799), 2
Sarfaty, Regina, 144
Savage English Opera, 41, 114
Sayao, Bidu, 75, 103
Scala, La, 75, 108, 126, 129
Schipa, Tito, 58, 94
Schumann-Heink, Ernestine, 90
Schwarzkopf, Elisabeth, 81, 110, 131
Scott, Elmer L., 114
Scott, Sir Walter, 129
Scotti, Antonio, 41, 92–93, 115
Scotti Opera Company, 94, 115
Scotto, Renata, 80
Sears Roebuck, 148
Sebastian, Georges, 112
Secret, Le, 3
Secret of Suzanne, The, 47
Sembrich, Marcella, 90, 93
Semiramide, 7, 23
Serafin, Tullio, 81
Serva Padrona, La, 144
Shakespeare Festival (Stratford, Connecticut), 119
Shakespeare, William, 138
Sherman and Clay Music Company, 89
She Stoops to Conquer, 135

Shostakovich, Dmitri, 110
Shreveport, 34, 152
Simionato, Giulietta, 75, 76, 77, 80, 81, 110, 122
Simoneau, Leopold, 139–140
Slezak, Leo, 41
Smetana, Bedrich, 138, 150
Solti, Georg, 81
Sonnambula, La, 23, 37, 41, 85
Spangler, George, 55–56
Spanish-American War, 90–91
Spectacle de la Rue St. Pierre, Le, 1–3
Spoleto, 132
Spontini, Gasparo Luigi, 7, 8
Stanford University, 94–95
"Star-Spangled Banner, The," 51, 91
State Fair Musicals, 113
State Fair Music Hall, 117, 120, 121, 123, 125
Steber, Eleanor, 75, 118, 139
Stella, Antonietta, 132
Stevens, Risë, 103, 118, 149
Steward, Leroy T., 45
Stignani, Ebe, 108
Strakosch, Maurice, 37–38
Strauss, Johann, 140
Strauss, Richard, 44, 110, 115–117, 140, 145, 146, 150, 152
Stravinsky, Igor, 144–145, 146
Streich, Rita, 81
Sullivan, Louis, 39
Summer and Smoke, 113
Sunday, Billy, 57–58, 116
Suor Angelica, 132
Susannah, 33
Sutherland, Joan, 131–132
Sutter's Fort, 84
Swarthout, Gladys, 138

T

Tabarro, Il, 152
Tabary, Louis, 2, 4
Taddei, Giuseppe, 110, 122, 131
Tales of Hoffmann, The, 140
Tamagno, Francesco, 40
Taming of the Shrew, The, 77
Tampa, 34
Tannhäuser, 38, 111, 149, 154
Taylor, Zachary, 7
Teatro Massimo, 132

Tebaldi, Renata, 78, 79, 80–81, 108, 113, 118
Teller House, 136, 139
Ten Nights in a Bar Room, 135
Tetrazzini, Luisa, 46, 47, 92, 114–115
Texas Steer, A, 135
Teyte, Maggie, 46, 115
Thaïs, 44, 45, 57, 81, 115, 132, 133
Théâtre d'Orléans, 5–14, 15, 35
Théâtre de la Rue St. Pierre, Le, 3
Théâtre St. Philippe, 4–5
Thomas, Ambroise, 20
Tibbett, Lawrence, 103, 118
"Tiger Rag," 30
Tivoli Opera House, 88, 91–92, 93, 94
Tolstoi, Leo, 62
Tosca, 25–26, 52, 55, 102, 146, 151
Toscanini, Arturo, 41, 52
Tostée, 39
Tower, The, 144
Toymaker, The, 91
Traubel, Helen, 103, 118
Traviata, La, 23, 33, 34, 38, 46, 50, 76–77, 88, 89, 90, 103, 108–109, 121, 123, 124, 146, 149, 152
Treigle, Norman, 34
Tremont House, 37
Trip Across the Ocean, A, 135
Tristan und Isolde, 58, 103, 149
Troilus and Cressida, 110
Trovatore, Il, 18, 26, 31, 38, 78, 90, 103, 111–112, 141, 149, 151, 152
Tsarouchis, John, 125
Tucci, Gabriella, 110
Tucker, Richard, 81, 118
Tulane University, 27, 29
Tulsa Opera, Inc., 152, 153
Turandot, 150, 152

U

University of California, 98
University of Denver, 137

V

Valda, Giulia, 40
Valdengo, Giuseppi, 152
Valletti, Cesare, 110
Van Buren, Martin, 7
Vanderbilt family, 83
Van Gordon, Cyrena, 48, 54, 56, 66
Vanni-Marcoux, 48

178   INDEX

Varnay, Astrid, 150–151
Venice, 131
Verande, Louis P., 27
Verdi, Giuseppe, 18, 23, 26, 32, 38, 43, 49, 66, 76, 81, 85, 87, 88, 90, 108, 120–121, 123, 124, 148, 150
Vespri Siciliani, I, 121
Vestale, La, 8
Veterans' Memorial Building, 99–100, 102
Vickers, Jon, 126
Vienna, 126
Vittandini, 97
Volksoper (Vienna), 31
Vries, Rose de, 37

W

Wächter, Eberhard, 81, 131
Wade, Thomas, 88
Wagner, Richard, 38, 49, 50, 53–54, 102, 114, 149
Waldorf Astoria Hotel, 74
Walküre, Die, 54, 66, 103, 115
Wall Street crash, 66, 68
Walska, Ganna, 54
Walton, Sir William, 110
Ward, Robert, 141
Warfield, William, 113
War Memorial Fund, 98–99
War Memorial Opera House, 98–112
Warren, Leonard, 103, 118, 149, 152
Washington Ballroom, 5
Washington, George, 1
Watkin, Will A., 114
Weber, Carl Maria von, 86

Weber, Henry, 70–71
Werther, 33
West, Mae, 140
White, Carolina, 47
Whitehill, Charles, 115
Whitney, John Hay, 127
Wigwam, 65
Wilde, Oscar, 44
Wilkinson, Hugh M., 32
Williams, Tennessee, 113
William Tell, 15
Wilson, Dolores, 140
Wise Maiden, The, 111
Witherspoon, Herbert, 68
Wolf-Ferrari, Ermanno, 47, 53
Wolf, Peter, 149–150, 152
World's Fair (Chicago 1893), 41
World War I, 27, 48–51, 98
World War II, 31, 71–72, 106–107, 118, 138–139, 148
Wright, Frank Lloyd, 113
Wuthering Heights, 145–146

Y

Yeoman of the Guard, The, 138

Z

Zaccaria, Nicola, 131
Zampa, 90
Zanetto, 92
Zaza, 54
Zeffirelli, Franco, 119, 122, 123, 127, 128–129, 131, 154
Zingari, 48